THE FAITH
WE SING

THE FAITH
WE SING

by

S. PAUL SCHILLING

90-2479

THE WESTMINSTER PRESS

Philadelphia

First edition

Published by The Westminster Press®
Philadelphia, Pennsylvania

PRINTED IN THE UNITED STATES OF AMERICA
9 8 7 6 5 4 3 2 1

Library of Congress Cataloging in Publication Data

Schilling, S. Paul (Sylvester Paul), 1904–
    The faith we sing.

    Includes bibliographical references and index.
    1. Hymns, English—History and criticism. 2. Public worship. I. Title.
BV310.S34   1983   264'.2   82–21749
ISBN 0–664–24434–3 (pbk.)

ACKNOWLEDGMENTS

Grateful acknowledgment is made to the following, who have granted permission for the reprinting of lines from copyrighted material:

Agape, A Division of Hope Publishing Co., Carol Stream, Ill. 60187, for "Thanks to God, whose Word was spoken," by R. T. Brooks, copyright © 1954, renewal 1982 by Agape. Also for the following by Tom Colvin: "Christ the Worker," copyright © 1964, and "Fill us with your love," copyright © 1969. Also for the following by Fred Kaan: "Christ is crucified today," "Committed to Christ," and "Today I live"; all copyright © 1975. International copyright secured. All of the above are copyright © by Agape. All rights reserved.

American Ethical Union, for "Divinity is round us." Copyright 1955: The American Ethical Union Library Catalog Number 54:11625.

Augsburg Publishing House, for "Earth and all stars!" by Herbert F. Brokering. Copyright 1968, Augsburg Publishing House.

Albert F. Bayly, for "Lord of all good, our gifts we bring to thee," "Lord of the boundless curves of space," "Praise and thanksgiving, Father, we offer," "Rejoice, O people, in the mounting years," and "Your love, O God, has all mankind created." Copyright Albert F. Bayly.

J. E. Bowers, for " 'Glory to God!' all heav'n with joy is ringing." Copyright J. E. Bowers.

Celebration Services (International), Ltd., Millport, Isle of Cumbrae, Scotland, for "How beautiful the morning and the day," by Owen Barker, copyright © 1975; "Look around you, can you see?" by Jodi Page Clark, copyright © 1976; "Lord, give us your Spirit that is love," by Sandy Hardyman, copyright © 1978; and "I will rejoice in the Lord alway," by Jan Harrington, copyright © 1973, 1975. Also for "God is our Father," copyright © 1977. From *Cry Hosanna.* Also for "Wind, wind, blow on me," by Jane and Betsy Clowe. Copyright © 1975. From *Fresh Sounds.* Also for "Fear not, rejoice, and be glad," by Priscilla Wright, copyright © 1971, and for "We really want to thank you, Lord," copyright © 1973. From *Sound of Living Waters.* All of the above are copyright by Celebration Services (International), Ltd. All rights reserved.

Emily Chisholm, for her translation of Kurt Rommel's "O who can tell me where Jesus Christ is born today?" © 1973.

Christian Conference of Asia, Singapore, for "On a day when men were counted," by Daniel T. Niles.

Stewart Cross, for "Father, Lord of all creation."

Margaret Pleasant Douroux, for "Trees" ("Trees don't want to be mountains"), copyright © 1979, and "Clean Heart" ("Give me a clean heart"), copyright © 1970 by Margaret Pleasant Douroux.

Ruth Duck, for "Lead on, O cloud of Presence," copyright 1974 by Ruth Duck.

EMI Music Publishing, Ltd., for "We turn to you, O God of every nation," by Fred Kaan. © 1967 B. Feldman & Co., Ltd. Reproduced by permission of EMI Music Publishing, Ltd., 138–140 Charing Cross Road, London WC2H 0LD.

Faber Music, Ltd., for "Lord, as I wake I turn to you," by Brian Foley. Reprinted from *New Catholic Hymnal.*

Norman O. Forness, for "Rise up, O saints of God." Copyright 1978 by Norman O. Forness.

Franciscan Communications Center, for "Make me a channel of your peace," by Sebastian Tem-

ple, composer and adapter of words. © 1967 Franciscan Communications, Los Angeles, Calif. 90015.

Robert J. Fryson, for permission to quote from "God is."

Galaxy Music Corp., for the following by Sydney Carter: "Lord of the dance," copyright © 1963 by Galliard, Ltd., and "When I needed a neighbour," copyright © 1965 by Galliard, Ltd. Also for "When the bells chime noon in London" ("The Clock Carol"), by Paul Townsend, copyright © 1965 by Galliard, Ltd. Also for "God of concrete, God of steel," by Richard G. Jones, copyright © 1966 by Galliard, Ltd. Also for "Am I my brother's keeper?" by Ian Ferguson; "The World He Loves," by David S. Goodall; "Song and Dance," by Michael Hewlett; and "All who love and serve your city," by Erik Routley. All copyright © 1969 by Galliard, Ltd. Also for "O God of the eternal now," copyright © 1972 by Galliard, Ltd., and for "Sing we of the modern city" and "We meet you, O Christ, in many a guise," by Fred Kaan, copyright © 1968 by Galliard, Ltd.; and for "The love of God is broad," by Anders Frostenson, translated by Fred Kaan, copyright © 1976 by Stainer & Bell, Ltd. Also for "Moses, I know you're the man," by Estelle White. Published by Mayhew-McCrimmon, Ltd., Great Wakering, Essex, England. All rights reserved. All of the above are used by permission of Galaxy Music Corp., New York, sole U.S. agent.

H. C. A. Gaunt, for "Dear Lord, to you again our gifts we bring."

Gooi en Sticht, B.V., for "We who once were dead," by Muus Jacobse. Copyright 1963 Gooi en Sticht, B.V., Hilversum, The Netherlands.

John Webster Grant, for "O Holy Spirit, by whose breath."

James H. Hargett, for "From the shores of many nations." © 1973 by James H. Hargett.

Harper & Row, Publishers, Inc., for "O holy city, seen of John," by Walter Russell Bowie.

David Higham Associates, Ltd., for "Morning has broken," by Eleanor Farjeon, from *The Children's Bells,* published by Oxford University Press.

Hope Publishing Co., Carol Stream, Ill. 60187, for the following by Richard K. Avery and Donald S. Marsh: "Every morning is Easter morning," copyright © 1972, and "Male and female," copyright © 1974. Also for "God, who stretched the spangled heavens," by Catherine Cameron, copyright © 1967. Also for "Great is thy faithfulness," by Thomas O. Chisholm, copyright 1923, renewal 1951 extended by Hope Publishing Co. Also for the following by Fred Pratt Green: "Christ is the world's light," copyright © 1969; "For the fruits of his creation," copyright © 1970; "Of all the Spirit's gifts to me," copyright © 1979; "The Church of Christ in every age," copyright © 1971; "When in our music God is glorified," copyright © 1972; and "When the church of Jesus," copyright © 1969. Also for the following by Brian Wren: "Christ is alive," copyright © 1968; "I come with joy," copyright © 1968; "Lord Christ, the Father's mighty Son," copyright © 1962; "There's a Spirit in the air," copyright © 1969. Also for "There's a quiet understanding," by Tedd Smith, copyright © 1973. International copyright secured. All of the above are copyright © by Hope Publishing Co. All rights reserved.

House of the Resurrection, Mirfield, West Yorkshire, for "O crucified Redeemer," by Timothy Rees.

H. Trevor Hughes, for "Beyond the mist and doubt" and "Creator of the earth and skies," by Donald Hughes.

The Hymn Society of America, for "God of the Ages," by Elizabeth Burrowes, copyright © 1958; "Creating God, your fingers trace," by Jeffrey Rowthorn, copyright © 1974; "God in his love," by Fred Pratt Green, copyright © 1973; and "O God of every nation," by William W. Reid, Jr., copyright © 1958. All of the above are copyright © by the Hymn Society of America, Wittenberg University, Springfield, Ohio 45501. All rights reserved.

Hymns Ancient and Modern, Ltd., for "O thou who at thy eucharist didst pray," by William Harry Turton.

Willard F. Jabusch, for "The King of glory comes." © 1967 by Willard F. Jabusch.

Derwyn D. Jones, for "Now thank we God for bodies strong."

Richard G. Jones, for "God of concrete, God of steel," "God who created this garden of earth," and "The God who rules this earth." Copyright by Richard G. Jones.

Judson Press, for "Renew thy church, her ministries restore," by Kenneth L. Cober, copyright 1966 by K. L. Cober. Also for "O God whose love compels us," by Daniel B. Merrick, Jr., copyright © 1967.

Fred Kaan, for his translation of "Let all who share our bread and cup," by J. A. Cramer. Copyright by Fred Kaan.

Lexicon Music, Inc., for "Soon and very soon," by Andraé Crouch, © copyright 1976 by Lexicon Music, Inc., ASCAP, and Crouch Music, ASCAP. Also for "Goin' up yonder," by Walter Hawkins, © copyright 1976 by Libris Music, BMI. For both of the above: All rights reserved. International copyright secured. Used by special permission.

The Liturgical Conference, for "It's a long, hard journey," by Nick Hodson. Copyright © by Nick Hodson. With permission of The Liturgical Conference, 810 Rhode Island Ave., N.E., Washington, D.C. 20018. All rights reserved.

Joel W. Lundeen, for "Now we join in celebration." Copyright Joel W. Lundeen.

Manna Music, Inc., for "Lord, don't move that mountain," by Doris Akers, © copyright 1958 by Manna Music, Inc., 2111 Kenmere Ave., Burbank, Calif. 91504. International copyright secured. All rights reserved.

Martin & Morris, Inc., for the following by Kenneth Morris: "Christ is all," copyright 1946, and "Yes, God is real," copyright 1944 by Kenneth Morris.

Mayhew-McCrimmon, Ltd., for "Moses, I know you're the man," by Estelle White. Reproduced by permission of the publishers: Mayhew-McCrimmon, Ltd., Great Wakering, Essex, England.

Moody Press, for "Spirit of the living God," by Daniel Iverson, copyright 1935, 1963. Moody Press, Moody Bible Institute of Chicago.

A. R. Mowbray & Co., for "God is love: let heaven adore him," by Timothy Rees. Copyright by A. R. Mowbray & Co.

Oxford University Press, for "Strengthen for service, Lord," from the Syriac Liturgy of Malabar, translated by C. W. Humphreys and Percy Dearmer; from *The English Hymnal* (alt.). Also for "Sing to him in whom creation," by Michael Hewlett; from *English Praise.* Also for "Christ is the King! O friends rejoice," by G. K. A. Bell; "Christ is the world's true light," by G. W. Briggs; "As the disciples, when thy Son had left them," "O Father above us, our Father in might," and "Sing praise to God, who spoke through men," by Percy Dearmer; and "Lord of all hopefulness, Lord of all joy," by Jan Struther; all from *Enlarged Songs of Praise.* Also for "Now is eternal life," by G. W. Briggs; "O God of earth and altar," by G. K. Chesterton; "Forgive our sins as we forgive," by Rosamond E. Herklots; "Father eternal, Ruler of creation," by Laurence Housman (alt.); and "A man there lived in Galilee," by S. C. Lowry.

Kenneth L. Patton, for "We journey with a multitude." Copyright by Meeting House Press.

Mrs. M. E. Peacey, for "Filled with the Spirit's power," by John R. Peacey. © Mrs. M. E. Peacey.

The Pilgrim Press, for "Broken bread and outpoured wine," by Scott McCormick, Jr. Copyright © 1969 by the United Church Press.

Roger K. Powell, for "Lord, we thank thee for our brothers."

Theodore Presser Co., for "Lord God, by whose creative might," by Rosamond Herklots, © 1962, Theodore Presser Co.

Rightsong Music, Inc., for the following by Thomas A. Dorsey, copyright © by Hill & Range Songs, Inc.: "Lord will make a way some how," copyright © 1943; "Old ship of Zion," copyright © 1950, 1951; and "Take my hand, precious Lord," copyright © 1938. The above copyrights renewed, assigned to Unichappel Music, Inc. (Rightsong Music, Inc., Publisher). International copyright secured. All rights reserved.

The Royal School of Church Music, Croydon, Surrey, England, for "O holy Father, God most dear," by G. A. Tomlinson, © St. Martins Publications, Ltd.

R. B. Y. Scott, for permission to use "O Day of God, draw nigh."

Scottish Churches' House, Dunblane, Scotland, for "Am I my brother's keeper?" by Ian Ferguson. © 1969.

Hugh Sherlock, for "Lord, thy church on earth is seeking."

J. W. Shore, for "Morning glory, starlit sky," by W. H. Vanstone.

Colin P. Thompson, for "Christian people, raise your song."

Josef Weinberger, Ltd., for "O Lord, all the world belongs to you," by Patrick Appleford, copyright 1965 Joseph Weinberger, Ltd., London. Reproduced from *27 20th Century Hymns.*

The Westminster Press, for new stanza 3 of "Beneath the cross of Jesus," by Elizabeth C. Clephane, written by Dalton E. McDonald and Donald D. Kettring. Also for "Walk tall, Christian," by Miriam Drury. Both of the above are copyright 1972 by The Westminster Press. From *The Worshipbook—Services and Hymns.*

World Library Publications, Inc., for "Where charity and love prevail," ninth-century Latin, paraphrased by Clifford Evers, copyright 1961, 1962; "Cup of blessing that we share," by Bernard Mischke, copyright 1966; and "Sent forth by God's blessing," by Omer Westendorf, copyright 1964. The above are copyright by World Library Publications, Inc.

Worship, published by the monks of St. John's Abbey, Collegeville, Minn., for Erik Routley's revised wording of "In Christ there is no east or west," which appeared in the Jan. 1979 issue.

FOR MARY

Treasured partner in
worship and life

CONTENTS

Acknowledgments   5

Preface   15

PART ONE
ORIENTATION

1   Why Do the Words Matter?   23

2   Hymn Tunes and Theological Meaning   31

3   Criteria of Evaluation   41

PART TWO
MAJOR BELIEFS VOICED IN HYMN TEXTS

4   God   55

5   Humanity   78

6   Jesus Christ   88

7   The Holy Spirit   110

8   The Church and Its Mission   117

9   The Christian Life   141

10   Consummation   160

continued

PART THREE

SPECIAL TOPICS

11   Gospel Hymns   177

12   Folk Hymnody   196

13   Inclusive Language   213

Key to Abbreviations Used in Notes   229

Notes   233

Index of Authors and Translators of Hymns   249

Index of First Lines of Hymns   254

PREFACE

Let ev'ry instrument be tuned for praise;
let all rejoice who have a voice to raise;
and may God give us faith to sing always:
Alleluia, alleluia, alleluia!

With these lines Fred Pratt Green closes his jubilant hymn "When in our music God is glorified" (1972). They make a fitting beginning for this discussion. Every hymn witnesses to some aspect of the faith of those who sing it. Yet worshipers frequently pay little attention to what they affirm when they sing, and may even sing lustily what they don't believe at all.

Churches are now widely and rightly concerned about liturgical renewal. However, the rich benefits promised can hardly be attained unless understanding is joined with feeling in all aspects of worship, including the hymns. This book is a modest effort to deepen this understanding. In relation to historic and contemporary Christian thought, it attempts to identify, interpret, and evaluate the theological convictions voiced in representative hymns. It aims to stimulate thoughtful awareness of their meaning, discrimination in their use, and appreciation of their contribution to the enrichment of Christian faith and life.

Such an inquiry confronts immediately the question: Which hymns are representative? This question in turn resolves itself into two: (1) To what sources shall we turn? Especially, which of the many published collections should be consulted? (2) Within the collections chosen, which hymns should be selected for study?

With regard to the first problem, our exploration utilizes mainly the following materials:

1. The standard current hymnals of major Christian communions in Great Britain, Canada, and the United States, along with those of several smaller denominations that have published hymnbooks in the past decade or so. These sources include seven produced in Great

Britain, one in Canada, and eleven in the United States.

2. Recently published supplements to standard hymnals, seven British and three American. These aim to make available much new and worthy material without the prohibitive costs of complete revisions of existing books.

3. Roman Catholic hymnbooks. The Catholic Church does not have a long history of congregational singing. However, since Vatican II, partly because of its call for more active lay participation in the liturgy, interest in hymn-singing among Roman Catholics has greatly increased. Some unofficial publications of high quality have resulted. These make use of the hymnodic treasures of the centuries, including many Protestant hymns, and also of significant contemporary contributions. The four hymnals listed include two each from Great Britain and the United States, dating from 1971 to 1975.

4. Ecumenical hymnals, of three main types:

a. Hymnals published jointly by two or more different communions, such as the *Hymnbook for Christian Worship* (1970), produced by the Disciples of Christ and the American Baptist Convention, and *The Hymn Book* of the Anglican Church of Canada and the United Church of Canada (1971). The most notable instance of such cooperation is *With One Voice: A Hymn Book for All the Churches* (1979), first published as *The Australian Hymn Book* (1977). This is a compilation by a committee representing the Anglican, Congregational, Methodist, Presbyterian, and Roman Catholic churches. It contains 571 hymns, with a Catholic supplement including 59 more. *Cantate Domino* (1980) has been in successive editions a valuable resource for ecumenical worship, especially for groups meeting under the auspices of the World Council of Churches. The *E.A.C.C. Hymnal*, published in 1963 by the East Asia Christian Conference, manifests strong Western influence, but includes in its 200 entries an Asian section of 97 hymns either written in or translated into English.

b. Hymnals published jointly by several bodies of the same tradition. Examples are the *Lutheran Book of Worship* (1978); the Presbyterian *Worshipbook* (1972); and *The Church Hymnary* (1973), produced by five Presbyterian bodies in the British Isles.

c. Two independently edited supplemental hymnals, designed to encourage creative innovation in church music while utilizing some of the best classical hymns: *Ecumenical Praise* (1977) and *Songs of Thanks and Praise* (1980).

5. Nondenominational independent hymnbooks that aim to meet the needs of theologically conservative congregations. Their contents present a broad spectrum, including many hymns in the gospel song tradition, hymns from the common heritage covering many centuries, and some in contemporary folk idioms. Of special interest are *Hymns II* (1976), published for use by the Inter-Varsity Christian

Fellowship; *Hymns for the Living Church* (1974); and *Hymns for the Family of God* (1976).

6. Collections of "songs of celebration" in folk idioms. Marked by wide variety, these reflect the interests of various intentional communities, the charismatic movement, groups influenced by rock and other secular music, and persons dedicated to the search for justice and peace. They appear in paperback, often wirebound or looseleaf, and frequently print only the melody with guitar accompaniment. Examples include *Sound of Living Waters* (1974), *Fresh Sounds* (1976), *Cry Hosanna* (1980), *Songs of Praise*, Vol. I (1975), the Avery and Marsh songbooks, the faith and folk series edited by Peter Smith, *Sisters and Brothers Sing* (1977), *Everflowing Streams* (1981), several collections by the Benedictine Monks of Weston (Vermont) Priory, and disposable leaflets like the Roman Catholic monthly *Missalette*.

7. Collections designed to fill the needs of particular ethnic groups, largely overlooked in traditional hymnals: *Songs of Zion* (1981), a United Methodist publication that includes hymns with new arrangements by black musicians, upbeat gospels, anthems, spirituals, and Afro-American freedom songs; and *Lift Every Voice and Sing* (1981), a collection of Afro-American spirituals and other songs published by the (Episcopal) Church Hymnal Corporation.

In addition to the above, Erik Routley's *A Panorama of Christian Hymnody* (Liturgical Press, 1979) and *An English-speaking Hymnal Guide* (Liturgical Press, 1979) have been valuable resources. The former makes available the texts (without tunes) of 593 hymns, including the original texts of many hymns translated into English from Latin, French, and German.

The second procedural question concerns the selection of particular hymns to be explored. Which should be regarded as characteristic? I have found it best to examine carefully the texts in each collection in a search for the beliefs they express. This means asking of each hymn: What does it say on the themes it touches? How do its assertions relate to those of other hymns on the same subject or subjects? Various emphases emerge as dominant. Hymnic statements of these are then interpreted in the context of the witness of the biblical writings, the historic faith of the church, and the experience and thought of Christians today.

This approach obviously requires a choice of themes to be explored. In this I have been guided by the major divisions of systematic theology as historically understood. The topics are indicated by the chapter headings of Part Two. While these are not comprehensive, I believe they are representative of the belief content of our hymnody.

Hymn writers often touch on different facets of Christian faith in the same poem. For example, affirmations of the goodness and grace of God appear not only in hymns of thankful praise but also in lyrics on the saving activity of Jesus Christ or the sinfulness or worth of humanity. Hence we shall range widely in our search for the meanings of hymns on any particular theme.

The method followed admittedly runs the risk of subjectivism. However, this ever-present danger can be minimized by a constant effort really to listen to what is being said. I have tried not to include or exclude hymns and ideas simply because of my own likes and dislikes.

Part Three departs from the topical organization of Part Two. Three areas deserve more attention than they could receive if considered only incidentally under doctrinal headings: the gospel hymns of praise and personal experience still widely sung, along with the currently influential black gospel songs; the popular songs of celebration in folk idioms that have proliferated in the past several decades; and the problem of sexist language.

The book devotes relatively little attention to tunes. Since hymns are meant to be sung, tunes cannot be ignored, and in a good hymn words and music are mutually supportive. The close connection between text and tunes is discussed in Chapter 2 and assumed throughout. Yet theological meaning is conveyed chiefly by words; hence, for the purpose of this study, tunes must be secondary. This circumstance may be felt by some readers to involve a serious lack, and it is regrettable. However, it will enable us to concentrate on our central concern with what hymns have to say about the fundamental affirmations of Christian faith.

In quoting stanzas or multilinear passages of hymns I am departing from the custom of beginning every line of poetry with a capital letter. The older form is often distracting, artificially interrupting the thought of the words. This is especially true when a sentence carries over from one stanza to the next, as in the fifth and sixth stanzas of "Where cross the crowded ways of life." If we open lines with lowercase letters, except when they begin new sentences, we better preserve the continuity of thought and hence the meaning of the passage. This style of printing poetry is followed in translations of Job, The Psalms, Proverbs, and Isaiah in both the Revised Standard Version of the Bible and the New English Bible.

To assist the reader in locating the full texts of hymns and securing information regarding tunes, notes are provided listing specific sources. With few exceptions, if hymns are found in 15 or more collections, no references are given. However, data are cited for hymns that are omitted from some standard hymnals, and for new or recently discovered texts. A key to the abbreviations used precedes the Notes.

The discussion that opens Chapter 1 appeared as an article in *The*

Hymn, quarterly journal of the Hymn Society of America, in July 1981, and is used by permission.

My work on this project has benefited greatly from discussion and correspondence with colleagues and friends. Particularly helpful on the issues raised in Chapter 2 were the observations of Max Miller of Boston University, Roy A. Reed of the Methodist Theological School in Ohio, and Margaret Torgersen of Newton Centre, Massachusetts. Pearl Williams-Jones of the University of the District of Columbia rendered valuable aid through her critical comments on the section dealing with black gospel hymnody. William B. McClain of Wesley Theological Seminary, chairman of the editorial committee of *Songs of Zion,* and Carlton R. Young of Emory University, editor of the *Supplement* to the United Methodist *Book of Hymns,* graciously provided information regarding the contents of these hymnals in advance of their publication. A course on Theology in Hymnody at Andover Newton Theological School and local church study groups in Osterville, Massachusetts, and Lakeland, Florida, provided useful laboratories for exploring and testing ideas. The libraries of Andover Newton and Boston University School of Theology were invariably helpful in securing and lending books needed for research.

My son Robert, minister of music at North United Methodist Church, Indianapolis, and a member of the music faculty of Butler University, has guided me to important sources and made many constructive suggestions. The contribution of my wife, Mary, in typing, perceptive criticism of style and content, proofreading, and constant encouragement has been invaluable.

To all of the above and many others who cannot be listed here I am deeply grateful.

S.P.S.

Centerville, Cape Cod
Massachusetts

PART ONE
ORIENTATION

1

WHY DO THE WORDS MATTER?

A simple prayer, found in a hymn "for younger children" by Edith Florence Boyle Macalister (1873–1950), reiterates effectively the apostle Paul's appeal in I Cor. 14:15 for intelligence as well as spirit in both prayer and song:

> And when we sing, and when we pray,
> Help us to mean the words we say.[1]

If we are to sing and pray (often we do both at the same time) with spirit and understanding, we must mean what we say and know what we mean. Unless the hymns we use in worship express our real convictions, we might as well sing the stock market reports, the real estate ads from the daily newspaper, or a list of names from the telephone directory.

Yet there is widespread evidence of lack of attention to the ideas uttered in hymns. Few persons, it is to be hoped, will go so far as the organist who recently wrote, "In hymn-singing, words are important only to the extent that they stay out of the way of the music." But the practice of many leaders and congregations betrays an attitude disturbingly similar. Not all of the discords in church music are struck audibly by singers and accompanists. Many are produced by theological concepts out of harmony with Christian truth, by religious ideas contradictory to the actual experiences and beliefs of the worshipers, by unexamined clichés, or by words that lack any clear meaning whatever.

HYMNS AS EMBODIMENTS OF CHRISTIAN BELIEFS

Just why are understanding and coherence of thought so important? We must of course avoid overrationalizing attitudes and intentions which, defying precise formulation, are expressed in poetic

23

metaphor. We must also recognize the indispensable role of suitable and singable tunes; after all, hymns are meant to be *sung!* Yet there are solid grounds for expecting hymn texts to convey clear meanings, and for thoughtful awareness in those who sing them of what those meanings are.

1. The attainment of a sense of reality in worship requires understanding of the beliefs articulated in the hymns sung as well as in other parts of the liturgy. If the words used do not say what those who utter them really believe, the whole proceeding becomes a sham. If the words are needlessly ambiguous, they cannot mediate effectively a consciousness of the divine presence. Truly to "worship the Lord with gladness" (Ps. 100:2) requires that what we say accord with the character of the God believed in and God's aims for human life.

Søren Kierkegaard, in his comparison of worship to a drama, declares that the chief actors are not the minister or the members of the choir. Though they perform a necessary function, it is akin to that of prompters. The central action is carried out by the members of the congregation as they seek to relate their lives in praise, prayer, and commitment to the divine Spirit. If this analogy is fitting, how essential it is that we give heed to the meaning of the lines we utter! The best actors and actresses do not stop with memorization, but think and feel their way into the content of their lines until in a profound way they *become,* during the play, the characters they portray. Such identification is not too much to expect in the singing of hymns in worship, but it demands effort to grasp and appropriate the meanings expressed, and also to select hymns that articulate the real beliefs of the singers.

2. Hymns provide a singularly appropriate medium for communicating the central meaning of the Christian life as the believer's response to God. They can do this most adequately only if they reflect accurately the worshipers' perception of God's action and the quality of life it calls forth. Christian faith arises as a joyous, grateful response to the creative and redemptive action of God, and the life that results is the believer's continuing answer in trust, love, and obedience to God's manifold activity. Thus the whole life of the Christian centers in and issues from his or her relation to God, particularly to God as disclosed in the life, teachings, death, and resurrection of Jesus Christ.

The same motivation is operative in Christian worship, including hymnody. This understanding of the divine-human relationship had much to do with Isaac Watts's trailblazing departure from the previous assumption of English Calvinists that Christians are expected merely to sing the Bible, especially the psalms. As Louis F. Benson has shown, for Watts the Bible is God's word to us which we are personally to appropriate. Our hymns, then, represent our response to God's utterance, "our word to God." This can be expressed in biblical language only as we make that language our own. Thus Watts "laid the ground for the free hymn of human composure."[2]

A fascinating parallel is found in the thought and practice of Nicolaus Ludwig von Zinzendorf (1700–1760), who wrote: "The hymnal is a kind of response to the Bible, an echo and an extension thereof. In the Bible one perceives how the Lord communicates with mankind; and in the hymnal how mankind communicates with the Lord."[3]

3. Theology, good, bad, or indifferent, is present in all hymns, making it important to identify just what we are upholding when we sing. The beliefs involved may be affirmed or denied, explicit or implicit, intentional or incidental, eloquently or crudely formulated. In any case, all hymns make some kind of theological statement; they have something to say about God, the divine character and purpose, the nature and destiny of human life, the way of salvation, human responsibility before God, and related matters. When we are voicing concerns as ultimate as these it is important that we pay attention to the content of our words.

If we sing with Samuel Rodigast (1649–1708),

> Whate'er our God ordains is right, . . .
> wherefore to him we leave it all,[4]

we are clearly asserting a view of God's work in history quite different from that stated by William DeWitt Hyde (1858–1917):

> Creation's Lord, we give thee thanks
> that this thy world is incomplete,
> that battle calls our marshaled ranks,
> that work awaits our hands and feet.[5]

Elizabeth C. Clephane (1830–1869), taking her stand "beneath the cross of Jesus," is "content to let the world go by"; whereas Ian Ferguson, writing in 1967, accepts responsibility for the hungry and oppressed:

> I am my brother's keeper,
> I dare not wash my hands.[6]

Can thoughtful Christians avoid noticing the widely divergent understanding embodied in these verses? Can we ignore the apparent contradictions and sing as though they did not exist?

4. Precisely because hymns express religious convictions in a form used by large numbers of people, they are an indispensable vehicle for teaching Christian faith and life. Both defenders and critics of orthodox faith have used hymns to express their ideas. Arius of Alex-

andria (ca. 250–336) sought through song to popularize his view of
Christ the Son as a created being subordinate to the Father, while
supporters of Nicene Christology such as Ambrose of Milan (340–397)
countered with hymns like:

> O splendor of God's glory bright,
> from light eternal bringing light.[7]

The history of the church presents many witnesses to the pedagog-
ical effectiveness of church music. Augustine bears eloquent testimony to the contribution of the church's hymns to his own spiritual
life: "How greatly did I weep in Thy hymns and canticles, deeply
moved by the voices of Thy sweet-speaking Church! The voices
flowed into my ears, and the truth poured forth into my heart."[8]

Martin Luther, in the preface to his *Geystliche Gesangk Büchleyn*
(Spiritual Hymn Booklet) of 1524, identifies his aim with that of Paul
in I Cor. 14:15 and Col. 3:16: "to sing spiritual songs and Psalms
heartily unto the Lord so that God's word and Christian teaching
might be instilled and implanted in many ways."[9]

Reliable clues to the representative theological emphases of the
Wesleyan evangelical revival are found in the hymns of Charles
Wesley and those translated by John Wesley. The Arminian doctrine
of the God-given freedom of all persons to respond to divine grace
appears unmistakably when Charles sings:

> Come, sinners, to the gospel feast;
> let every soul be Jesus' guest;
> ye need not one be left behind,
> for God hath bidden all mankind.[10]

The characteristic Wesleyan stress on the possibility of "holiness of
heart and life" comes to expression repeatedly, as in Charles Wesley's
familiar lines:

> Finish, then, thy new creation;
> pure and spotless let us be.
> Let us see thy great salvation
> perfectly restored in thee.

The effectiveness of hymns as teaching instruments springs not
only from the fact that they embody basic beliefs but from the form
or manner of that embodiment. Here three considerations deserve
mention. First is the cumulative power of repetition. The reiteration,
over the years, of affirmations concerning God, Jesus Christ, the
human situation, and the way of salvation affects powerfully if imper-
ceptibly the real beliefs of the singers.

Secondly, the fact that hymns link ideas with emotion gives them special teaching power. Music has a distinctive capacity to touch the feelings, and this is accentuated when music is a channel for meanings expressed in poetic language, especially when those meanings concern the rich common heritage of Christian faith, with its personal experiences of sorrow and joy, sin and deliverance, defeat and victory, disappointment and hope, and human and divine love. Questionable as well as true ideas may be strengthened when sung. A recent hymn by Fred Pratt Green (b. 1903) witnesses eloquently to the profound positive contribution of the musical idiom:

> When in our music God is glorified,
> and adoration leaves no room for pride,
> it is as though the whole creation cried:
>   Alleluia, alleluia, alleluia!
> So has the Church, in litany and song,
> in faith and love, through centuries of wrong,
> borne witness to the truth in ev'ry tongue:
>   Alleluia, alleluia, alleluia![11]

Thirdly, the frequent use of poetic imagery, especially metaphorical language, enables hymns to deepen insight and enrich understanding in ways not readily accessible through literal prose alone. Without disparaging reason, one can say that metaphors provide a valuable extrarational means of conveying the richness of the faith given to the church.

An additional aspect of the teaching function of hymnody is the opportunity afforded by new hymns to show the contemporary relevance and significance of Christian faith. Recent publications include a variety of hymns that deal seriously with the challenge of, or the bearing of Christian insights on, such problems as the space age, technology, ecology, human oppression and exploitation, atomic energy, and nuclear war. Hymns like "God of concrete, God of steel," by Richard G. Jones (b. 1926),[12] "Earth and all stars," by Herbert F. Brokering (b. 1926),[13] and "O God of every nation," by William W. Reid, Jr. (b. 1923),[14] relate faith in God illuminatingly to industry, scientific research, higher education, and the threats of materialism, militarism, and racism in human relations.

5. Closely linked to the teaching function of hymns is the fact that when they voice the gospel effectively they play an important part in the church's evangelistic witness. Among those present whenever Christians gather for worship are likely to be not only the fully engaged but also the lukewarm and the half convinced, as well as some honest skeptics and sincere seekers, including children and youth who have not yet made any basic value commitments. What the hymns say to such persons may make a real difference in their re-

sponse to the appeal of the message declared. The important role of
hymn-singing in the major evangelistic campaigns of the past century is well known.

However, the very power of hymnody to win a hearing makes it
imperative that heed be given to the content of what is heard. Frequently multitudes are attracted by a message in song and sermon
that promises individual comfort and peace, makes the Christian way
falsely easy, and ignores the wholeness of the New Testament gospel.
Hymns that offer a partial, truncated version of the good news may
win converts, but not responsible Christians equipped to embody the
healing, transforming love of God in a sick and broken world.

Fortunately, there are many hymns old and new that can and do
offer a wholistic, positive witness. Christian hymnody has demonstrated its ability to strengthen the faith of believers, to move the
almost persuaded, and to deepen as well as to symbolize the love that
the Christian community exists to incarnate.

THE FOCUS

The considerations just urged should make clear the need for the
kind of exploration attempted in these pages. It has six overlapping
aims that combine theoretical and practical interests.

1. It seeks to heighten awareness of the thought content of hymns,
to alert the reader to the fact that they do make or imply theological
affirmations.

2. It attempts to make plain that these affirmations play an important role in hymnody, worship, and life.

3. It aims to identify the major beliefs expressed in typical hymns.

4. It endeavors to interpret the beliefs embodied in hymns in order
to increase awareness of their meanings, the experiences they reflect,
and the insights they contribute to Christian understanding.

5. It ventures to evaluate the truth content of representative
hymns. With regard to any given hymn or passage at least two questions should be raised: Does it express what the singer really believes
and means? Is it consistent with historic Christian faith?

6. Interwoven with these concerns are several others that might
be regarded as relatively—but only relatively—more practical:

   a. To enhance the contribution of hymns to corporate worship.

   b. To facilitate mutual understanding and a cooperative relationship between pastors, church musicians, and other worshiping
Christians with regard to the function and quality of music in worship.

   c. To increase the service that hymns can render in heightening
faith in and personal awareness of the transforming presence of God.

d. To enable hymns to play their part in equipping Christians for caring relationships with other persons and responsible participation in society.

BASIC DEFINITIONS

In a discussion that seeks maximum clarity of understanding, an author is responsible for stating just what he or she means by essential words repeatedly used. A few definitions are therefore in order.

Derived from the Greek *hymnos,* a hymn broadly understood is simply a song of praise honoring a god or gods, a hero, a nation, or some other entity or reality. Strictly speaking, in Christian worship it has God as its object. Thus for Augustine a hymn is "a song with praise to God." However, this is too narrow a conception to cover accurately what hymns are in actual practice. Though most are explicitly or by implication addressed to God, many take other forms; cases in point are "O holy city, seen of John," "Book of books, our people's strength," and "O day of resurrection." Some refer to God in the third person: "All my hope in God is founded." Others are calls to decision or action, such as "Once to every man and nation" and "O brother man, fold to thy heart thy brother." Still others express aspiration: "O for a closer walk with God." Nevertheless, in all of these there is a reference to or an orientation toward God; they seek to link the lives of the singers to the divine purpose, so that God does become the central point of reference. Like the Colossian Christians (Col. 3:16, RSV), Christians today, in singing worship, may encourage and teach one another the meaning for life of their common relation to God.

As a literary form, a hymn is usually a lyric poem with a metrical and strophic text. Literally, a lyric is a poem suited for singing to the accompaniment of a lyre or harp, but, more broadly, it is simply a poem appropriate for singing. As distinguished from epic or dramatic poetry, a lyric poem is one that gives voice to the poet's feelings rather than dealing with external events. Hymns are therefore good examples of lyrics, since they express the feelings, attitudes, needs, and commitments of their authors and those who use them.

This use by persons other than the author calls attention to another important mark of a hymn, its fitness for singing by groups of people. By no means do all lyrics qualify as hymns in this respect. Those that do so may also have rich value for devotional use by individuals, but only poems that can be readily used by small or large assemblies of broadly like-minded persons can be regarded as hymns.

In summary, therefore, we may say that a hymn is a lyric poem that is suitable for singing in corporate worship and that voices the worshipers' feelings and attitudes toward God and God's intention for their lives.

The term "hymnody" is the English form of the Greek *hymnōidia*, a combination of *hymnos* with *ōidia*, a song or a singing (cf. English "ode"). Thus etymologically, hymnody means the singing or composition of hymns. However, it has taken on the additional meaning of hymns considered collectively. We shall use the word primarily in this sense, to designate the totality of the Christian heritage of song.

What, then, is theology? Also Greek in origin, it is *logos* of *theos*, thought or thinking about God, "God-talk." But since God for Christian faith is the ultimate ground of all that is, theology has to do with the relation of God, as known or believed in, to the whole of life. Hence any exploration of the meaning of God for any aspect of our experience is theological. When we think theologically, we try to see all of life in the perspective of our relation to God.

More precisely, Christian theology is the thoughtful inquiry into the meaning of the faith called forth by God's self-disclosing activity, especially in Jesus Christ. It seeks through critical examination to discover the truths implied in the history and experience of the Christian community and to interpret them in the most intelligible and persuasive manner.

With reference to hymnody, the theologian—and this should include every serious Christian—wants to find out what the songs used in worship say about such themes as God and God's active presence in the world; the significance of Jesus Christ; the worth, alienation, and re-creation of human beings; the church and its mission; the Christian life; and human destiny. Further, she or he asks whether these assertions make sense, whether they express authentically the basic convictions of the Christian community, and whether they fit what we know from the scientific study of the physical order and the lives of persons in society.

Theology in hymnody, therefore, is the study of the meaning and truth of the faith we sing. The increased understanding thus gained, in addition to being valuable in itself, should enrich our worship and deepen our sensitivity to the divine presence in the whole of life.

2

HYMN TUNES AND THEOLOGICAL MEANING

When we focus attention on the text of hymns, the question of music inevitably arises: Is the music then of little or no importance? What is the contribution of the tune? What does it have to do with what the words "say"? Does the tune itself "say" anything? Is there any theological meaning in the music to which hymn texts are set?

The role of music in the Hebrew-Christian tradition has not been solely that of an accessory to words. Psalm 149 calls on the faithful to praise the Lord by singing a new song, but Psalm 150 continues:

> Praise him with fanfares on the trumpet,
>   praise him upon lute and harp;
> praise him with tambourines and dancing,
>   praise him with flute and strings;
> praise him with the clash of cymbals,
>   praise him with triumphant cymbals.

In this spirit the church has for centuries enriched its life with instrumental music, often with no reference whatever to words. Whether in worship services or in special musical events, the organ, many other instruments played individually or in various combinations, and sometimes full orchestras have been utilized for their religious value. What is that value? Does instrumental music without voices simply evoke a mood conducive to prayerful meditation, or does it somehow also make listeners aware of that mysterious reality on which their finite lives ultimately depend? Can music as such, hence hymn tunes without texts, mediate truth?

MUSIC, REALITY, AND RELIGIOUS FAITH

When Voyager II was launched into space it carried, in a packet of items exemplifying our human culture, a recording of the

31

Cavatina of Beethoven's *Quartet in B-flat Major,* Opus 130, performed by the Guarneri String Quartet. The Cavatina, writes Robert
McAfee Brown, "is an evocation of transfigured sorrow—purified,
cleansed, and shared—a creation that communicates more of whatever is the nature of ultimate reality than any theological prose I
have ever read."[1] Since theology seeks to discover and share truth
about the ultimate, Brown seems to be asserting that the Cavatina
communicates truth. However, he makes no attempt to describe
what the music conveys—perhaps because the "whatever" defies
translation into theological prose. Had he made the attempt, he
might have interpreted transfigured sorrow in terms of a cross at the
heart of reality—a suffering love that cleanses, renews, and brings
victory over sin and death. Yet it seems unlikely that Beethoven
would have aroused such reflections had not Brown brought to his
listening his own enlightened faith.

Thoughtful persons differ considerably in their responses to sublime music. The humanist Corliss Lamont, facing along with theists
the certainty of death, prepared a funeral service for those who wish
to affirm the worth and dignity of human life but do not believe in
a more-than-human God. His service makes use of choice poetry and
exalted instrumental music, but it offers no suggestion that the music
communicates anything whatever about ultimate reality.[2] Apparently the same music may deepen in the committed Christian a
consciousness of God and in the humanist a heightened sense of the
tragic nobility of human life, with no reference to God.

A similar conclusion is reached if we note the impossibility of any
sharp differentiation between "sacred" and "secular" music. As is
well known, frequently the melodies of familiar secular folk songs,
even barroom ballads, have been taken over as settings for religious
texts, thus becoming part of the church's hymnodic tradition.

The tune PASSION CHORALE, which appears five times in Bach's
St. Matthew Passion, and which provides the setting for the hymn
"O sacred Head, now wounded," first appeared as the tune of a love
song, "My heart is distracted by the charms of a gentle maiden." The
carol "What child is this?" uses a melody from an old English ballad
about the "Lady Greene Sleeves." Charles Wesley's "Come, O thou
Traveler unknown" is set in the United Methodist *Book of Hymns* to
the traditional Scottish melody "The Caledonian hunt's delight," to
which Robert Burns wrote the song "Ye banks and braes o' bonnie
Doon." The frequency and readiness with which secular tunes have
been adapted to hymnodic use argues strongly against assigning any
definable theological meaning to music as such.

There seems to be no discernible line of demarcation between
sacred and secular music. A New England clergyman who thought
otherwise once asked a Moravian youth, who had just joined in per-

forming some chamber music by Haydn on a Saturday afternoon, whether he would use the same instruments the next day to worship God. The young man replied, "And should you, sir, pray with the same mouth tomorrow with which you are now eating sausages?" The Moravian refusal to divide music neatly into secular and religious is a good model for others to follow. Music without words unquestionably has power to move, disturb, or bring emotional assurance, but its explicit theological significance depends on the beliefs of those who compose, hear, or perform it. Believers in God will relate their experience to the divine presence. Others will ascribe it to some impersonal reality or simply enjoy it or be disturbed by it without referring it to anything beyond themselves. It may be given, but does not require, a theistic interpretation, and it does not in itself tell us who God is or what God's purposes are for human life.

Nevertheless, there is evidence that music may shed some light on the nature of what is, and therefore on the reality that Christians address when they worship. Neither Arthur Schopenhauer (1788–1860) nor Friedrich Nietzsche (1844–1900) believed in a personal Creator God, but both devoted much attention to music, and in different ways they regard it as a symbol of the dynamism of reality. Schopenhauer maintains that music, unlike the other arts, speaks of "the will itself"—the universal will-to-be.[3] In Nietzsche's view "music symbolizes the primordial pain in the heart of the Primal Unity, . . . a sphere which is beyond and before all phenomena."[4] It is "a repetition and a recast of the world."[5]

These philosophers thus agree with Brown that music discloses something at the heart of things, but the three do not agree on what that something is. In this regard there are two main traditions in Western thought. The dominant one, at least until the nineteenth century, takes its cue from the mathematical aspects of music, and stresses the order, rationality, harmony, and stability of the world as expressed in musical compositions. The other, more impressed by the elements of movement, vigor, feeling, and uninhibited vivacity in music, emphasizes the energy, creative freedom, and unforeseeable novelty in the universe. The former tradition is represented by Confucius, Pythagoras, Plato, Gregory of Nyssa, Augustine, and Boethius; by the medieval inclusion of music with arithmetic, geometry, and astronomy in the division of the seven liberal arts known as the quadrivium; and in modern times by Kepler and Leibniz, and in Thomas Browne's "music of the spheres." The latter tradition appears in Schopenhauer and Nietzsche and in modern composers like Igor Stravinsky, Arnold Schönberg, Sergei Prokofiev, Béla Bartók, and Maurice Ravel, in whose works new scales, harmonies, dissonance, and other tonal effects reflect the agitation, ferment, and restlessness of contemporary life.

Nietzsche himself thought that in the last analysis order, form, and reason serve freedom and life—not the other way around. Yet for him both principles are essential, and both are "artistic tendencies which burst forth from nature itself."[6] Here I believe he points us in the right direction. Though individual pieces of music do not yield conceptual truths concerning reality, music as an art form does provide data that help us to understand our world. The musical evidence suggests a universe of free activity, generating change and novelty, within an enduring structure of rational, dependable order.

The connection between music and mathematics is inescapable. The relations of notes and octaves in the scale, the correlation between pitch and wavelengths, rhythm as the ordered alternation of contrasting elements, the uniformly recurring beats and accents that comprise meter, and the laws of harmony all seem to manifest a pattern which human composers do not make but find, and which all must acknowledge. Even the variations represented by the chromatic, diatonic, heptatonic, hexatonic, and pentatonic scales, along with the different divisions found in the twelve-tone and seven-tone scales, and the five-tone scale used for centuries by Chinese composers, are diversified arrangements within a generally recognized structure. They represent an effort by composers to break with the past by introducing something new in music. Yet the use of the twelve-tone row is one of the most intellectually constructed techniques of musical composition. Further evidence of the mathematical structure of music is found currently in electronic music and the music produced by synthesizers.

However, within the framework observed by all composers are elements that defy any neat, placid arrangement. The sounds of music exhibit dynamic activity, unpredictable movement, and energetic expressions of unrestrained emotion. Dissonance as well as consonance is displayed. Music may "soothe a savage breast," but it may also excite both the savage and the allegedly civilized breast to savage acts. Possibly there is operative in music something akin to Werner Heisenberg's principle of uncertainty in physics or the emergence of random mutations in biological evolution. Whatever else reality may be, it is not cut-and-dried but dynamic and open-ended. It is not surprising if music manifests the indeterminacy-within-order discernible in other areas.

One positive aspect of this indeterminacy is the creativity disclosed in musical composition and performance. Like other artists, composers of music are constantly producing works that did not exist before. Similarly, performers are always offering new interpretations; no two performances of the same composition are identical. Such novelty lends support to the notion of creativity in the nature of things.

We may conclude, then, that music provides dependable data on which a defensible interpretation of reality may be based. It is one of the aesthetic values, which along with intellectual, moral, religious, and other values comprise an indispensable basis for any thoughtful inquiry into the kind of universe we live in. Such investigation must of course utilize the methods and results of the physical, biological, and social sciences, but it must be equally concerned to learn all that can be learned from the whole range of our human experience of value or worth, in which music plays an important role.

Musical compositions without words cannot warrant specific statements regarding God's goodness or love, God's purpose for human life, or the extent of God's power or wisdom. However, the orderly structure and dynamism of music may justly be taken, along with other empirical data, as a basis for critical thought about God. So great are our human differences—genetic, geographical, social, economic, political, and philosophical—that persons of religious faith will interpret the data differently from those with a nonreligious orientation, and religious believers themselves may not see eye to eye. Nevertheless, people of faith may find in music support for some beliefs; for example, in God's intelligence, creativity, eternity, or temporality. Faith is not inevitably produced—but it may be enhanced—by musical sensitivity.

Caution must be exercised with respect to the relation to reality of music in the form of hymn tunes. Such tunes provide only a limited basis for judgment. This is true because of their miniature length, their strophic repetition, and the regularity required for ease in group singing. Yet they cannot be isolated from other musical forms. They provide part of the evidence, and the data they yield do not contradict what we learn elsewhere. Rather, hymn tunes manifest in their own way both the order and the freedom noted in music as a whole.

THE RELATION OF TUNE AND TEXT

Though hymn tunes do not in themselves convey definite theological ideas, when they are joined with texts they may strengthen or undermine the meanings expressed. In three important respects they influence the impact of the words sung.

1. Like other music, they are capable of stirring and expressing deep emotion. In a classic passage John Milton describes how pealing organ and full-voiced choir unite to

> dissolve me into ecstasies,
> and bring all Heaven before mine eyes.[7]

Fear, hope, anger, gratitude, sympathy, love, enthusiasm, courage—
these and many other feelings find in music appropriate avenues of
expression. Romantic music may mediate passion. Martial music may
arouse patriotic feeling. Emotional conflict may be indicated musi-
cally by contrasting motifs. In Baroque music, formations utilizing
the chromatic scale are used to express grief or lament, as in the
repetitions of the bass in the "Crucifixus" of Bach's *B-Minor Mass.*
Music may also give voice to widely varying degrees of depth and
intensity.

By linking feeling with ideas stated in words, religious song provides a medium by which emotions are directed and ideas are
charged with power. The time-encompassing faith of Isaac Watts's
"Our God, our help in ages past" is perfectly phrased in the stately
cadences of the tune ST. ANNE. The music of "There is a balm in
Gilead" voices effectively the cry of the wounded sinner and the
affirmative answer of the gospel. The tune HAMBURG is peculiarly
suited to express both the repentance and the commitment aroused
in those who with sensitivity "survey the wondrous cross." Beethoven's HYMN TO JOY is a superb vehicle for the words of Henry van
Dyke's "Joyful, joyful, we adore thee." The courage called for in John
Bunyan's "He who would valiant be" is heightened by the moving
melody of the tune ST. DUNSTAN.

2. Equally clear is the contribution of music to the moods evoked
by hymn texts. A mood may signify a pervasive attitude, the totality
of the dispositions that comprise the dominant emotional character
of a person, or it may refer to a particular temper or quality of mind
as affected by emotion. Music may express moods in either sense, and
different forms of music serve different moods. Alexander L. Ringer
points out that the rhythmic balance of medieval monophonic plainsong breathes an atmosphere of faith and inward peace, while the
strictly metrical rhythm and mathematically definable structures of
most eighteenth-century music mirror the rational temper of the
Enlightenment.[8]

In hymns it is obvious that the mood of the music should fit that
of the words. When it does, the tune sustains or intensifies the mood
of the text and serves to reinforce its message. A valued musician
friend, Margaret Torgersen, illustrates this by reference to the aspiration expressed in the tenor line of CWM RHONDDA (used in both
"God of grace and God of glory" and "Guide me, O thou great
Jehovah"); the somber, reflective mood of "I wonder as I wander,"
furthered especially by the low tone at the end; and the gladness
occasioned by the story of "The first Nowell" and excitingly voiced
by the crescendo of the four Nowells in the refrain.

3. Hymn tunes may fortify or weaken the convictions embodied in
the words. Though Louis G. Nuechterlein regards the text of a hymn

as inherently more important than the tune, he acknowledges that the tune is likely to be the dominant factor in the acceptance and use of a hymn. Most often it is the tune that "determines the fate of the text. An appealing tune can sustain poetry of poor quality; an unappealing tune, however, is rarely able to give much help even to a first-rate text." Therefore, though a text ought not to be evaluated wholly on the basis of its linkage with a particular tune, it is most likely to reach and move congregations "if it is matched with a tune that sustains, heightens, and intensifies its theological message as well as its poetic mood."[9]

The truth of this judgment is illustrated both positively and negatively in the tunes of *Hymns Ancient and Modern* (1861), the representative hymnal of the Oxford movement. Its new tunes, intended to infuse new life into Christian worship, were chiefly the work of the editor, William H. Monk, and three others, John B. Dykes, Joseph Barnby, and Sir John Stainer. Louis F. Benson writes that these tunes are "beautiful music of their kind," with a "distinctly spiritual message," but that they do not notably exhilarate our feelings or nourish our Christian virility.

> The new melodies were sentimental rather than strenuous, and often plaintive. . . . They express more the feeling of the Oxford Revival than its resolution, the spiritual sentiment of the individual rather than the sense of corporate worship. . . . They have a curious gift of suggesting to the imagination that a yearning after holiness is the way to God's peace.[10]

Most of the tunes referred to by Benson are no longer used. However, the four tunes of Dykes that survive in the majority of present-day hymnals are strong tunes happily linked with the thought of the words: NICAEA, MELITA, LUX BENIGNA, and ST. AGNES, which provide settings respectively for "Holy, holy, holy," "Eternal Father, strong to save," "Lead, kindly Light," and "Jesus, the very thought of thee."

Hymn texts with shallow or theologically questionable content have sometimes been given long life through their connection with lively, easily singable tunes. Thus "Savior, like a Shepherd lead us," a children's hymn, continues to be sung by adult congregations who enjoy the melody despite the childish words. It seems unlikely that many Methodists would still sing Charles Wesley's "Arise, my soul, arise," with its substitutionary penal view of the atonement and its unscriptural "My God is reconciled," were it not joined to the stirring tune LENOX, by Lewis Edson.

Erik Routley calls attention to tunes that fail to express the newness, affirmation, and tension of the gospel, being marked instead by a complacency and dreamy sentimentality, and by a world denial that is also essentially faith denial because of its reliance on security. Some tunes are marked by "a kind of dull negation" that overlooks the demands involved in acceptance of the good news of God's redemptive action. The sheer liveliness of many of the gospel songs of the Sankey era, which rely heavily on musical platitudes and clichés of rhythm and phrase, involves "a resurrection without passion: factitious sentiment generated by quickly-resolved discords in the harmony is substituted for Passion."[11]

Many such tunes are joined with texts that are equally defective. The glibness and triviality of the tune CONVERSE fit well the words of "What a friend we have in Jesus," which conceives of Jesus solely as one who bears our sins and griefs, shields us from care, and provides solace and refuge from trouble. This message was no doubt appropriate for the author's sorrowing mother, for whom it was written, but it omits completely the responsibility that should be shouldered by Christian worshipers who are true disciples of Jesus.

Happily, there are in church music many outstanding examples of a mutually reinforcing connection between tune and text. Routley notes that while some tunes miss the tension of the gospel, others by using counterpoint—interweaving with the main melody another independent but related melody—impart an awareness of "the controversy of the gospel"—and of the conflicts encountered in real life. He mentions the works of W. K. Stanton and Herbert Murrill as examples.[12] In hymnody, as indicated by Louis F. Benson, this quality is exhibited by some of the old psalm tunes,[13] though in the nature of the case music written for singing by the average congregation will rarely be contrapuntal.

A moving example of a positive relation of music to words appears in Bach's *St. Matthew Passion* at the point where the Evangelist tells how Peter, hearing the cock crow a third time, "went out and wept bitterly" (Matt. 26:75; Luke 22:62). The musical accompaniment, with its descending chromatic notes, is a perfect expression of overwhelming guilt and sorrow.

In hymnody, among many notable historic instances of tune-text harmony is Johann J. Schütz's "Sing praise to God who reigns above," set to a tune of the Bohemian Brethren well named MIT FREUDEN ZART (with tender joys). Contrasting illustrations of pairings of text and tune are found in the traditional "Just as I am, without one plea" and the youth hymn "Just as I am, thine own to be." In the former, William B. Bradbury's plaintive WOODWORTH provides a fitting accompaniment for the repentant spirit of persons who, "poor, wretched, blind," accept with grateful assurance the offer of one who comes to "welcome, pardon, cleanse, relieve." In the latter a vigorous, buoyant tune by Joseph Barnby reflects the unreserved dedication of those who "in the glad morning of their day" commit all their capacities to the service of the Lord of their lives.

Several twentieth-century hymns manifest a similar congruity. The strong Irish traditional melody SLANE, most familiar as the tune of "Be thou my vision," is also the setting for "Lord of all hopefulness, Lord of all joy," by Jan Struther (1901–1953), which in beautiful poetry asks for the bliss, strength, love, and peace of God at the break, the noon, the eve, and the end of the day.[14] Both freshness and strength mark LOMBARD STREET, by Frederick George Russell (1925), which accompanies Albert F. Bayly's "O Lord of every shining constellation" (1950, alt. 1968).[15]

Two other quite recent hymns exemplify superlatively the effectiveness of a happy marriage of music and words. The searching lines beginning, "God who created this garden of earth," by Richard G. Jones, six stanzas in all, are set to QUEDLINBURG, from a chorale by J. C. Kittel (1732–1809). They move the singer, identified with the first and second Adam, from disobedience through a fervent prayer for forgiveness to liberation and newness of life.[16]

In "Walk tall, Christian," by Miriam Drury (1969), the believer is admonished to walk tall, true, free, and proud, but he or she is saved from arrogance by reliance on divine grace. The tune WOOSTER, by Richard T. Gore (1969), breathes confidence based not on human self-righteousness but on the strength of God gladly accepted:

> Walk true, Christian, / keep faith come weal or woe;
> to upright, pure, forgiving souls, / his bounties overflow.[17]

In commending the wedding of music and words I do not mean to suggest that a particular tune must be linked with one text "as long as they both shall live." Here bigamy and even polygamy are sometimes quite legitimate. Some tunes can be sung in different styles and tempos with different texts and thereby project a variety of moods. A good example is OLD 113TH, probably by Matthäus Greiter (ca. 1500–1552). Most familiar as the setting of Isaac Watts's hymn based on Psalm 146, "I'll praise my Maker while I've breath,"[18] it was used earlier by Lutherans for their chorales and by Calvinists for their metrical psalms. It appears in the Genevan Psalter (1551) for Psalm 113, and in the Ainsworth Psalter (1612), brought to Plymouth by the Pilgrims, for Psalm 136. It is the tune used in Lutheran hymnals in Germany for "O Mensch, bewein dein Sünde gross" (O man, bewail your grievous sin), by Sebald Heyden (1494–1561). Bach's chorale prelude for organ on this theme is quiet, meditative, poignant, fluid, and rather slow, evoking a mood far removed from the joyful exuberance of "I'll praise my Maker."

Fortunately, the linkage of a strong text to a weak, difficult, or unsingable tune need not mean that the value of the words must be lost. Individuals may use the text in private devotion, and leaders of worship may have it read as poetry without feeling compelled to urge that singing be attempted.

In succeeding chapters we shall focus attention almost entirely on the meaning of hymn texts. Yet we cannot afford to forget that the words are intended to be sung, and that the musical settings often determine whether the message, however worthy it may be, will win a hearing. We shall therefore look constantly for tunes that reinforce and enhance the import of the words, and rejoice when we find them.

3

CRITERIA OF EVALUATION

If the beliefs voiced in hymns are important, we need to identify them, to ask whether they express our real convictions, and to inquire how they relate to the beliefs of the Christian community, past and present. Such questions may lead us to reexamine our own beliefs and those taken for granted by other Christians; hence we shall need to be open to the possibility of new insights gained through the hymns we study. Our primary concern, however, will be to discover hymns that offer defensible, coherent, and life-enriching interpretations of Christian faith.

Such a process involves evaluation, which if carried out intelligently entails the use of consciously adopted norms. The introductory statements of many hymnal committees state clearly the norms that guided their painstaking work, and ordinarily these include theological guidelines. Congregations also need to exercise discrimination in using the resulting collections. To some degree they do this constantly, if tacitly, by singing some hymns frequently, others rarely, and still others never. The concern of this book is that such choices be made more thoughtfully and related to the Christian faith of those who make them.

"Test everything," urges the apostle Paul; "hold fast what is good" (I Thess. 5:21). Such testing requires criteria. If these criteria can be clearly stated and applied, the resulting judgments should be more honest, intelligent, and objective. We need a better basis for judgment than our own likes and dislikes. Subjectivity is hard enough to avoid at best, but it is certain to increase in the absence of explicit standards.

It is important, however, that evaluation be primarily constructive. It is easy to find fault with hymns in wide use, and sometimes negative criticism is appropriate and necessary, but our chief aim must be that of increasing appreciation for the hymns that express authentic Christian faith. We should likewise keep in mind that most hymnals are used by very diverse constituencies. They must therefore include some hymns that will not meet the needs of, and may even be objectionable to, considerable numbers of persons for whom the books are published. Respect for sincere differences in preference can be maintained, not by elitist elimination of all questionable songs from publication, but simply by omission from use of those which particular congregations or groups find unacceptable.

SUGGESTED GUIDELINES

General

Though our primary guidelines will be theological, we should remember that hymns are lyric poetry and therefore subject to judgment according to the canons of good literature. Questions having to do with literary merit need to be raised. The following are pertinent questions to ask of a particular hymn:

1. Is it structurally sound? Does it have a central theme and organic unity of ideas? Does it manifest progression of thought rather than repetitiveness or circularity? Is it brief enough to be sung as a unit in worship?

2. Are its lines poetic, euphonious, and aesthetic; or trite, grating, and slipshod?

3. Are its words and phrases put together in orderly, connected fashion, or does it disregard generally accepted laws of grammar and syntax?

4. Do the accented syllables conform to a regular rhythm suitable for singing, and do the units of thought end with the ends of lines, avoiding "run-ons"? These conditions do not apply to poetry as such, but they do disqualify many poems of superior quality for use as hymns.

5. Is its language simple, concrete, and direct, using mainly words in common use; or stiff, archaic, ornate, or florid?

6. Does its verbiage balance the intellectual and the emotional, avoiding both dry abstraction and effusive sentimentality?

7. Does it say something clearly and coherently without being coldly and precisely propositional?

In the preface of *The Hymn Book* of the Anglican Church of Canada and the United Church of Canada, the editors state that hymns must be of such quality that "they are worthy of being offered to God in praise and reverence with integrity." Observance of the above criteria should ensure such worthiness from the standpoint of literary merit. However, songs intended to relate worshipers to God "with integrity" need to heed standards of religious truth as well as those of good literature. These will now claim our attention.

Theological

Before we look at criteria that apply to hymns alone, it should be helpful to relate to hymns norms that are basic to the entire Christian quest for truth. Here the four doctrinal guidelines adopted by The United Methodist Church may prove suggestive, since they are ecumenical rather than narrowly denominational: Scripture, tradition, experience, and reason.[1] These will be weighted differently by different communions and individuals, but all of them are recognized to some degree by all Christian groups. They are offered here not as a rigid pattern, but as a constructive basis of thoughtful appraisal by all who wish to reflect theologically on the texts of our hymns.

Since the Scriptures are the church's earliest witness to the creative, redemptive, renewing, and fulfilling activity of God in human life and history, they constitute our primary point of reference. With regard to any hymn, therefore, we need to ask whether it is in harmony with the testimony of the biblical writings. This means not looking for proof texts, but relating the basic message of a hymn to relevant biblical passages interpreted in the context of the Bible as a whole, in the light of the inquiries of competent scholars, and with openness to the guidance of the Holy Spirit. Our hymnody is full of biblical language and imagery and informed by biblical faith. Hence we shall want to ask how authentically a particular hymn reflects some facet of the truth contained in the Scriptures.

The New Testament writings themselves were the product of the primitive Christian community, and the determination of the canonical books was the work of the church. Hence church tradition, the deposit of the experiences and beliefs of successive Christian communities, becomes another important doctrinal norm. This conviction assumes that God continues to manifest self-giving love throughout the history of the movement begun through the coming of Jesus Christ. Therefore hymns may be expected to embody what has been given to and learned by the church through the centuries, and their claim to truth may rightfully be judged in part by their relation to that heritage. Both the traditions of particular communions and the totality of the ecumenical tradition must be carefully considered.

Christian faith involves not only intellectual assent to biblical testimonies or church creeds but personal religious experience as well. No claims to truth about God are likely to win more than token support apart from some firsthand awareness of the divine presence. For Christians this means especially "living through" an assurance of the forgiving and transforming love of God disclosed in Jesus Christ and witnessed to by the indwelling of the Holy Spirit. Such experience is corporate as well as individual; it is not exclusive but shared.

Hence it relates the Christian to the total community of faith, and it brings that community into responsible relation to the larger human community. Since hymns reflect the needs, aspirations, and spiritual victories of their authors, the experiences out of which they grow must be taken seriously. By the same token, they may register personal idiosyncrasies and passing moods, and so need to be examined in the light of the experiences of others. It is always pertinent, therefore, to inquire whether what a hymn asserts is in harmony with the experience of the Christian community as a whole. It may add something precious to that experience, or it may need to be modified or corrected by it.

If we are to follow the apostolic admonition to "sing intelligently" (I Cor. 14:15), we shall use reason as one criterion in hymn evaluation. Here we may need to rid ourselves of a frequent misunderstanding: reason does not entail a cold, barren, one-sided intellectualism that stifles warmhearted feeling and subjects the rich fullness of human life to its autonomous, imperious authority. Reason is simply the thinking activity of the whole person which seeks to discover truth by criticizing, relating, ordering, and interpreting coherently the data of our conscious experience. Hence when we examine a hymn from the perspective of reason we ask whether its assertions are internally consistent and whether they are connected harmoniously with one another and with other affirmations of Christian faith.

Further, remembering that the God we worship is the source of all truth, we shall be ready to examine the connections between the understanding of the world manifest in the hymn with what has been discovered through the truth-seeking endeavors of natural and social scientists. If the faith we sing is to appeal to thoughtful people, it must be able to show that the truths it upholds do not contradict what is known on other grounds. Actually it does much more than this; it illuminates the whole of life and gives to life enduring worth. If we look at human experience as a whole in the light shed by faith in God's creative, reconciling, and liberating activity, we discover that our total existence becomes more understandable and deeper in meaning. In the words of Walter Marshall Horton, we may find the Christian revelation "confirmed by its power to unify and crown all other truth."[2] But we cannot discover this unless we relate it to other truth, and this is the work of synoptic reason. Our appreciation of hymns will therefore be heightened, not diminished, as we study them with full use of our thinking capacity.

These four doctrinal norms are intimately interrelated. None of them can claim exclusive sovereignty. However, when they are used together, complementing one another, they are the best guides we have in our quest for religious truth. In the more specialized area of study of the truth content of our hymns they are of basic importance.

We turn now to guidelines relating specifically to hymnody. I suggest four that seem to be applicable to all hymns, whatever their particular content.

1. There is a central theological question to ask of any hymn text: Is it in essential accord with the basic faith of the Christian community? Each of the chapters in Part Two will raise this question with specific reference to the doctrinal area being considered. One multifaceted query will run like a thread throughout the discussion: Are the attitudes and convictions expressed in a hymn consistent with New Testament teaching as a whole and with our own highest Christian experience and insight?

2. Does the poetic and often metaphorical language characteristic of hymns express convictions that are essentially consonant with Christian beliefs? Hymn writers typically communicate their ideas less in propositional, discursive prose than in a more imaginative, symbolic idiom. But by means of that idiom they aim to state truth. It is pertinent to ask whether or not they succeed.

Anyone familiar with the literature of the Bible knows the richness of its imagery and the effectiveness of its authors' use of narration, symbol, metaphor, and parable to convey their message. In Genesis 1 the action of God on each of the successive days of creation is introduced with the words "God said." In Hosea (11:3, 8, RSV) we learn of a God who "taught Ephraim to walk," whose "heart recoils" from executing anger, and whose "compassion grows warm and tender." Isaiah sounds a similar note when he confesses that we have "all strayed like sheep" (Isa. 53:6), yet rejoices in declaring:

> Before they call me, I will answer,
> and while they are yet speaking, I will listen.
> (Isa. 65:24)

Job tells of hearing "a sound of roaring" as God "thunders with the voice of majesty" (Job 37:4).

The psalms are especially colorful in their metaphors. God is portrayed as standing far off and hiding himself (Ps. 10:1), as forgetting his worshipers and hiding his face (13:1). Smoke rises from his nostrils and devouring fire comes from his mouth (18:8). "His right hand and holy arm have won him victory" (98:1). So all people are summoned to break into songs of joy, while even the sea and its creatures are invited to roar their gladness and the rivers are urged to clap their hands and the hills to sing (98:7–8).

Though Jesus knew how to use incisive logic, he taught primarily in the language of parable and metaphor, with telling employment of concrete illustrations drawn from nature and the daily experiences of ordinary people. The vivid imagery of the gospel narratives speaks eloquently of the power of figure and story to express truth.

It is in such literature that the language of our hymns has its roots. Particularly close is the linkage of hymnody with the psalms, the earliest musical expression of Hebrew and Christian faith. Like the Hebrew poets, the authors of our hymns praise God as shepherd, king, lawgiver, light, rock, refuge, shield, defender, home, father, deliverer, and friend. In New Testament imagery they adore God as Alpha and Omega, comforter, advocate, and dove, and they describe God's saving activity disclosed in Christ through the use of metaphors like ransom, defeat of the powers of darkness, blood, penalty, and price. Many hymns on God's creative work use anthropomorphic metaphors like these:

> Clouds arise, and tempests blow
>   by order from thy throne.

> Soon as the evening shades prevail,
> the moon takes up the wondrous tale;
> and nightly, to the listening earth,
> repeats the story of her birth.

> The earth in mute narration
>   reveals its Maker's ways.

Some hymns are cast wholly in figurative language, as are the five stanzas of "As the bridegroom to his chosen," paraphrased by Emma F. Bevan in 1858 from a Latin hymn attributed to John Tauler (1300–1361). In each stanza four vivid similes are followed by the line: "So, Lord, art thou to me."[3] Two modern counterparts using mostly different comparisons are "As water to the thirsty," by Timothy Dudley-Smith (b. 1926), and "As the lyre to the singer," by Narayan Vaman Tilak (tr. by Nicol Macnicol).[4]

The sensitive interpreter of hymnody will cherish the values conserved by its symbolic language and be grateful for the way in which its images free us from bondage to literal, prosaic statements. Often we are able to penetrate beneath the words themselves to depths of meaning that ordinary propositional forms of expression cannot adequately communicate. Poetic words, writes Frederick Buechner, "set echoes going the way a choir in a great cathedral does, only it is we who become the cathedral and in us that the words echo."[5]

We err, therefore, when we unimaginatively find only precise descriptions in expressions meant to convey truth figuratively. At the same time, we have the right and the responsibility to determine what the intention of the imagery is, and whether it is in accord with the beliefs associated with it. What does the writer aim to say? In what direction do the words point? Metaphorical as well as literal language may distort truth, hide it, or express it ambiguously.

Lines that speak of divine wrath, the power of the blood, or a ransom paid in our behalf may contain elements of profound truth or they may encourage false or misleading understandings of God. Routley says correctly that the modern reader must exercise "imaginative forbearance" on encountering phrases like "an interest in the Savior's blood" and other formulations of traditional atonement theologies,[6] but it is fair to ask whether such forbearance is enough. Some imagery gets in the way of truth. Hymns occasionally mix metaphors in a helter-skelter fashion that hinders full appreciation of their meaning, as does the one which in quick succession refers to Jesus as "the lily of the valley, the bright and morning star."

The inner meaning and the direction of figurative no less than prosaic forms of expression must be carefully explored. An important criterion will be the degree to which the images employed in hymns communicate illuminatingly some aspect of authentic Christian faith.

3. Is the hymn in harmony with present-day scientific knowledge? To answer this question affirmatively is not to say that all hymns that praise the God "who reigns above," or sing of angelic beings, or look to heaven as the ultimate destiny of the righteous must be rejected. Many such references, though they exhibit the influence of prescientific views of the physical world and use terms that cannot now be taken literally, still contribute through their vivid symbolism to the enrichment of both faith and understanding. Indeed, many authors who utilize such language never intended it to be interpreted in other than a symbolic sense.

Nevertheless, whether or not hymns use words influenced by now-abandoned conceptions of the cosmos, their language must be capable of interpretations that do not contradict what is firmly known today about the physical order. It is hardly accidental that though the United Methodist *Book of Hymns* still includes William Walford's "Sweet hour of prayer," it has deleted the stanza in which the redeemed soul, "while passing through the air," shouts farewell to the hour of prayer.

Until the past few decades, however, most English hymns have used highly traditional language in relating faith in God to nature. Hymnody has not kept pace with the momentous changes wrought by modern technology in the thinking of ordinary people who have little theoretical understanding of new developments but are influenced by them in every aspect of their thinking and living. It is imperative that hymn writers no less than theologians seek to articulate Christian faith in terms that make sense in our scientific era, and with an acute awareness of both the achievements and the limits, the promises and the threats of scientific investigation. We also need hymns that take account of the fact that Western culture is no longer predominantly agricultural, but urban and industrial. How many people in the United States have ever seen a shepherd or had any firsthand acquaintance with a sheep?

It is encouraging to note that a significant number of hymns that meet the needs just mentioned are now appearing in new hymnbooks and supplements. In "God, who stretched the spangled heavens," Catherine Cameron (b. 1927) prays for guidance for those who have

> known the ecstasy of winging
>   through untraveled realms of space;
> probed the secrets of the atom
>   yielding unimagined pow'r,
> facing us with life's destruction
>   or our most triumphant hour.[7]

Similarly Albert F. Bayly (b. 1901), seeing both the shining constellations and "the atom's hidden forces" as alike fulfilling the laws of God, asks for illumination, that in our relation to both we may fulfill the divine will.[8] For Richard G. Jones (b. 1926) in "God of concrete, God of steel," the God worshiped by Christians as love is equally Lord of art, industry, travel, and scientific research.[9]

4. Is the hymn inclusive and universal in outlook? *The Hymnal 1940 Companion* (3d ed. rev., 1967) states succinctly the norm here proposed: "Among the outstanding characteristics of the *Hymnal* are its inclusiveness and universality. Race, nationality, religion, learning are barriers which sometimes divide men. When we praise God we become aware of the unity which underlies our differences." Self-evidently no one hymn can achieve the breadth possible in a collection, but a hymn can and should be free of divisive elements and phrases indicating attitudes of superiority or indifference toward people outside the circle of the singers.

With respect to universality several subquestions need to be asked. Does the hymn reflect the needs, aspirations, and experiences common to, or at least open to, all human beings, or is it provincial and limited, with a bias toward one segment of humanity? Is it nationalistic in spirit, or marked by condescending attitudes toward other peoples, races, or religions, as were some of the missionary hymns of the early twentieth century? Is it inclusive with regard to sex, or cast in language that assumes or unconsciously implies male dominance? Does the hymn voice some enduring element of Christian faith that can be shared rather than the transitory feelings of one or a few individuals?

THE QUESTION OF ALTERATIONS

Most of the standards proposed have actually been applied over the years by editorial committees in abridging texts or altering words, phrases, or lines. The right of hymnbook committees to make carefully considered changes in uncopyrighted original texts or translations can hardly be questioned. But regard for the intention of the writer and the danger of distortion of meaning require special attention to the criteria that should guide amendments and deletions. A few examples of revision of original materials will indicate the reasons why alterations have been made and perhaps shed light on the guidelines that should be followed. A major form of alteration is that of omission of stanzas too numerous for use in their entirety. "Jesus, the very thought of thee" is a selection from a twelfth-century Latin poem, the earliest manuscript of which contains 42 stanzas. *De Contemptu Mundi,* a twelfth-century poem of 2,966 lines by Bernard of Cluny, which begins with the words "Hora novissima," has provided texts for at least four hymns, including "Jerusalem the golden." The sections omitted concern mainly the evils of medieval society, while those retained extol the joys of heaven. "These things shall be: a loftier race" opens with the fourth stanza of a 17-stanza poem by John A. Symonds (1840–1893). "Immortal Love, forever full" was extracted from a poem of 38 stanzas by John Greenleaf Whittier (1807–1892). "Strong Son of God, immortal Love" is one of several selections from the 11 stanzas of the Prologue of *In Memoriam,* by Alfred, Lord Tennyson (1809–1892). The original of "O for a thousand tongues to sing," by Charles Wesley (1707–1788), had 10 stanzas. Obviously alteration in original texts through reduction in length is a fact. Theological concerns have clearly affected some retentions and deletions of stanzas.

Another long-standing practice is that of amending words, phrases, and lines. Some revisions occur because certain words have acquired meanings that offend aesthetic sensibilities today. In other changes doctrinal influences are apparent. When Isaac Watts in the opening stanza of "Alas! and did my Savior bleed" described himself as a worm, he probably meant not a loathsome creature but one of no importance—a typical eighteenth-century usage. Later editors, not content with either interpretation or simply concerned to avoid ambiguity, have amended the line to "for sinners such as I." The opening words of "Before Jehovah's awful throne" have undergone similar editing. The 1978 *Lutheran Book of Worship* changes *awful* (awe-full) to *awesome;* while the Presbyterian *Worshipbook* amends the first line to become "Before the Lord Jehovah's throne."

The third stanza of "Faith of our fathers" originally stated una-
bashedly the Roman Catholic theology of its author, Frederick W.
Faber (1814–1863):

> Faith of our fathers! Mary's prayers
>   shall win our country back to thee;
> and through the truth that comes from God
>   England shall then be truly free.

In most hymnals the opening couplet has been changed to:

> Faith of our fathers! We will strive
>   to win all nations unto thee,

and in the fourth line *England* has become *mankind.*

Charles Wesley's "Love divine, all loves excelling" has undergone
various changes reflecting both Arminian belief in free will and
changing views of the Wesleyan doctrine of Christian perfection. In
the second stanza Wesley wrote, "Let us find that second rest." Very
soon several collections changed *second* to *promised,* and this alteration is found in most hymnbooks today, though the United Methodist
Book of Hymns has reinstated *second.* In the same stanza Wesley's
line "Take away our power of sinning" underwent change in several
late eighteenth-century collections; *power* became *love,* or *power of*
was altered to *bent to.* Most recent hymnbooks prefer *love of,* though
The Book of Hymns retains *bent to.*

The closing lines of the first stanza of "Rock of Ages," by Augustus
M. Toplady (1740–1778) prayed that the Rock would "let the water
and the blood"

> be of sin the double cure,
> save from wrath and make me pure.

The majority of hymnals that still include this hymn have changed
the wording to "cleanse me from its guilt and power."

The traditional use of masculine nouns like King, Father, and Lord
to refer to God, of *man* and *mankind* to designate both men and
women, and of masculine pronouns for both God and human beings
has come under attack in the past decade as implicitly affirming male
dominance. Various efforts are being made to substitute nonsexist,
inclusive language in hymns while preserving meter and singability.
Chapter 13 will explore this issue.

A few hymnbooks or supplements are now appearing which consistently modernize the language of older hymns to accord with that
used in some contemporary songs of high quality. Thus in the Presbyterian *Worshipbook* the archaic *thee, thou,* and *ye* are changed to
you; thy becomes *your,* and *hast* becomes *have.* These alterations

too are partly theological, since they reflect a conception of God as permeating the world rather than above or separated from it, and as actively involved in day-by-day earthly life—hence to be referred to by the same language used in ordinary speech.

Alterations like those cited are inevitable, and in the main they are to be welcomed. However, they entail real dangers, especially from carelessness, subjectivity, and lack of due regard for the rights and the purpose of the author. It is therefore important that alterations be made in accord with guidelines carefully worked out. The following are suggested as pertinent for both published collections and particular occasions.

1. An author's own text is to be preferred unless there are convincing reasons for change. Often it is better for singers to exercise freedom of interpretation than to attempt changes that may meet only transitory interests. But where doctrinal positions are expressed that cannot be honestly embraced or that on critical examination seem patently untrue, alterations should be sought.

2. Permissions must be secured from holders of copyrights still in effect, and from living authors.

3. The integrity of the author's message must be scrupulously preserved. Mutilation must be avoided and thematic sequence maintained. If changes proposed fail to meet these conditions, it is better not to use the hymn.

4. Alterations may rightly be made when they promise after careful examination to yield a clearer, more coherent statement of some aspect of Christian faith in terms that will commend what is said to the persons for whom the hymn is intended.

5. The general and theological criteria proposed in this chapter for hymn evaluation apply equally to alterations. A conscientious attempt to appraise hymns according to standards like these should contribute to a heightened appreciation of hymns and deepened meaning in Christian worship.

PART TWO

MAJOR BELIEFS

VOICED IN HYMN TEXTS

4

GOD

Late in the second century A.D., Clement of Alexandria declared: "Where there is an unworthy conception of God, passing into base and unseemly thoughts and significations, it is impossible to preserve any sort of devoutness either in hymns or discourses or even in writings or doctrines."[1] What we think about God is fundamental to all our other religious convictions. Hence our exploration of the beliefs voiced in hymn texts begins with what they say about the one who is praised.

GOD IN AFFIRMATIONS OF FAITH

The Apostles' Creed opens with the confession, "I believe in God the Father almighty, maker of heaven and earth." The Nicene Creed inserts *one* before *God* and adds after *earth,* "and of all things visible and invisible." Both creeds go on to affirm the redemptive action of God in human history in Jesus Christ and the life-giving work of God as Holy Spirit.

Various modern affirmations attempt to express these meanings in contemporary language. A creed formulated by Edwin Lewis and widely used among United Methodists declares faith in the infinite wisdom, power, and love of God, "whose will is ever directed to his children's good." The Statement of Faith of the United Church of Canada affirms belief in God, "who has created and is creating," who has come in Jesus to reconcile and renew, and who works in human life "by his Spirit." The Statement of Faith of the United Church of Christ testifies to the *deeds* of the God believed in, and in gratitude traces God's creating, saving, renewing, strengthening activity through the whole of human life, including "the struggle for justice and peace."

Explicit in these affirmations, but also implied in the ancient creeds, is the faith that God is the ultimate source and ground of both power and goodness, existence and worth, the natural order and the whole realm of value. All that is ours owes its being ultimately to God, and the norms of the good life, as well as the resources for living it, root in the divine character.

Uppermost in Christian thought of God is faith in one who is worthy of our highest praise and hence elicits our adoration and devotion. Christians find their supreme manifestation of the divine in the events centering in the life, teachings, death, and resurrection of Jesus Christ. It is this disclosure of self-giving love at the heart of reality, conceived as Christlike personality, that moves men and women to trust and the commitment of their lives. But inseparably linked with this is the faith that God is also the ultimate power in the universe, that holy love is not an adjunct to the creativity on which all existence depends, but its innermost nature. The Rock of our salvation is the Maker of heaven and earth. God the Redeemer and God the Creator are one and the same.

Two implications of this two-faceted belief need to be stressed today. First, the reality of God should not be conceived abstractly, but in terms of creative process. In the light of what we know of evolutionary changes in the created order, we can no longer embrace the traditional Thomistic view of God as a static, timeless Absolute, an impassive First Cause or Unmoved Mover. Far more illuminating is the interpretation that sees the divine life as intimately involved in the experienced realities of dynamic change and movement toward the new.

Second, it is misleading to think of God as a being above or outside creation. God does not stand over against the world, acting on it from without like a carpenter, wood-carver, or potter. Rather, the divine activity that creates and redeems underlies, permeates, and sustains the universe. God is the ground or matrix of all the being and becoming of the world, the dynamic personal Spirit who in unbounded love seeks to form a community of mutually supportive persons who freely strive with God and one another for the maximum realization of values.

GOD IN OUR HYMNS

Hymns that focus attention on God cannot be neatly classified, since each hymn ordinarily expresses multiple convictions. However, if we look for their major emphases, we can without distortion group most of them, or units within them, broadly under the three headings of the Trinitarian formula. Hence we shall concentrate on hymns, stanzas, or lines that voice faith in God as creativity, redemptive love, and transforming, life-giving power.

If this threefold division, following historic expressions of Christian faith, seems to depart from the twofold characterization of God just given, the incongruity is only apparent. Actually, the two approaches converge, or rather crisscross. God understood as Father, Son, and Holy Spirit is both the dynamic ground of all that is and the conserver and enhancer of all value. Likewise, the God who is both the source of all existence and the advancer of all good is active as Creator, Redeemer, and Life-giver.

God as Creative Power

Speaking on Mars Hill in Athens, the apostle Paul proclaimed that in God "we live and move, in him we exist" (Acts 17:28). This truth is beautifully stated in the third stanza of the hymn by Walter Chalmers Smith (1824–1908), "Immortal, invisible, God only wise":

> To all, life thou givest,
>   to both great and small;
> in all life thou livest,
>   the true life of all.

These lines are an especially fitting way of presenting a Christian view of creation, since they interpret it not as a one-time occurrence in the distant past, but as the constant dependence of all things on the creative activity of God. Fred Kaan (b. 1929) likewise recognizes that divine creation sustains as well as originates our world. The first stanza of his "God who spoke in the beginning" closes with the lines:

> He who calls the earth to order
> is the ground of what we are.[2]

One of the most eloquent hymns of adoration of God as Creator of the natural order is "The spacious firmament on high," by Joseph Addison (1672–1719), set to moving music from Haydn's *The Creation*. Addison exults in the faith that both "the blue ethereal sky" by day and the "spangled heavens" by night proclaim in silent movement "their great Original," the power of a divine hand.

Christopher Wordsworth (1807–1885), in his "O Lord of heaven and earth and sea," goes beyond Addison by adding to the beauties of nature the bounties of human life, and by responding in grateful love to these manifold expressions of the love of God. Asking how we can show our gratitude "for all the blessings earth displays," the hymn offers the answer of faith. "What can to thee, O Lord, be given . . . ,"

to thee, from whom we all derive
our life, our gifts, our power to give;
O may we ever with thee live,
who givest all.[3]

The twentieth century, especially in the past three decades, has
witnessed the birth of a remarkable number of hymns relating a
Christian view of creation to our rapidly expanding knowledge of the
physical world and the problems it raises. Increasing numbers of
writers see the amazing new developments in science, invention,
and technology as human utilization of divinely given resources, but
note their potential for good or evil and pray for wisdom and
strength to control them constructively.

No hymn captures the excitement and promise of contemporary
research and industry so vividly as one by Herbert F. Brokering (b.
1926) that begins:

Earth and all stars!
Loud rushing planets!
Sing to the Lord a new song!

Three stanzas call on the forces of nature and a variety of musical
instruments to sing a new song. Another urges "engines and steel,"
"loud pounding hammers," "limestone and beams," and "loud building workers" to join in the singing. Still another addresses the univer-
sities:

Classrooms and labs!
Loud boiling test tubes! . . .
Athlete and band!
Loud cheering people!
Sing to the Lord a new song![4]

Richard G. Jones has given us a more sober but equally contemporary hymn which begins:

God of concrete, God of steel,
God of piston and of wheel,
God of pylon and of steam,
God of girder and of beam,
God of atom and of mine,
All the world of power is thine.

The succeeding three stanzas laud the

Lord of rocket, Lord of flight,
Lord of soaring satellite,

as well as the

> Lord of science, Lord of art,
> God of map and graph and chart,

identifying the creative source and sustainer of such activities with
the God who

> loosed the Christ with Easter's might,
> saves the world from evil's blight.

All stanzas have the same closing ascription as the first, except that
the words *speed, truth,* and *love* are successively substituted for
power.[5]

For Albert F. Bayly (b. 1901) in "Lord of the boundless curves of
space," the created world understood in contemporary terms is the
context for God's purposive work in history and Christ's liberation of
human beings who have marred the divine image. The hymn traces
to God's creative might the energy active alike in galaxies and atoms
as well as the mysteries of life at all levels:

> Your Spirit gave the living cell
>   its hidden, vital force;
> the instincts which all life impel
>   derive from you, their source.[6]

"God, who stretched the spangled heavens," by Catherine Cameron (b. 1927), prays that our Creator, who has made us in the divine
image and granted us "inventive powers," will "show us what we yet
may do." Recounting the achievements of human beings in space
exploration and scientific research, the hymn highlights the grave
responsibility this newfound mastery entails. It faces us with either
utter destruction or unprecedented achievement. Appropriately,
the closing stanza is a prayer that we may use our powers and our
freedom aright:

> As each far horizon beckons,
>   may it challenge us anew;
> children of creative purpose,
>   serving others, hon'ring you.
> May our dreams prove rich with promise;
>   each endeavor well begun;
> great Creator, give us guidance
>   till our goals and yours are one.[7]

The somber warning sounded briefly by Cameron appears more
urgently in a hymn by Rosamond E. Herklots (b. 1905):

> Lord God, by whose creative might
> the human race on earth was born,
> direct our way lest hope's new morn
> be darkened in destruction's night.[8]

> © 1962, Theodore Presser Co.
> Used by permission.

She goes on to stress the worthlessness of successful explorations in outer space, ocean depths, and nuclear power if the people of the earth suffer from poverty, famine, and war. The hymn closes with a prayer for light and strength to find the way to brotherhood and peace.

A recurring theme of contemporary hymns on creation is that God's work is unfinished, and that it is carried forward partly through men and women as co-creators. The sheer wonder of God's continuing creation in nature is the inspiration of the popular "Morning has broken / like the first morning," by Eleanor Farjeon (1881–1965). Each new sunrise and birdsong, rainfall and dewfall is seen by the author as "springing fresh from the Word." So she invites us to

> praise with elation, / praise every morning,
> God's re-creation / of the new day.[9]

An earlier twentieth-century hymn by William DeWitt Hyde (1858–1917) relates continuing creation to human responsibility to share in it. Hyde voices thanks that the Creator's world is incomplete, hence that "work awaits our hands and feet." God is seeking to replace "wrong's bitter, cruel, scorching blight" with "the blessed kingdom of the right"; and this provides for human beings "a field for toil and faith and hope."[10]

Thomas Curtis Clark (1877–1953) treats this theme Christologically, beginning with the declaration that "Our faith is in the Christ who walks" with us today. In this faith,

> We serve no God whose work is done,
>   who rests within his firmament;
> Our God, his labors but begun,
>   toils evermore, with power unspent.[11]

Supported by divine love, we too are summoned to go forward to fulfill God's purpose for our time.

God as Reconciling Love

Since creation for Christian faith roots in love, and since God is one, it is not surprising that many hymns join adoration of the Creator with grateful praise for the God who acts in love to restore a creation broken by sin. Thus Joachim Neander (1650–1680) opens a hymn found in virtually all standard collections with the lines:

> Praise to the Lord, the Almighty, the King of creation!
> O my soul, praise him, for he is thy health and salvation!

Other hymns have more to say about the meaning of salvation. For instance, Henry F. Lyte (1793–1847), in his well-known "Praise, my soul, the King of heaven," offers in four participles a summation unsurpassed in brevity and content by anything found elsewhere in either hymnody or treatises on theology. Those who are called to praise are "ransomed, healed, restored, forgiven." Father-like, God "tends and spares us," "gently bears us," and "rescues us from all our foes."

In another widely-used and much-loved hymn, Johann J. Schütz (1640–1690) begins by relating the reign of God in the cosmos to the redeeming love of God in human life:

> Sing praise to God who reigns above,
>   the God of all creation,
> the God of power, the God of love,
>   the God of our salvation.

Remarkably, this seventeenth-century composition is one of the very few in all hymnody to use the mother figure to describe God's care, even though the simile reverts to the masculine in the pronoun and the adjective that follow:

> As with a mother's tender hand,
> he leads his own, his chosen band.

Closely related to this understanding of God's love is the belief that it fulfills its ends without suppressing human freedom. Alfred North Whitehead emphasizes his conviction that God acts by "persuasion," through "the worship he inspires." God is "the poet of the world, tenderly leading it by his vision of truth, beauty, and goodness."[12] Almost two centuries earlier Robert Robinson (1735–1790) voiced a similar idea in his evangelical "Come, thou Fount of every blessing":

> O to grace how great a debtor
>   daily I'm constrained to be!
> Let thy goodness, like a fetter,
>   bind my wandering heart to thee.[13]

In quite different language Daniel B. Merrick, Jr. (b. 1926), conveys the same message in his "O God whose love compels us." The com-

pulsion is to obey God's will, yet "in perfect freedom." In the final
stanza Merrick prays that divine love may control us "with wisdom,
faith and power," then offers a similar prayer for the church and
humanity.[14]

Hymns portraying God as redemptive love will be further explored in Chapter 6, on the meaning of Jesus Christ.

God as Life-giving Presence

In Christian hymnody, as in Christian faith in general, God is not
only Creator and Redeemer but spiritual Presence. We cannot separate creative power and saving, forgiving love from the divine activity that in every "now" works to create life anew. The God who
brings the world into being and acts to heal its brokenness also strives
unceasingly within it to bring forth a new creation.

A perceptive hymn by Michael Hewlett (b. 1916) begins with a call
to "sing to him, in whom creation / found its shape and origin"; but
it quickly moves to another summons:

Sing to God, the close companion
of our inmost thoughts and ways.[15]

God can be personally known and experienced. The term used by
Christian faith—though not alone by Christians—to express this
nearness is *Spirit.* Both the Hebrew *ruach* and the Greek *pneuma*
can be accurately translated into English as either wind (or breath)
or spirit—an unmistakable indication of the capacity of God, in biblical thought, to interpenetrate human life—"closer than breathing,
nearer than hands and feet." Hymn writers, following Scripture,
use a rich variety of images to convey this meaning, while also making plain the function and character of the divine reality they portray. A recurring theme is the continuing activity of God within
individuals and groups, in church and world, to guide, empower,
enliven, renew, and transform. Since such actions have been historically identified with the work of God as Holy Spirit, we
shall defer further examination of hymns on this theme until Chapter 7.

THE THREEFOLD ONENESS OF GOD

The hymns explored so far in this chapter have focused attention
on three main manifestations of the divine activity, while assuming
that the God so portrayed is one. Historic Christian faith has expressed this threefold oneness in the doctrine of the Trinity. Unfortu-

nately, the teaching has often been stated in terms that strike many critical minds as incomprehensible.

Hardly any language is more frequent in Christian liturgy and hymnody than the Trinitarian formula. The Gloria Patri and the Doxology are sung or said in practically every service of worship, and both praise the God whom we come to know and love in three ways. In *The Church Hymnary* many hymns based on the psalms close with the same supplementary stanza in italics:

> To Father, Son, and Holy Ghost,
>   The God whom we adore,
> Be glory as it was, and is,
>   And shall be evermore.[16]

Hymns almost too numerous to mention have a Trinitarian structure. The anonymous "Come, thou almighty King" addresses God as King, Word, and Comforter in successive stanzas, and in a fourth stanza praises the "great One in Three." Even the Unitarian Universalist *Hymns for the Celebration of Life* uses the same three nouns, though the Word is creative rather than incarnate, and the fourth stanza is omitted.

Exhibiting the same parallelism is the majestic "Eternal Father, strong to save," by William Whiting (1825–1878). The first three stanzas open respectively with the couplets:

> Eternal Father, strong to save,
>   whose arm has bound the restless wave . . .
>
> O Christ, whose voice the waters heard,
>   and hushed their raging at thy word . . .
>
> O Holy Spirit, who didst brood
>   upon the chaos dark and rude . . .

The fourth stanza unites the thought of the preceding ones in addressing the "Trinity of love and power." The differentiation is not carried through distinctly, however, for the initial stanzas all stress the power of God to calm storms and replace "wild confusion" with peace; and all close with the prayer: "O hear us when we cry to thee / for those in peril on the sea."[17]

Probably the most familiar hymn with a Trinitarian focus is "Holy, holy, holy," by Reginald Heber (1783–1826), which in both its opening and closing stanzas praises "God in three persons, blessed Trinity." It may also be one of the most misleading, since its use of the word *person* exposes worshipers to the danger of a tritheism which was not implied when the Latin *persona* was first used to designate three forms of divine activity.

Even the justly popular "Now thank we all our God," by Martin
Rinkart (1586–1649), points in the same direction at the beginning
of its third stanza:

> All praise and thanks to God
> the Father now be given,
> the Son, and him who reigns
> with them in highest heaven.

Even though the three are referred to in the next line as "the one
eternal God," the fact that they are said to rule with one another
suggests a triumvirate rather than a triunity.

Worshipers who think of God according to the analogy of personality understandably have difficulty with the notion of three divine
persons. To meet this problem various revisions have been tried.
Hymns for the Celebration of Life changes the last line of both the
opening and closing stanzas of "Holy, holy, holy" ("God in three
Persons, blessed Trinity") to read "Who wert, and art, and evermore
shalt be"—words used by Heber in his original second stanza. The
1941 edition of the Baptist-Disciples *Christian Worship* renders this
line "God over all, and blest eternally," but its successor, the *Hymnbook for Christian Worship* (1970) restores the original.

We shall find greater meaning in hymns on the Trinity—and
deeper understanding of our faith—if we recall how the doctrine
grew up and what it intends to say. Belief in God as somehow both
one and three was not invented by ivory-tower theologians. Rather,
it grew out of the concrete experience of Christian people who met
in their own lives one who was active in three main ways: as the
source and sustainer of their existence; as the forgiving love that,
made known through Jesus, lifted the crushing burden of their sins
and made them new persons; and as the life-giving presence that
continued with them after the earthly life of Jesus and empowered
the community of his followers.

At first the church made no effort to explain the precise relation
between the three. The word "Trinity" appears nowhere in the New
Testament. In succeeding centuries, however, as the church faced
conflicts within and competing religions and philosophies without, it
felt the need to clarify and formulate its belief. The form of words
which became dominant in the fourth and fifth centuries in the West
was that God is one substance (Latin *substantia*) in three persons
(personae).

By this language the church did not mean that God is composed
of three persons in the same sense in which Ethel, Harry, and Elaine
are three individual identities. The word *persona* in the ancient
Roman world underwent several changes in meaning. It meant ini-

tially a mask worn or held by an actor in a drama; later, the part or role played; and still later, the actor himself in day-by-day life. When the word was used to interpret what God meant for Christians it was probably in the second of these stages. God in three "persons" meant God fulfilling three great roles, becoming manifest in three main forms of expression.

The dramatic analogy may still be useful, as long as we avoid the Sabellian heresy, which treated the parts played as merely temporary, successive appearances. We shall want to affirm that God truly is the reality who acts in the ways experienced. We may also find in human psychology a helpful clue to a better understanding of God. Feeling, thinking, and willing are distinguishable activities of the person as a center of consciousness, yet the whole person is in each of them. Similarly, we may think of God as one reality who is constantly creating, loving, and renewing. Actually, no list of three verbs or nouns can do more than hint at the fullness of the divine life, but the three familiar names, or their equivalents, may be our most eloquent symbols.

Four twentieth-century hymns merit special attention because of the fresh ways in which they express such faith. Reginald T. Brooks (b. 1918) has voiced gratitude to God in five stanzas:

> Thanks to God whose Word was spoken
> in the deed that made the earth. . . .
>
> Thanks to God whose Word incarnate
> glorified the flesh of man. . . .
>
> Thanks to God whose Word was written
> in the Bible's sacred page. . . .
>
> Thanks to God whose Word was published
> in the tongues of every race. . . .
>
> Thanks to God whose Word is answered
> by the Spirit's voice within. . . .

The unity is provided by the Word, which acts in this hymn in five ways—or four if the writing and the published translation of the Bible are treated as one; and each stanza closes with the invitation: "Praise him for his open Word." Several hymnals omit the third and fourth stanzas, and the result is a very good hymn in the Trinitarian mold.[18]

In "Lord of all good, our gifts we bring to thee," Albert F. Bayly lists the talents offered to God by those who respond to divine love, then in a closing stanza addresses the Giver in lines that are a lucid summary of Trinitarian doctrine:

Father, whose bounty all creation shows,
   Christ, by whose willing sacrifice we live,
Spirit, from whom all life in fullness flows,
   to thee with grateful hearts ourselves we give.[19]

Two other hymns make explicit a social reference that remains implicit in the two just cited—the work of the Triune God in breaking down barriers and uniting in love peoples created for community. Stewart Cross (b. 1928) addresses three stanzas to "Father, Lord of all creation, / Ground of Being, Life, and Love"; "Jesus Christ, the Man for Others"; and "Holy Spirit, rushing, burning / wind and flame of Pentecost." The hymn closes with a prayer to the Spirit:

May your love unite our action,
   nevermore to speak alone:
God, in us abolish faction,
   God, through us your love make known.[20]

In "Creating God, your fingers trace" (1974) Jeffery Rowthorn devotes two stanzas to the creative work of God in the physical world and the maintenance of life, then addresses successively the redeeming and indwelling God. The oneness of the divine action is implied by the way in which functions often assigned to Son or Spirit are intermingled. To the God who redeems, and whose "arms embrace / all now oppressed for creed or race," the petition is directed:

Let peace descending as the dove
make known on earth your healing love.

Recognizing that the one family of the indwelling God has "a billion names," the final stanza asks that each life be touched by grace.[21]

ETERNITY AND TEMPORALITY

Two additional aspects of Christian faith in God merit special attention because of the frequency with which they appear in hymnody and life, and also because of the ambiguity and dubious nature of some assertions made about them. These are the eternity of God and divine providence.

A simple illustration of the problem of time and eternity in God presented by some hymns is Paul Townsend's charming "The Clock Carol," a carol hymn that begins, "When the bells chime noon in London." One stanza declares:

For he is there through nights and days,
   through rain and cold and heat;

behind the chatter of the clocks
we sense his timeless beat.[22]

Unfortunately, such contradictions as timeless beats are not confined to songs for children—which does not mean that they don't matter in these!

In an excellent hymn on the Christian mission, "Eternal God, whose power upholds / both flower and flashing star," Henry Hallam Tweedy (1868–1953) addresses the God of love, truth, beauty, righteousness, and grace as he prays for the coming of the kingdom on earth. The eternal God spoken to in the opening stanza is one "to whom there is no here nor there, / no time, no near nor far." With regard to space, the passage asserts that God is not confined to particular locations, but present everywhere. To be consistent with this, a temporal reference need only affirm that God is not restricted to certain times, but is always active. Instead, we are told that to God there is no time. Yet the following lines present a God who is constantly doing things that require time: sending us forth; helping us to spread God's gracious rule; and inspiring heralds of good news.[23]

A similar incongruity appears in "The God of Abraham praise," a nineteenth-century paraphrase of the fourteenth-century Yigdal (Doxology) of Daniel ben Judah Dayyan, which appears in most hymnals, sometimes with "Praise to the living God" as the opening line. The last lines of the first stanza speak of

the one eternal God, / ere aught that now appears;
the first, the last: beyond all thought / his timeless years.

Yet the Spirit of God is described as flowing free, "high surging where it will," and his love is "our strength and stay / while ages roll." What Daniel ben Judah and the nineteenth-century translators probably meant is expressed in the affirmation made in both the first and the third stanzas, which sing of the God of Abraham, "who was, and is, and is to be, / and still the same!"[24]

"Eternity" in its literal etymological meaning does of course connote timelessness, but it can also describe that which transcends time or endures through all time. The former view has often been upheld in classical theism, strongly influenced by Aristotle and Neoplatonism. Here God has been conceived as the changeless Absolute who exists above the world in timeless perfection, and for whom there can be neither before nor after but only an eternal now. Obviously none of the hymns just cited seriously thinks of God in this way. A deity "who was, and is, and is to be" would seem to be one for whom past, present, and future are real, but who does not change in character with the passing years.

Like the Hebrew-Christian Scriptures (see Ps. 102:26–27; Mal. 3:6;

Heb. 13:8; James 1:17), our hymn writers often contrast the tran-
sitoriness of created things with the permanence of their Creator,
and stress the changelessness and everlastingness of God. However,
in both cases the primary aim is to declare that God is not subject to
the perishability of finite things, that unlike vacillating human beings
God is utterly reliable and trustworthy. God's Word is eternal—true
at all times, and the steadfast love of the one who utters it abides
forever.

One of the best expressions of this temporalistic understanding of
eternity is found in the opening lines of the hymn by Ernest N.
Merrington (1876–1953), an Australian:

> God of eternity, Lord of the ages,
>   Father and Spirit and Saviour of men!
> Thine is the glory of time's numbered pages;
>   thine is the power to revive us again.

The hymn goes on to praise God's faithfulness, mercy, and grace

> shown to our fathers in past generations,
>   pledge of thy love to our people and race;

and closes with this prayer:

> As thou hast blessed us through years that have ended,
>   still lift upon us the light of thy face.[25]

In the closing lines of "How shall I sing that majesty," John Mason
(1645–1694) moves us to share his awe and wonder as he contem-
plates the greatness of God in both time and space:

> Thou art a sea without a shore,
>   a sun without a sphere;
> thy time is now and evermore,
>   thy place is everywhere.[26]

Christian hymnody bears witness to the faith that the God who
creates, sustains, heals, renews, and transforms life can be counted
on through all change.

PROVIDENCE

Perhaps no aspect of Christian faith in God touches our lives more
intimately than belief in divine providence. Broadly understood, this
is the conviction that the natural order, human history, and the lives
and destinies of individuals fall within the wise and righteous rule of
God, who can be counted on to provide for our well-being. Faith in

providence means trust that, whatever evils may assail us, we are kept in God's love. "There is nothing . . . in all creation that can separate us from the love of God in Christ Jesus our Lord" (Rom. 8:38–39).

Concretely, *what does it mean to say that we are in God's care*, especially in view of the fact that persons who trust God, as well as those who don't, are often called on to endure intense physical pain and mental anguish, and that all of us face the inevitability of our own death? *In what ways, specifically, does God keep us?* How do our hymns respond to questions like these?

Defective Views

Two traditional views, reflected in hymns that are still frequently sung, will not bear critical scrutiny. The popularity of several of these hymns indicates that those who sing them either accept the understanding of providence expressed in them or pay little attention to the words.

1. Some devout Christians hold that all the events of our lives, even those distressing to us, are ordained by the omnipotent God who rules all that happens in both nature and human life in accord with his holy purposes. In a hymn based on Psalm 148, "The Lord Jehovah reigns," Isaac Watts relates this conception of divine sovereignty particularly to human history, where God's wrath, justice, law, truth, and love are determinative:

> Strong is his arm, and shall fulfill
> his great decrees and sovereign will.[27]

A similar faith moves Josiah Conder (1789–1855) to rejoice. In "The Lord is King! Lift up thy voice" he summons earth and heaven to join him.

> The Lord is King! Who then shall dare
> resist his will, distrust his care,
> or murmur at his wise decrees,
> or doubt his royal promises?[28]

Consistent with this understanding of God's action is the conclusion that godly men and women should perceive even the ills encountered as actually furthering their true welfare. Joachim Neander (1650–1680), in his widely used "Praise to the Lord, the Almighty, the King of creation," asks:

> Hast thou not seen
> how thy desires e'er have been
> granted in what he ordaineth?

Various hymnbook editors, apparently detecting a lack of realism in the implied answer to Neander's question, have amended "desires" to read "entreaties," "heart's wishes," "all that is needful," or the like, but have retained the assumption that these are granted or sent in what God "ordains."[29]

In "If thou but suffer God to guide thee," Georg Neumark (1621–1681) states positively this view of providence, counseling willing resignation to God's righteous will:

> Only be still, and wait his leisure
>   in cheerful hope, with heart content
> to take whate'er the Father's pleasure
>   and all-discerning love hath sent.[30]

Benjamin Schmolck (1672–1737) joins to this trusting acceptance of the divine will the belief that occurrences which seem to us evil are only apparently so; actually the bitterness of losing lesser goods brings us closer to God, our only ultimate good.

> What God hath done is done aright,
>   in gifts withheld or sent us;
> and what sufficeth in His sight,
>   should always well content us:
> 'tis for our sakes He gives or takes;
>   then humbly bowed before Him,
>   in silence we adore Him.[31]

2. Some writers go so far as to declare that God not only supplies all the needs of men and women of faith but grants them immunity from harm. In "Sometimes a light surprises," William Cowper (1731–1800) makes the sweeping claim:

> Beneath the spreading heavens,
>   no creature but is fed;
> and he who feeds the ravens
>   will give his children bread.[32]

On occasion such faith is so far-reaching that it regards those who make God their refuge as wholly protected from deadly shafts, pestilence, and fatal strokes—indeed, from all forms of evil. Mirroring accurately the promises of Psalm 91, an anonymous hymn from the *United Presbyterian Book of Psalms* (1871) concludes:

> Because thy trust is God alone,
> thy dwelling place the Highest One,
> no evil shall upon thee come,
> nor plague approach thy guarded home.[33]

In "Children of the heavenly Father," Caroline V. Sandell Berg (1832–1903) of Sweden centers attention on the assurance of Romans 8 that "neither life nor death shall ever / from the Lord his children sever." In one stanza, however, she agrees with the passages just quoted:

> God in his own doth tend and nourish,
> in his holy courts they flourish.
> From all evil things he spares them,
> in his mighty arms he bears them.[34]

It is understandable that many persons can find comfort in ascribing all events to the secret counsels of the divine will. This recourse to mystery and utter trust evokes a sense of security amid the bafflements of life. But to maintain that an absolute Sovereign purposes for our well-being even the evils that assail us raises difficult questions for many reflective Christians. If we inquire whether, as Neander says, our desires or needs are granted in what God ordains, would not most of us in honesty have to reply negatively? Must we really be content with what happens as sent by God's "all-discerning love"? Open-eyed Christians can hardly regard the hopeless poverty of Calcutta, the agony of terminal victims of leukemia, or the parental abuse of terrified but helpless children as part of God's good plan; and it is a sham to pretend otherwise.

The moving assurances of Psalms 91 and 121, and the hymns inspired by them, may be making use of vivid metaphors and poetic hyperbole to voice the profound faith that God never forsakes us, that no evil can remove us from the divine presence, and that our destiny is in the hands of one who loves us. So they have been understood by many generations of Jews and Christians, to whose faith calamities are not ultimately calamitous. But if they are interpreted literally, they run counter to observable facts. Multitudes of God's children have so little bread (or rice) that they suffer and die of starvation. Persons who are sustained by faith in God are threatened in about the same proportion as unbelievers by disease, accident, and natural disaster.

Thanksgiving for needs met and evils avoided is understandable and commendable when it springs from the actual experience of an individual. But to claim that everyone is so protected is naive and insensitive to the anguish that multitudes endure. Both realism and regard for the implications of our professed belief in the divine goodness demand that we look farther in our effort to understand what it means to be kept by God.

Affirmations Consistent with Realistic Faith

The views of providence thus far considered, though fairly frequently expressed in hymnody, can hardly be regarded as dominant. A careful study of representative hymns discloses several other interpretations that are much more in accord with the biblical witness as a whole, Christian experience, and reasonable faith. An examination of these should bring us closer to the understanding we seek.

1. God keeps us by providing a dependable natural order that makes life possible and affects all people impartially. Because nature functions according to uniform "laws" that we can discover and count on, we are able to grow crops, make plans, avoid many dangers, write music, and invent efficient means of transportation and communication. This belief is implied in the many hymnic references to the regular processes of nature, and in the appeals to sun, moon, and stars, along with natural forces like fire and rain, to adore the Creator. The familiar hymn by Francis of Assisi (1182–1226), "All creatures of our God and King," is a prime example of this.

In a few instances belief that the regularities of the physical order manifest the care of God is more explicit. For example, in a seldom-sung hymn, "How gentle God's commands!" Philip Doddridge (1702–1751) asserts, "That hand which bears all nature up / shall guard his children well."[35] Still more plain is the second stanza of a hymn by Thomas O. Chisholm (1866–1960), "Great is thy faithfulness":

> Summer and winter and springtime and harvest,
>   sun, moon, and stars in their courses above,
> join with all nature in manifold witness
>   to thy great faithfulness, mercy, and love.[36]

2. God keeps us by giving us the strengthening, sustaining power of the divine presence. This is of course the deepest meaning of Psalms 91 and 121 (see also Ps. 27:10; 94:14). It is also the core of the message of Second Isaiah as he promises the return of exiled Israel to its homeland. The Deliverer proclaims:

> I have called you by name and you are my own.
> When you pass through deep waters, I am with you,
>   when you pass through rivers,
>   they will not sweep you away. . . .
> Have no fear, for I am with you.
>   (Isa. 43:1, 2, 5)

This is the theme of some of our greatest hymns. The assurance of "How firm a foundation, O saints of the Lord," is no facile pledge of exemption from trouble, but the far more helpful promise that when we face difficulties and dangers, as we know we must, we are not alone but supported by one whose strength will enable us to bear whatever is demanded.

Both Georg Neumark and Joachim Neander, some of whose lines spurred critical comment above, in other passages sound this deeper note. In his hymn already cited, Neumark declares:

> He'll give thee strength, whate'er betide thee,
>   and bear thee through the evil days.
> Who trusts in God's unchanging love
> builds on the rock that naught can move.

Neander's "All my hope on God is founded," freely translated by Robert Bridges (1844–1930), contrasts the frailty of human potentates and institutions with the strength of the Eternal:

> Pride of man and earthly glory,
>   sword and crown, betray his trust;
> what with care and toil he buildeth,
>   tower and temple, fall to dust.
> But God's power, hour by hour,
> is my temple and my tower.[37]

The temple and tower analogies remind us of Martin Luther's "A mighty fortress is our God," or in the translation by Thomas Carlyle (1795–1881), used in most British hymnbooks, "A safe stronghold our God is still." Sometimes we urgently need a secure citadel. During the Nazi occupation of Norway in World War II, thousands of Christians gathered in the cathedral square in Oslo to defy an edict banning public assemblies. Luther's sturdy hymn proved just the right vehicle for declaring their faith in their true stronghold. With a stirring sermon by Bishop Eivind Berggrav, it inspired them with the strength to face the years of hardship and lost freedom.

At other times, however, the image employed by John Bunyan (1628–1688) is more appropriate. Percy Dearmer's adaptation of Bunyan's "He who would valiant be" portrays the Christian life as a pilgrimage on which the traveler is defended not by the walls of a castle but by the Spirit that accompanies him in the open country where he is exposed to attack. But the greater the danger, the greater is his strength for meeting it:

> No foes shall stay his might, / though he with giants fight;
> he will make good his right / to be a pilgrim.[38]

A refreshing hymn on the constancy of God's providential care throughout our earthly journey is "A gladsome hymn of praise we sing," by Ambrose Nichols Blatchford (1842–1925). He speaks of the

God "whose providence is our defence, / who lives and loves forever," then continues:

> Full in his sight his children stand,
>   by his strong arm defended,
> and he whose wisdom guides the world
>   our footsteps hath attended.
> For nothing falls unknown to him,
>   or care or joy or sorrow,
> and he whose mercy ruled the past
>   will be our stay tomorrow.[39]

3. God keeps us by guiding us on life's journey. Many hymns that perceive life as a hazardous passage across ever-changing terrain portray God as leading the traveler. God guides us by equipping us with reliable internal charts—norms for living abundantly and the capacity to read them aright—and also by helping us through thought and prayer to clarify choices and make sound decisions.

In some hymns it is individuals who acknowledge or ask for the guiding hand of God, although with reference to experiences that other people share. Thus William Williams (1717–1791) in "Guide me, O thou great Jehovah" prays that "the fire and cloudy pillar" will lead him on his journey "through this barren land" and across the Jordan to a safe arrival in Canaan. Though for Williams—and for many others since his time—the barren land was probably an apt metaphor, it hardly reflects accurately the experience of many who sing the hymn today. When it was used in a recent worship service, the cover of the bulletin was resplendent with blue iris in a summer garden, and the faces and garb of the congregation were not those of weary pilgrims.

More universal and enduring in its appeal is the ancient Irish hymn "Be thou my vision, O Lord of my heart." Confronting the uncertainties, problems, and choices that every day brings, people of all ages and circumstances can join trustfully in the plea:

> Be thou my wisdom, and thou my true word;
> I ever with thee and thou with me, Lord,

and pray honestly, "Still be my vision, O Ruler of all."

Many "we" hymns that invoke God's guidance move from grateful acknowledgment of past help to appeals for light in the present and the future. Thus "God of our fathers, whose almighty hand," by Daniel C. Roberts (1841–1907), asks the God whose love has "led us in the past" to be "our ruler, guardian, guide, and stay."[40]

The same pattern is followed in the noble hymn "God of our life, through all the circling years," by Hugh T. Kerr (1871–1950). The second stanza prays for God's continuing guidance today and tomorrow:

> God of the past, our times are in your hand;
>   with us abide.
> Lead us by faith to hope's true Promised Land;
>   be now our guide.

Acknowledging that God's presence sheds on our way the light we need, the hymn makes the fitting commitment:

> God of the coming years, through paths unknown
>   we follow you.

The closing lines state eloquently the attitude of faith in all stages of life:

> Be now for us in life our daily bread,
>   our heart's true home when all our years have sped.[41]

A recent hymn (1956, alt. 1971) by Elisabeth Burrowes (b. 1885) relates providence to the space age. It begins:

> God of the ages, by whose hand,
>   through years long past our lives were led,
> give us new courage now to stand,
>   new faith to find the paths ahead.

The reference in the concluding stanza to the unknown vastness of space hints also of the mysteries that face us always in the unknown future, but with the assurance that in both uncertainties we are led by the light of God's grace:

> Though there be dark, uncharted space
>   with worlds on worlds beyond our sight,
> still may we trust your love and grace
>   and wait your word, "Let there be light."[42]

4. God keeps us by participating in our anguish and overcoming evil through self-giving love. Nothing speaks more convincingly of the meaning of providence than the gospel of the Word made flesh, dwelling with us, sharing the whole range of human experience, suffering for and with a broken world, and thereby restoring it and saving it for fulfillment of the divine intention.

Part of this caring action consists simply in the fact of God's "being there" where people are hurting. Fred Kaan (b. 1929) brings out this truth vividly in his "We meet you, O Christ, in many a guise," where Jesus symbolizes the divine presence in all forms of human struggle today:

In millions alive, away and abroad,
involved in our life, you live down the road.
Imprisoned in systems, you long to be free,
We see you, Lord Jesus, still bearing your tree.[43]

Timothy Rees (1874–1939) relates this message more directly to providence, while asserting graphically the reality of both human and divine suffering. In his "God is love: let heaven adore him," he affirms:

God is love: and he enfoldeth
    all the world in one embrace;
with unfailing grasp he holdesth
    every child of every race.
And when human hearts are breaking
    under sorrow's iron rod,
then they find that selfsame aching
    deep within the heart of God.

However, the aching heart is not the last word. That belongs to the power of God, which "holds and guides" us by sacrificial love.[44]

In an extraordinary new hymn, "Morning glory, starlit sky," W. H. Vanstone (b. 1923) contrasts the "openness" of God's gifts in nature and in human experiences of beauty and truth with the hiddenness of "love's agony, love's endeavor, love's expense." Yet the nails and crown of thorns of one who hangs helpless on a tree "tell of what God's love must be":

Here is God: no monarch he,
    throned in easy state to reign;
here is God, whose arms of love
    aching, spent, the world sustain.[45]

5. God keeps us by giving eternal life to persons of faith and love, and by controlling the outcome of creation as a whole. The God whose suffering love shares and conquers the travail of our earthly lives also guides us toward the consummation of the divine purpose.

This trustful attitude regarding our ultimate destiny is expressed in very different ways by two writers separated by seventeen centuries. In "Sunset to sunrise changes now," Clement of Alexandria (ca. 170–ca. 220) declares:

Here in o'erwhelming final strife
    the Lord of life hath victory;
and sin is slain, and death brings life,
    and sons of earth hold heaven in fee.[46]

Fred Kaan addresses the same theme in his hymn "Committed to Christ, / who died, but who rose," based on Rom. 8:31–39:

> No danger or death, / no future how grim,
> no hatred or rule / can part us from him
> whose promise enfolds us / wherever we move;
> for nothing can fetter / the flow of his love.[47]

One of the most beloved of the many hymnic versions of the Twenty-third Psalm is that by Isaac Watts, "My Shepherd will supply my need." After paraphrasing the psalm in five stanzas, Watts adds a sixth of his own, which in touching simplicity voices much of what we have found our hymns saying about God's providential care. Referring to the Shepherd's house, the poet concludes:

> There would I find a settled rest,
>   while others go and come;
> no more a stranger, or a guest,
>   but like a child at home.[48]

Rest, it should be borne in mind, need not mean passive repose in sheltered safety. It can connote the inner sense of well-being of one who even in struggle knows he is upholding the right, the calmness of the person who is "in tune with the universe," living in harmony with God. Since we are discussing poems set to music, it may be well to recall that a rest in music is an interval of rhythmic silence, an integral part of the movement. Home, moreover, may be less a secure and static haven than the direction in which God is leading us. Our home is where we belong—on the way toward ever-new fulfillments of the divine purpose. If we believe God is keeping us, we are at home with the Alpha and the Omega of our being, and we are sustained by trust that the accomplishment of God's righteous will is on the way.

5

HUMANITY

According to Hebrew and Christian belief, human beings are children of God, created in the divine image. Capable of knowing God, they are responsible to God for lives harmonious with the divine purpose. Made for companionship with God and one another, they are called to respond freely in growth toward mature personality. Yet repeatedly they distort the image and break the relationship. Ignoring or denying their responsibility to their Creator, they trust their own insights rather than the divine will, and they center their lives in themselves. Hence they are alienated from God, one another, and themselves. However, in spite of their sin they remain capable of reconciliation and transformation by divine grace. God is constantly acting to restore the severed relationship. Hence the way is open for the prodigals to return home, and when they do they are received by a love that makes them whole again and restores them to healthy relations with God and one another.

THE HUMAN SITUATION IN HYMNODY

We need not expect this threefold understanding of humanity to appear in our hymns in this neat order. Hymnists are not writing textbooks in theology; and in the Christian experience they portray, the consciousness of sin and the possibility and reality of healing are closely connected. Few authors are moved to extol the worth of humanity without mentioning its shortcomings, and no Christian wants to sing about how sinful he or she is without praise of God's redeeming love. So what we find in the main is hymns that confess our failure to fulfill the divine intention, call us to repentance, and celebrate our forgiveness and renewal.

Hymns and hymnals have not always balanced the negative and positive aspects. It is therefore important to ask whether a given hymn recognizes the self-centeredness, difficulties, and anguish of human existence without succumbing to a dismal view that overlooks its creativity, joys, and values. The editors of *The New Catholic Hymnal* state their desire "to convey a general spirit of happiness and joy, though not complacency, so that while there are hymns on the subject of penitence, sorrow and of urgent supplication, there is no pervasive atmosphere of guilt, gloom, and dejection, which has been hanging over hymnody as a legacy mainly from the Victorian period."[1] The gospel our hymns celebrate is good news addressed to people who need it. We cannot expect every hymn to affirm both the sinfulness and the redeemability of human beings, but we can justifiably ask that either emphasis be stated in a manner consistent with the other.

Human Worth

Mention should be made of some hymns, to the left of the central Christian tradition, which extol the greatness, nobility, freedom, and promise of humanity. Thus Sophia Lyon Fahs (1876–1978) sings:

> Divinity is round us—never gone
>   from man or star,
> from life or death, from good or even wrong—
>   in all we are.[2]

Fahs goes on to acknowledge explicitly the reality of human error, anger, and faulted virtue, while insisting that "God" is present not only in our noblest actions but "in all men's anguished needs." We are called as it were to help God's ways to "unfold" by freeing love in human life.

In the poetry of Kenneth L. Patton (b. 1911), humanism is less restrained. He extols human life as the highest product of nature, with a noble heritage and a nobler future:

> O man, acclaim your heritage,
>   your noble history of fire.
> You are the heavens come of age,
>   the bearer of the sun's desire,
> a prophet come to life at last,
>   a thinker from the molten streams,
> a valiant poet of the vast
>   to dream the universe's dreams.[3]

Such confidence in virtually boundless human powers finds no support from authors who, writing from an avowedly Christian perspective, see men and women as creatures of a more-than-human God. However, these writers do not therefore denigrate humanity, but rather affirm its unique worth and dignity, precisely because of its relation to God as its Source and Sustainer.

Frank Edwards (1898–1968), for example, grounds human life along with the physical order in the creative action of God:

> God of earth and sea and heaven;
>   by thy power are all things made;
> man, created in thine image,
>   lives nor breathes without thine aid.

Because of this relation to God, men and women can discern the divine witness "in saint and seer" and in ordinary human lives sensitive to the divine presence. Yet the freedom it entails opens the way to misused gifts and self-centeredness. So the poet prays, "Purge our pride and our vainglory," and in grateful response to forgiving mercy offers "talents, time, and treasure" for the service of God.[4]

Two other twentieth-century hymns are noteworthy because of the differing ways in which they affirm the value of human personality. Both uphold, along with their belief in divine revelation, a kind of natural theology, since they assume that clues to the divine reality, hence some dependable knowledge of God, can be found through the patient use of our God-given capacity to think coherently about our experience as a whole.

Percy Dearmer (1867–1936) portrays God as working through human beings to disclose the divine purpose and lead them toward realization of the highest values:

> Sing praise to God, who spoke through man
>   in diff'ring times and manners.

Seers who have blazed the path to truth, prophets like Amos who have shown the way to faith in one good God, Socrates and Plato who by critical examination of ideas have molded "our ways of thinking," and poets and artists with their vision of beauty—all of these evoke the repeated response, "To God be thanks and glory."

In the closing stanza, however, Dearmer calls in question the real significance of the human quest when he lauds those

> who bring our highest dreams to shape
> and help the soul in her escape.[5]

This approval of a Platonic dualism between the shadow world of matter that we now inhabit and the spiritual realm that alone is real, and to which we must as disembodied spirits escape, is in line with a long-held and still-influential view of human existence, but one which requires critical scrutiny. At best such dualism is difficult to reconcile with the belief that the physical world manifests the creative activity of God, and especially with faith in God's self-incarnation in human history.

In sharp contrast to Dearmer in this respect is a hymn by Derwyn Dixon Jones (b. 1925) that sees bodies and minds alike as expressions of the creative activity of God. It is the only hymn I know that explicitly thanks God for sex:

> Now thank we God for bodies strong,
> vitality and zest,
> for strength to meet the day's demands,
> the urge to give our best,
> for all our body's appetites
> which can fulfilment find,
> and for the sacrament of sex
> that recreates our kind.

The second stanza thanks God for the capacity of human minds to seek and find truth, and the awareness that "in searching out life's ways" we "but discern his mind." Finally, the poet gives thanks that with all our powers we can "respond to Spirit's call"—a gift that makes us unique in creation.[6]

Human Sinfulness and Divine Grace

Most hymns that stress the positive capacities of human beings recognize also the degree to which these capacities remain unrealized because of sin. In other hymns the emphasis is placed on the patent reality, and in many cases the extremity, of human evil, combined with the promise of, or a prayer for, forgiveness.

Thus Charlotte Elliott (1789–1871) in her well-known "Just as I am, without one plea" is "tossed about" by conflicts, fears, and doubts, and burdened with a sense of her wretchedness and blindness; yet she responds to the invitation to come for pardon and cleansing to the Lamb of God. Similarly, Isaac Watts, in the original text of his "Alas! and did my Savior bleed," marvels that his Redeemer could willingly give his life "for such a worm as I." Later revisions have changed this to "sinners such as I," but the painful consciousness that crimes like his have caused the crucifixion remains, along with corresponding wonder at grace so incomparably great that it would sacrifice all for the sake of unworthy sinners.[7]

Other hymns exhibit an equally vivid consciousness of the gravity of sin, but lay relatively greater emphasis on the divine grace that makes the sinner whole. The black spiritual "There is a balm in Gilead" is a notable example of this mood. So also is Charles Wesley's "Jesus, lover of my soul," in which he rejoices that though "false and full of sin" he receives plenteous grace that makes and keeps him pure within.

John Newton's "Amazing grace" is so widely used today in purely secular settings that its profound religious meaning can be readily overlooked. However, from start to finish it celebrates the forgiving love that can find the lost, give sight to the blind, and lead sinners from wretchedness to their true home in God. Two things should be borne in mind before this hymn is dismissed because of the demeaning connotation of the word "wretch." First, the term no doubt expresses accurately Newton's self-assessment as he looks back on his role as a crewman on a slave ship. Secondly, by definition a wretch may be not only a person sunk in vice or degradation, but a banished person, an exile, or one who is miserable because of great poverty. So the word was probably the best Newton could find to express how he felt about himself. Surely many of us today, in spite of our fancied sophistication, know what it means to be estranged from God and one another, and to be poor in soul if not in things.

Curtis Beach (b. 1914) shifts the focus from the individual to humanity. In "O how glorious, full of wonder," based on Psalm 8, he confesses to God his astonishment that in spite of our being a

> mixture strange of good and ill,
>   from thy ways so often turning,
>   yet thy love doth seek us still.

We have misused our God-given dominion over nature, but can still be reclaimed for the divine purpose:

> Soaring spire and ruined city,
>   these our hopes and failures show.
> Teach us more of human pity,
>   that we in thine image grow.[8]

One of the most perceptive and arresting hymns from any century on the renewal of sinful humanity is a new composition by Richard G. Jones (b. 1926).

> God who created this garden of earth,
> giving to Adam in all of us birth,
> what have we done with the dangerous tree?
> Lord, forgive Adam, for Adam is me.

The next three stanzas describe Adam's desire to be equal to God, the comparable thirst of proud humanity for status and fame, and the cursing of the earth that results from misused stewardship, followed in each case by a prayer that Adam might be freed from his sin, "for

Adam is me." The fifth stanza celebrates the renewal of human life through the death of the second Adam on another tree, and the hymn concludes with a shout of victory:

> Rises that Adam the master of death,
> pours out his spirit in holy new breath;
> sheer liberation! With him I am free!
> Live, second Adam, in mercy in me![9]

Possibilities Open to Renewed Humanity

Some of our hymns go beyond the experience of forgiveness to celebrate also the exciting possibilities open to those who are healed, renewed, and made whole. On the individual level this was of course a central emphasis of the Wesleyan revival, and long before that, of Eastern Orthodoxy. The Greek fathers' doctrine of "theosis" or "christification" of humanity found classical expression in the declaration of Athanasius that "Christ became man that we might become divine."[10] "Theosis" points primarily to three realities: (1) the reestablishment of communion between God and human beings; (2) the communication of divine grace to human beings through the Holy Spirit; and (3) the genuine re-creation and transformation of human nature by the power of God.[11]

Closely akin to this are the Wesleyan doctrines of sanctification, or "holiness of heart and life"; and perfection, or the attainment of maturity in Christian love by the empowerment of the Spirit of God. John Wesley's expectation that a Christian can become "so far perfect, as not to commit [voluntary] sin" is easily dismissed today as hopelessly unrealistic, but such rejection should not obscure the central concern and abiding truth of his teaching—that human beings can by the indwelling power of the Spirit grow continually in grace and Christlike love.

This understanding of what life can become when centered in God is a recurrent theme in Charles Wesley's hymns, as in "Love divine, all loves excelling" and "O for a heart to praise my God." Every stanza of the latter voices the yearning for "a heart from sin set free,"

> a heart in every thought renewed
>   and full of love divine,
> perfect and right and pure and good,
>   a copy, Lord, of thine.

That the aspiration toward Godlike character in hymnody is a genuine part of our ecumenical heritage is indicated by the fact that "Love divine" appears in virtually all hymnals, Protestant and Catho-

lic, and that "O for a heart to praise my God" is found in the great
majority of British hymnbooks and in a considerable number of those
published in the United States.

A comparable affirmation of the quality of life open to persons
strengthened by the Spirit is found in the refreshingly different language of a hymn by Miriam Drury (b. 1900) written in 1969:

> Walk tall, Christian,
>   walk tall and have no fear;
> the Christ of God whose child you are,
>   he holds you in his care.

Succeeding stanzas admonish Christians to walk true, free, and
proud, trusting not in their own unaided powers, but assured that

> to upright, pure, forgiving souls,
>   his bounties overflow.

In the closing stanza Christians are called on to be Christ's ambassa-
dors in the realization that

> his gospel and his church are judged
>   by what his people are.[12]

Other hymns extend to society the promise of what life can become when empowered by God. Enthusiasm for "Rise up, O men of
God," by William P. Merrill (1867–1954) has declined, partly because
of realism regarding the coming of a "day of brotherhood" to "end
the night of wrong," and partly because the masculine language of
the hymn leaves many women feeling excluded. It may well be
replaced by a new hymn by Norman O. Forness (b. 1936), found so
far only in the *Lutheran Book of Worship.* Far more than a revision
or a paraphrase, it begins:

> Rise up, O saints of God!
>   from vain ambitions turn;
> Christ rose triumphant that your hearts
>   with nobler zeal might burn.

Later stanzas urge the saints of God—presumably persons committed to divine purposes—to speak out God's word of hope amid
today's despair and to act in love to heal the pain of creation. They
are not expected to "bring in" the kingdom but to embrace its tasks,
not to end wrong but to "give justice larger place." They are not
simply people who strive mightily toward the heights, but persons
centered in and strengthened by God:

> Commit your hearts to seek
>   the paths which Christ has trod,

and quickened by the Spirit's power,
rise up, O saints of God![13]

Another hymn that combines realism and hope for society is "Turn back, O man, forswear thy foolish ways," by Clifford Bax (1886–1962). Reversing the usual imagery, he pictures earth's "tragic empires" as built by human beings in an agelong dream; they are now called to awaken from their "haunted sleep" and join in striving for a world that accords with the reality of "God's whole will." When that occurs, "Earth shall be fair, and all her folk be one!"[14]

DIVINE AND HUMAN AGENCY

With few exceptions, Christian hymn writers agree that human beings cannot realize their potential unless they are "quickened by the Spirit's power." In their own strength alone they are unequal to the task, but when they are open to the divine leading and supported by the divine presence they can live as sons and daughters of God.

The part played by men and women in salvation has often been the subject of vigorous theological controversy. Strict Calvinists have held that fallen humanity has lost all power to choose the good, but that God has elected some for salvation, and divine grace acts in them to carry out his sovereign will. On the other hand, thinkers influenced by Jacobus Arminius (1560–1609) have maintained that election is conditioned by the human response and that even fallen human beings retain sufficient freedom to reject or accept the divine initiative. This belief obviously grants to humanity an essential role in the fulfillment of the divine will, though it still asserts the centrality of unmerited grace.

Hymnists do not deal theoretically with this question of human versus divine agency, but their poems are practical expressions of discernible theological positions. Thus when ordinary Christians who may never have heard of Calvin or Arminius are asked to sing certain hymns, they are in effect called on to embrace one of the alternatives mentioned.

Several hymns previously cited affirm explicitly or implicitly the sole agency of God.[15] Similarly, in "Jesus, the sinner's friend, to thee," Charles Wesley, burdened by the consciousness of his inability to rise above his fallen condition, pleads for the divine action which alone can save him. The third stanza states clearly the Calvinistic position:

At last I own it cannot be
that I should fit myself for thee;
here, then, to thee I all resign;
thine is the work, and only thine.[16]

However, in "Jesus, I look to thee" the same author speaks of "claim-
ing" the promised divine presence, and in the third stanza he writes:
"We meet, the grace to take / which thou hast freely given."[17] In
many other hymns he assumes the need for human action in accepting God's grace and turning to God for strength and guidance. The
same assumption underlay the lifelong evangelistic efforts of the
Wesleys, in which they appealed to sinners to exercise their freedom
to turn from their sinful ways. The apparent contradiction disappears
if we recognize that Charles Wesley's hymns are cast in the language
of devotion and personal experience. Conscious of his failure to heal
himself, he gratefully ascribes to divine grace the sole responsibility
for his deliverance.

Something of the same "paradox of grace"[18] may be at work in
Adelaide A. Pollard (1862–1934) when she writes:

> Have thine own way, Lord, have thine own way!
> thou art the potter, I am the clay.
> Mold me and make me after thy will,
> while I am waiting, yielded and still.

In the opening lines of the fourth stanza she reiterates her plea:
". . . Have thine own way! / Hold o'er my spirit absolute sway!"
However, in the intervening stanzas she appeals only for help,
cleansing, and healing; while in her closing couplet she asks to be so
filled with the divine spirit that observers will see "Christ only, always, living in me."[19]

If the potter-clay metaphor is strictly applied, it clearly excludes
all human choice in both the process and the product. Yet the
poem as a whole may be interpreted simply as expressing the
poet's fervent desire to fulfill in every aspect of her life the purpose
of God. It can be and often is sung with that intent. Nevertheless,
it is hard to translate "yielded and still" into active, responsible
human participation in the creative work God is doing in the
world. If Christians see themselves as clay in the hands of the potter, they can easily accept the status quo as what God wants, feeling no responsibility whatever for changing it. Quiescence too easily becomes acquiescence in evils that should be uprooted, not
ignored, in the rationalized trust that God will remove them in
God's own good time.

In contrast to hymns that ascribe an active role to God alone, there
are many that, while regarding divine grace as basic, portray human
beings as summoned to respond in active trust to the divine initiative. Here Charles Wesley may be cited again. In "A charge to keep
I have," after accepting his commission to "glorify God," he states
more specifically what this means:

> To serve the present age,
> my calling to fulfill;
> O may it all my powers engage
> to do my Master's will![20]

In "Take thou our minds, dear Lord," William H. Foulkes (1877–1961) in successive stanzas conceives Christians as offering their minds, hearts, and wills in service to the God who is the source of all human powers. The paradox involved in affirming both divine and human agency in the same act appears again here. God is invited to reign in our souls, to hold full sway in our wills, and to guide "our ordered lives" in the divine way, but human accountability is assumed throughout. The relationship emerges unmistakably in the closing stanza:

> Take thou ourselves, O Lord, heart, mind, and will;
> through our surrendered souls thy plans fulfill.
> We yield ourselves to thee—time, talents, all;
> we hear, and henceforth heed, thy sovereign call.[21]

Few hymns bring out the relation between divine and human agency more effectively than the one by Daniel Merrick (b. 1926) which begins:

> O God whose love compels us
> to be thy light and way,
> to stand in perfect freedom
> and yet thy will obey.

The compulsion is clearly not that of a dictator, but the persuasive power of self-giving love. We live in a "decisive hour" and need help to make the right choices. Depicting the pride, greed, and bloody warfare that corrupt life on earth, the hymn prays that God will "make sensitive our spirits, / with love to intercede." The closing prayer asks:

> O give thy church new courage;
> renew her heart and mind,
> that flames of love's compulsion
> may kindle all mankind.[22]

The hymns just considered can hardly fail to remind us of the counsel of Paul to the Philippians: "You must work out your own salvation in fear and trembling; for it is God who works in you, inspiring both the will and the deed, for his own chosen purpose" (Phil. 2:12–13). This remains a central paradox of Christian faith.

6

JESUS CHRIST

THE PERSON OF JESUS CHRIST

God and humanity are never sharply separated in Christian faith. The God who is worshiped is the Creator and Liberator of human beings, and men and women find their highest fulfillment only in God. The fullest expression of this relationship is Jesus Christ. Hence the question of Jesus at Caesarea Philippi, "Who do you say that I am?" (Matt. 16:15–16; Mark 8:29; Luke 9:20) assumes basic importance for both theology and hymnody.

The longest articles of the Apostles' and Nicene Creeds are those affirming belief in Jesus Christ. The two foci of Christian worship, Word and Sacrament, proclaim in mutually enriching fashion the saving action of God in Christ. In hymnbooks arranged by topics the largest section is often that devoted to Jesus Christ, and sections or subjects like repentance, forgiveness, discipleship, and the Christian year add to this preponderance. The variety of images used by hymnists to refer to Jesus evidences further the special status accorded him: to mention a few, he is Light, King, Messiah, Prince of glory, Sun of righteousness, Immanuel, Word, priceless treasure, Lord, joy of loving hearts.

Through sheer repetition, the interpretations of Christ found in hymns may exert greater influence on the average Christian than any other medium. What do they say? This question can be answered best against the background of the New Testament witness and the church's later formulations.

Basic Affirmations

A careful reading of the Gospels and the epistles makes clear the belief of the early Christian community that somehow divine and human action were interwoven in Jesus.

88

"No man ever spoke as this man speaks," reported the Temple police (John 7:46). There was about him a quality of life and an inner authority that produced in those most closely associated with him an overwhelming awareness of the presence of God. Through him flowed a moral and spiritual power that exposed sham, convicted men and women of sin, and transformed those who committed themselves to his way. Even his crucifixion, regarded by the authorities as the ignominious death of a criminal, came to be seen as the supreme disclosure in history of the self-sacrificing love of God. Not even death could hold him. Soon after the initial shock of his death, his followers became joyously aware that the same Presence they had known in the days of his flesh was still with them, and they began to proclaim the good news of the risen Christ.

The New Testament accounts are equally clear about Jesus' humanness. He was conceived in a human womb and born of a human mother. He grew physically and in mental, moral, and spiritual insight. His life covered the whole range of typically human experiences: hunger and thirst; sleeping and waking; temptation; weariness and loneliness; suffering and sorrow; friendship, love, and joy. He felt the need for prayer and acted on it. He was subject to human limitations of space. Nor was he omniscient; he made inquiries to find out what he did not know, and disclaimed knowledge of some things he believed God knew. He even denied his own goodness: "No one is good except God alone." Finally, he endured physical cruelty, and died a real death.

Nevertheless, the Gospels portray Jesus as a thoroughly unified personality, a perfectly integrated life. Somehow the divine and the human were present not in alternation, but in complete oneness. He was all of one piece.

The earliest Christians did not attempt to construct careful theories concerning his person. However, they did testify that through him the transforming power of God had entered their lives, and was available to others. They began to say that God had become incarnate in him, as when the apostle Paul declared: "God . . . has caused his light to shine within us, . . . the revelation of the glory of God in the face of Jesus Christ" (II Cor. 4:6).

As the new faith spread throughout the Roman Empire, many efforts were made to comprehend the relation of Jesus the Christ to God, and later that between the divine and the human in his person. As various alternatives were rejected, the mainstream thought of the church answered the first question in the Nicene Creed (A.D. 325 and 381), and the second in the Definition of Chalcedon (451). Both statements were naturally formulated in terms of the dominant philosophy of the time, using the Greek notion of substance. The former asserted belief that the Son is "eternally begotten of the Father, God from God, Light from Light, true God from true God, begotten, not made, one in being [substance] with the Father." The latter rejected views that emphasized either the divinity or the humanity of Jesus Christ at the expense of the other, and declared that in him complete deity and complete humanity were merged, so that he was "of one substance" with each—one person "in two natures, without confusion, without change, without division, without separation."

Though the Chalcedonian formula offered no explanation as to how the two natures could be one person, it became the official doctrine of the early church. It is still widely regarded as the orthodox view, and its intention to safeguard both divinity and humanity in our conception of Jesus Christ is shared by most Christian bodies today.

Nevertheless, interpretations of Jesus Christ still differ as much as did those of the fourth and fifth centuries. Some lay primary if not exclusive emphasis on his divinity. Others regard him chiefly as a great teacher and a noble example of human life at its best. Still others attempt in various ways, using contemporary language, to maintain the balance of the Chalcedonian view. Thus the Statement of Faith of the United Church of Christ affirms simply that "in Jesus Christ, the man of Nazareth," God "has come to us and shared our common lot, conquering sin and death and reconciling the world to himself."

We turn now to ask what representative hymns have to say regarding the human and the divine in Jesus Christ. Four types of interpretation may be distinguished.

Conceptions of Jesus Christ in Hymnody

HYMNS THAT STRESS DIVINITY AND SUBORDINATE HUMANITY

"Jesus, thou joy of loving hearts!" is a paraphrase by Ray Palmer (1808–1887) of five stanzas of a twelfth-century poem dubiously attributed to Bernard of Clairvaux. Here Jesus in effect takes the place of God, who is not mentioned. Attributes normally identified with God in Christian faith are ascribed to Jesus; he is fount of life, source of unchanged truth, all-in-all, and living bread. The closing stanza prays:

> O Jesus, ever with us stay;
>   make all our moments calm and bright.

"Jesus, priceless treasure," by Johann Franck (1618–1677, tr. by Catherine Winkworth), makes a similar identification. The second stanza, addressed to Jesus, interchanges Jesus and God as our protector in danger:

In thine arm I rest me; / foes who would molest me
   cannot reach me here.
Though the earth be shaking, / every heart be quaking,
   God dispels our fear;
sin and hell in conflict fell
with their heaviest storms assail us;
   Jesus will not fail us.

In "Rise, my soul, adore thy Maker!" by John Cennick (1718–1755), the ascription of deity to Jesus is explicit, though contradictory, since Jesus/God is both prayed to and entreated to pray for the worshiper:

O my Jesus, God almighty,
   pray for me,
   till I see
   thee in Salem's city.[1]

The opening lines of a popular hymn by Joseph M. Scriven (1819–1886) likewise identify Jesus with the God we approach in prayer:

What a friend we have in Jesus,
   all our sins and griefs to bear!
What a privilege to carry
   everything to God in prayer.

An Asian Christian view of the incarnation is provided in a hymn written in 1963 by Daniel T. Niles (1908–1970), which relates the events of Jesus' birth to his resurrection and his significance as Savior. The equation of Jesus with God is clear in the opening stanza:

On a day when men were counted,
   God became the Son of man;
that his name in every census
   should be entered was his plan.
God, the Lord of all creation,
   humbly takes a creature's place;
He whose form no man has witnessed
   has today a human face.[2]

There is an important place in worship for hymns that lay primary stress on the action of God in Christ without explicitly and simultaneously recognizing Jesus' humanness. Yet hymns that confuse Jesus with God and either ignore or exclude his real humanity run counter to the New Testament witness. The very essence of Christian faith in the incarnation is that God has become manifest in a fully human life; the Jesus who disclosed God to men and women not only appeared to be but actually was human. Some hymn writers have

sought particularly to conserve this truth. A few examples will show
how.

HYMNS THAT FOCUS ON THE HUMAN LIFE OF JESUS

In sharp contrast to the hymns just cited are some that emphasize
Jesus' earthly life and teachings. These authors, mostly American,
may trace his insights and his strength to his personal relation to God,
but in these hymns they are inspired primarily by his vision of human
life and moved to follow his example. Thus in "O Master, let me walk
with thee" Washington Gladden (1836–1918) asks for patience, trust,
hope, and peace as he in company with Jesus shares the burdens of
others and seeks to guide the hesitant and the wayward in the paths
of true fulfillment.

Several hymns of John Greenleaf Whittier (1807–1892) are of this
type. His "O brother man, fold to thy heart thy brother" is mainly
a poem in support of the practical religion urged by James 1:27. The
third stanza identifies such outreach with the life of Jesus:

> Follow with reverent steps the great example
> of him whose holy work was doing good;
> so shall the wide earth seem our Father's temple,
> each loving life a psalm of gratitude.

Jay T. Stocking (1870–1936), taking his cue from the concern of the
twelve-year-old Jesus to be about his Father's work, addresses him as
the "Master Workman of the race" and the "Carpenter of Nazareth,"
and envisages our responsibility also as that of doing God's work.[3]
Milton S. Littlefield (1864–1934) likewise sees the Son of Man as
"Workman true" who shows us how to fulfill God's will by perform-
ing well our daily tasks:

> O Son of Man, thou madest known,
> through quiet work in shop and home,
> the sacredness of common things,
> the chance of life that each day brings.[4]

For some hymnists the humanness of Jesus is manifest not only in
his provision of an ethical example but also in his practice of prayer.
James Montgomery (1771–1854), for instance, is impressed by the
fact that Jesus himself felt the need to pray and became a model for
the prayer life of others. Note the appeal in the closing stanza of
"Prayer is the soul's sincere desire":

> O thou, by whom we come to God,
> the life, the truth, the way,

> the path of prayer thyself hast trod:
> Lord, teach us how to pray.[5]

Montgomery's lines are a salutary reminder that hymns which laud the human Jesus can be as one-sided as those which praise his deity. In honoring Jesus Christ as master teacher, skilled craftsman, and ethical example we have no warrant for overlooking his relation to the God whose love and purpose he disclosed.

Fortunately, we find in many hymns on Jesus Christ other interpretations than the contrasting emphases so far considered. Two approaches in particular preserve the balance exhibited in New Testament portrayals. One of these regards Christ as the eternal creative Word manifest in the man Jesus; the other conceives Jesus as the incomparable Revealer of God. Both views merit examination.

HYMNS THAT INTERPRET CHRIST
AS THE CREATIVE WORD ENACTED IN JESUS

A paraphrase by F. Bland Tucker (b. 1895) of the anonymous Epistle to Diognetus (second or third century) tells how "the great Creator of the worlds" gave "his holy and immortal truth" to people on earth:

> He sent no angel of his host
> to bear the mighty word,
> but him through whom the worlds were made.
> the everlasting Lord.
>
> He sent him not in wrath and power,
> but grace and peace to bring,
> in kindness, as a king might send
> his son, himself a king.[6]

The Spaniard Aurelius Prudentius (348–ca. 413), in "Of the Father's love begotten / ere the worlds began to be," presents Christ as the agent of both creation and redemption. With an allusion to Ps. 33:6, 9 the hymn declares,

> By his word was all created;
> he commanded and 'twas done.

It then goes on to affirm that the same love came in human form,

> that the race from dust created
> might not perish utterly.[7]

Two medieval Latin hymns of unknown authorship present Christ unequivocally as creator of the world. One of them, dating from the

eighth century, deals mainly with his saving activity, but opens with
these lines:

> O Christ, our hope, our heart's desire,
>   creation's mighty Lord,
> Redeemer of the fallen world,
>   by holy love outpoured.[8]

The other, a much more widely known hymn, probably from the
ninth century, ascribes both salvation and creation to Christ:

> Creator of the stars of night,
> the people's everlasting light,
> O Christ, the Savior of us all,
> we pray now, hear us when we call.[9]

In "At the name of Jesus / every knee shall bow," Caroline M. Noel
(1817–1877) extols Jesus rather than Christ as both the agent of creation and conqueror of sin and death. The closing lines of the first
stanza assert:

> 'Tis the Father's pleasure
> we should call him Lord,
> who from the beginning
> was the mighty Word;

and the second stanza opens with this declaration:

> At his voice creation
> sprang at once to birth.

Since Christians commonly believe that "God the Father" is "Creator of heaven and earth," what do these writers mean by ascribing
creation to the Word, or Christ, or even Jesus? They are influenced
mainly by several New Testament passages. The prologue to the
Fourth Gospel begins, "When all things began, the Word already
was. The Word dwelt with God, and what God was, the Word was.
. . . Through him all things came to be." Yet the world has not
recognized the source of its life and light. "So the Word became flesh;
he came to dwell among us, and we saw his glory, . . . full of grace
and truth" (John 1:1–3, 10, 14). The author borrows from Greek
philosophy the concept of the *Logos* (Word, Wisdom, Reason), which
brought the transcendent God into active relation to the created
order. John thereby asserts that the ultimate reality is not remote
from our world, but caringly involved in it. Indeed, God as the Word
has spoken, as it were, in history, becoming manifest in an actual
human life. The self-giving love that brought forth the world has now
acted decisively to save it.

Two other passages convey a similar message, though they use the imagery of the Son instead of the Word. The apostle Paul describes the Son as "the image of the invisible God," in whom all things were created. Through coming to dwell in him, "God chose to reconcile the whole universe to himself" (Col. 1:14–20). Likewise the author of The Letter to the Hebrews, after referring to God's speaking fragmentarily through the prophets, declares that God has now "spoken to us in the Son whom he has made heir to the whole universe, and through whom he created all . . ." (Heb. 1:1–3).

Passages like these, which use the images of Word and Son to point to God's active presence in both creation and the new creation, also support a distinction between the divine Word or Son and the man Jesus in and through whom God acts. It is clear that Jesus, if human in any recognizable sense, could not possibly be the creator of the universe, whereas the Word, conceived as God's self-utterance in relation to the world that owes its existence to God, can be so described. Most of the hymn writers who praise the Word recognize this distinction, and awareness of it on our part will deepen the meaning of our singing.

The distinction sheds light also on the question of "preexistence." Strictly speaking we cannot soundly affirm the preexistence of the man Jesus, who was born of a human mother on a specific date in a particular place. However, if we wish to use traditional language, we can quite legitimately speak of the preexistence of the Word, or the Son, or Christ, since all of these point to the eternal activity of the Spirit that was disclosed in Jesus—an activity that has been going on since the beginning of creation.

Here we are reminded again of the important difference between literal, factual statements and interpretative images, between metaphors and analogies and the realities to which they refer. Terms like Son, Word, Immanuel are not precise descriptions of the Eternal in time; they are rather our efforts to express the meaning of what God has done and is doing in human life and history. Physicists use "models" such as clusters of little balls to represent the structure and functioning of the atom, and such models fit the facts well enough to advance human knowledge, but those who build them do not claim that these constructs replicate the exact nature of reality. If this is true in scientific study of measurable entities, how much truer it must be of religious language where no quantitative investigation is possible. We have no charts or photocopies of the divine-human relation, but we have metaphors that advance understanding, fit the realities of religious experience, and furnish a dependable basis for the commitments of faith.

In *The Interpreter's Dictionary of the Bible* it is pointed out that, as used by Christians, the term "incarnation" was derived from the

Latin translation of John 1:14 and means "the revelation of God in the human life of Jesus of Nazareth."[10] This definition leads directly to the second of the ways by which hymnists try to maintain a balance between the divinity and the humanity of Jesus Christ.

HYMNS THAT VIEW JESUS CHRIST
AS THE UNPARALLELED REVEALER OF GOD

For many authors of hymns the way to understanding the relation of Jesus to both God and humanity is the simple awareness that through what they know of Jesus they have been led into the very presence of God. He is to them the supreme clue to the divine will and purpose.

In "We would see Jesus," J. Edgar Park (1879–1956) pictures modern people approaching Jesus much as did the Greeks who sought him during the Passover in Jerusalem (John 12:21). Most of the hymn describes the historical Jesus preaching, teaching, healing, and inviting women and men to follow him. Yet he is no ordinary leader. "Shining revealed" through his performance of lowly village tasks is a light which for Park is "the Christ of God,"

> divine and human, in his deep revealing
> of God and man in loving service met.

Such an appeal and authority are his that people respond with their lives:

> Let us arise, all meaner service scorning:
> Lord, we are thine, we give ourselves to thee.[11]

In "Christ is the world's light" Fred Pratt Green (b. 1903) depicts Christ as the world's light in whom we see God, the world's peace who unites us in God, and the world's life who redeems us for community in God's kingdom. He who is our brother is the unique disclosure of God our Father:

> Christ is the world's light, he and none other;
> born in our darkness, he became our brother.
> If we have seen him, we have seen the Father:
> Glory to God on high.[12]

For Alan Gaunt (b. 1935) Christ's voluntary acceptance of helplessness is both the mark of his true humanity and the key to his perfect revelation of God. The opening stanza of "Lord Christ, we praise your sacrifice" honors him for a love so great that he could forgive those who took the life he freely gave, thereby displaying perfectly the love and power of God. The third stanza, after acclaiming the now reigning Lord, continues:

> for ever by your victory
> is God's eternal love proclaimed.

The love which accepts death yet triumphs over it opens the way to hope and newness of life for all humanity.[13]

Hymns like these picture Jesus the Christ as a fully human person indwelt by the Spirit of God, thus enabled to reveal the divine character in unequalled fullness. The relationship does not entail the suppression or replacement of one consciousness by another, but the trustful, affirmative response of the man Jesus to the creative and redemptive initiative of the divine Spirit. Opening his life completely to God's loving intention, Jesus became spiritually one with his Father—in attitude, purpose, and will. His human center of consciousness was centered also in God. In him we see both the self-giving and compassionate love of God and God's norm for humanity —"the eldest among a large family of brothers" who are "shaped to the likeness of his Son" (Rom. 8:29).

The Question of Hymns Addressed to Jesus

Brief consideration should be given to a special form of the Christological question in hymnody—that of hymns addressed to Jesus. Ten of the standard denominational and ecumenical hymnals now in use contain between 10 and 24 hymns each in which Jesus is addressed in the opening line, and a good many others that begin with words or phrases like "O Jesus," "Lord Jesus," "Savior," or "Come, thou long-expected Jesus."

Many of these clearly or ostensibly think of Jesus quite literally as God. In addition to those already cited, examples include Sylvanus D. Phelps's "Savior, thy dying love," Charles Wesley's "Jesus, lover of my soul," "Jesus, the very thought of thee" (twelfth-century Latin), Thomas B. Pollock's "Jesus, with thy church abide," and Henry Collins' "Jesus, my Lord, my God, my all."

But what of hymns like Henry van Dyke's "Jesus, thou divine companion," John E. Bode's "O Jesus, I have promised," William W. How's "O Jesus, thou art standing," or Clement of Alexandria's "Shepherd of tender youth"? Some of these stress qualities and events in the human life of Jesus. Others focus on the claims made on our lives by the things he stands for. Clearly such hymns are not meant to be taken literally. How are they to be interpreted?

A considerable number of hymns and lines of hymns addressed to Jesus use a figure of speech known as apostrophe. In literature an apostrophe is a digression in the form of an address to a personified idea or object or person not literally present. The *Encyclopaedia Britannica* defines it as "a turning away from one's immediate audience to address another who may be present only in the imagination."[14] Examples in general literature are legion: "O liberty! what crimes are committed in thy name!" (attributed to Madame Roland on the scaffold, 1793); "Chillon! thy prison is a holy place" (Lord Byron); "Death, be not proud" (John Donne); the beautiful apostrophe to light at the beginning of Book III of John Milton's *Paradise Lost.* For a bit of comic relief note these lines from Oliver Herford's *Child's Natural History:*

> O Mongoose, where were you that day
> when Mistress Eve was led astray?
> If you'd but seen the serpent first
> our parents would not have been cursed.

Numerous instances may be found also in hymns that are not addressed to Jesus. Among them are "All creatures of our God and King"; "Faith of our fathers"; "O Zion, haste"; "O little town of Bethlehem"; "My country, 'tis of thee"; and "Watchman, tell us of the night." Hence it should occasion no surprise to find Jesus addressed apostrophically, as he is in hymns like Luther's "Ah, dearest Jesus, holy Child"; Henry F. Lyte's "Jesus, I my cross have taken"; and Patrick Appleford's "Jesus, humble was your birth";[15] along with hymn lines beginning "O holy Child of Bethlehem"; "What language shall I borrow / to thank thee, dearest Friend?"; and "Come, Prince of Peace, and reign."[16]

The recognition that some hymns and lines are apostrophes to Jesus, not addresses to him as God, will have value mainly for Christians who cannot honestly identify him with God. If they can address him in these hymns "as if" he were present in person when he is not literally there, possibly they can speak to him in similarly figurative manner in some other hymns intended quite literally by their authors. Indeed, such interpretation is not utterly different from that of worshipers who do not actually identify Jesus and God yet contentedly sing hymns addressed to "Lord Jesus" or "Savior," because the associations of these words impart to them the value of God. It is also likely that some Christians who do in words make the Jesus-God identification unconsciously accept it for this reason: they think of God in terms of Jesus.

In some hymns it is impossible to be sure whether the address to Jesus is literal or apostrophic. In such cases worshipers will follow their own best judgment. Many Christians, of course, have no problem with hymns that treat Jesus as God. Those who do have this problem may take one of three courses: (1) They can use the hymn in worship, trying to think of God in terms of Jesus, or as symbolized by Jesus. (2) They may address Jesus apostrophically, thereby conserving all the rich values suggested by his significance for faith. (3) If neither of these options is possible without distortion or artificiality, they can choose not to participate in singing the hymn. All three of these options may be followed by people in the same congregation, and with full mutual respect.

THE SAVING ACTIVITY OF JESUS CHRIST

The Atonement in Christian Thought

Christian faith centers in what God has done and is doing for human salvation. It is therefore not surprising that hymns concerned with Jesus Christ focus on his saving activity more often, and more directly, than on the more theoretical question of his person. Nevertheless, the church has never formulated a definitive statement on the redemptive work of Christ, or the atonement, comparable to those of the Nicene Creed or the Declaration of Chalcedon on his relation to God and humanity. None of the ecumenical councils preceding the split between East and West in 1054 produced a doctrine of the atonement, and there exists today no determinative or universally accepted view of the meaning of Christ for salvation.

The word "atonement" refers to the at-one-ment or reconciliation of human beings to God and one another through divine action in the life, suffering, death, and resurrection of Jesus Christ. It is the renewal of our relationship with God that has been broken by sin, and, derivatively, the restoration of personal wholeness and the reestablishment of right human relations. Just what is the role of Jesus Christ in this process?

If we begin with the New Testament, as we should, we find no carefully wrought answers, but a variety of metaphors drawn from the law court, the slave market, the home, temple worship, and the human experience of death and life. These became the basis for later thought. The divergent theories that emerged as the centuries passed can without injustice to any be grouped under three main types.

1. Among the ancient Greek fathers (Irenaeus, Origen, Athanasius, Gregory of Nyssa) Christ is portrayed as imparting to human beings enlightenment, incorruption, and victorious deliverance from sin and death. His life and sacrificial death provided knowledge of God and a needed example for human life. As the incarnate Logos who united divine and human natures, the immortal with the mortal, he purged humanity from corruption and mortality and made possible the renewed union of humanity with God. His death on the cross— understood as a supreme act of obedience, a recapitulation in reverse

of Adam's fall, and a ransom paid to Satan for the release of sinners
—was crowned by his resurrection, which demonstrated his supremacy over sin and death and destroyed their power. This type of
thought, centering in the notion of *Christus Victor,* has been called
by Gustaf Aulén the "classical" theory.

2. Medieval and orthodox Protestant thought produced various
theories which, though differing widely, agree in viewing the atonement as an objective transaction centering in satisfaction or penal
substitution. According to Anselm (1033–1109), Jesus Christ satisfied
the honor of God, which had been offended by human sin. Repara-
tion had to be made by a human being, since the sin was human, yet
made by God, since no finite being could make amends for the
offense against the infinite. Hence the necessity for the God-man,
whose vicarious death, crowning a perfect life, provided a super-
abundant satisfaction. According to the penal theory of John Calvin
(1509–1564), Christ took on himself the punishment demanded of
humanity by divine justice, thus appeasing God's wrath and making
forgiveness possible when Christ's work is accepted in faith.

3. The personal or moral theory formulated by Peter Abelard
(1079–1142), followed by Schleiermacher, Ritschl, Bushnell, and others, assumes that the barrier to salvation lies in humanity rather than
God, and finds the central meaning of the cross in its supreme revelation of God's self-sacrificing love, awakening in human beings repentance, love, and obedience. Jesus' life and teachings furnish men
and women with their perfect example; contemplation of his cross
moves them to want to serve the loving God there disclosed.

The Atonement in Hymns

GOD'S VICTORIOUS POWER OVER EVIL

Two widely loved hymns of praise accent the victory of Christ as
the key to salvation. In "O for a thousand tongues to sing" Charles
Wesley exults:

> He breaks the power of canceled sin,
>   he sets the prisoner free.

Edward Perronet (1726–1792) in "All hail the power of Jesus' name,"
invites all who have been "ransomed from the fall" to crown Jesus
Lord of all.

This conception appears frequently in hymns celebrating the liturgical year from Advent to Easter. In "Savior of the nations, come,"
Ambrose of Milan (340–397) calls on believers to raise the song of
triumph for him who came "captive leading death and hell." He then
salutes the Savior:

> You, the Father's only Son,
> have o'er sin the victory won.[17]

In English we have only one stanza of "Break forth, O beauteous heavenly light," by Johann Rist (1607–1667), but the light announces the child who will break the grip of sin:

> This child, now born in infancy
> our confidence and joy shall be,
> the power of Satan breaking,
> our peace eternal making.[18]

Familiar among other Advent hymns with this theme are Charles Wesley's "Come, thou long-expected Jesus" and Philip Doddridge's "Hark, the glad sound, the Savior comes."

The note of conflict and victory is sounded in hymns for Lent and Palm Sunday. In the second stanza of "Lord, who throughout these forty days" Claudia F. Hernaman (1838–1898) relates the struggles of Jesus to those of his followers, with a prayer for aid:

> As you with Satan did contend,
> and did the victory win,
> O give us strength in you to fight,
> in you to conquer sin.[19]

In "Ride on! Ride on in majesty!" Henry H. Milman (1791–1868) sees the triumphal entry as a promise of the decisive victory to follow:

> O Christ, your triumph now begin
> o'er captive death and conquered sin.

The harsh reality of the conflict with evil comes to the fore in hymns on the cross of Christ. Frederick W. Faber's "O come and mourn with me awhile!" stresses the sorrow and pain of the cross, but rejoices all the more that the love of God is triumphant. Faber's original refrain, "Jesus, our Love, is crucified," has been amended in most hymnals by the substitution of "Lord" for "Love." The closing stanza exclaims,

> O Love of God! O sin of man!
> In this dread act your strength is tried,
> and victory remains with Love,
> for he, our Lord, is crucified.[20]

It is in hymns on the resurrection that the affirmation of Christ's victory over sin and death reaches its climax. Three of these are representative. In Martin Luther's "Christ Jesus lay in death's strong bands" the triumph named is that over death alone, though the defeat of sin is implied. The second stanza paints a vivid picture of both conflict and conquest:

> It was a strange and dreadful strife
>   when life and death contended;
> the victory remained with life;
>   the reign of death was ended.
> Stripped of power, no more he reigns,
> an empty form alone remains;
> his sting is lost forever![21]

The joyous Easter hymn "Come, ye faithful, raise the strain," by John of Damascus (ca. 696–ca. 754), relates the triumph of Christ to both sin and death.[22] Little known but deserving of much wider use is the hymn of Clement of Alexandria (ca. 170–ca. 220) "Sunset to sunrise changes now." The poem as paraphrased by Howard C. Robbins is a message of the newness of life and "gleams of eternity" conveyed by the events of the cross and the resurrection. The final stanza is a succinct summary:

> Here in o'erwhelming final strife
>   the Lord of life hath victory;
> and sin is slain, and death brings life,
>   and sons of earth hold heav'n in fee.[23]

Few hymns are more jubilant than a new one by Brian A. Wren (b. 1936) that begins:

> Christ is alive! Let Christians sing.
>   The cross stands empty in the sky.
> Let streets and homes with praises ring.
>   His love in death shall never die.

Wren emphasizes the significance of Christ's conquest for "every place and time," and relates it to our ruinous divisions of color, nationality, and wealth. In all these "he suffers still," yet lives and "loves the more."

> Christ is alive! His Spirit burns
>   through this and every future age,
> till all creation lives and learns
>   his joy, his justice, love, and praise.[24]

The patristic notion of the death of Jesus as a ransom paid to Satan for the release of humanity from his control is too crude to be tenable today. One who is the epitome of evil could hardly have a claim on the human race that even God must respect, nor does the idea of a divine deception (since through the resurrection Satan lost the payment agreed upon) square with the character of God. However, bondage to Satan is an understandable way of expressing the helplessness of those who fall short in spite of their best efforts and intentions. Likewise, if taken metaphorically, the ransom motif—borrowed from the ancient slave market—may symbolize vividly the deliverance that faith attributes to Jesus Christ.

VICARIOUS PAYMENT OF THE PRICE OF SIN

Frequently expressed in hymnody is the conception that the atonement consists in satisfaction of God's honor offended by sin or payment of the penalty demanded of the sinner. According to these theories, God in mercy accepts the death of Christ in substitution for the deserved death of human offenders, making possible their forgiveness. Cecil Frances Alexander (1818–1895) writes in "There is a green hill far away":

> There was no other good enough
> to pay the price of sin;
> he only could unlock the gate
> of heaven and let us in.

This Jesus did by suffering and dying on the cross "that we might be forgiven."

In "Jesus, thy blood and righteousness," Nicolaus von Zinzendorf (1700–1760) rejoices that these offerings of the Savior have "fully absolved" him from sin, fear, guilt, and shame. The blood of Christ continually pleads for sinners at the mercy seat of God:

> Thou hast for all a ransom paid,
> for all a full atonement made.[25]

A similar emphasis is found in " 'Tis the most blest and needful part," by Christian Renatus von Zinzendorf (1727–1752) and Christian Gregor (1723–1801), set to a popular melody adopted at Herrnhut about 1740. For these writers the atonement is no merely objective legal transaction; it works a real change in the human heart:

> Naught in this world affords true rest
> but Christ's atoning blood;
> this purifies the guilty breast
> and reconciles to God.[26]

Whether or not the Wesleys' atonement theology was, like their understanding of faith, directly influenced by Moravian thought, their hymns are in tune with Moravian beliefs on this issue. John translated some of the hymns of Nicolaus von Zinzendorf, including the one just cited, and many of Charles's hymns uphold a penal substitutionary view. One example must suffice. In the second stanza of "Victim divine, your grace we claim," Charles Wesley addresses the Savior:

> You stand within the holiest place,
>   as once for guilty sinners slain;
> your blood for sinners intercedes
>   redemption for the world to gain.
> Your blood shall still our ransom be,
>   the payment made to set us free.[27]

The popular American hymn writer Fanny Crosby (1820–1915) stands also in this tradition. Among the 8,500 hymns she is said to have written is "To God be the glory! great things he hath done!" It is substitutionary but not legalistic, rooting the atoning work of Christ in the love of God asserted in John 3:16 and making faith a condition for the realization of the forgiveness won by Christ:

> O perfect redemption, the purchase of blood!
> To every believer the promise of God;
> the vilest offender who truly believes,
> that moment from Jesus a pardon receives.[28]

Finally, we may cite an early twentieth-century hymn by Somerset C. Lowry (1855–1932) which begins, "A man there lived in Galilee." The second stanza praises Jesus for his courageous and self-sacrificial action, and concludes:

> No thought can gauge the weight of woe
>   on him, the sinless, laid;
> we only know that with his blood
>   our ransom price was paid.[29]

These hymns suffer from a legalistic, abstract, mechanical idea of merit, guilt, and punishment, which are integral to personality and not literally transferable. The action of another person in paying a fine or serving a jail sentence that I have incurred might leave quite unchanged my truculent, hostile attitude toward society. Salvation is not essentially a change in our status before God from condemnation to justification. It is rather a dynamic process through which we enter new relationships with God, ourselves, and one another. It involves an internal transformation of personality in which love to God and those God loves becomes dominant in our lives.

Such hymns also tend to make justice or honor, rather than love, determinative in God, assuming an opposition inconsistent with belief in the divine unity. The assumption seems to be that the demands of divine justice must be met before the love of God can function effectively. Implicit likewise is the supposition, contrary to New Testament teaching, that Jesus' death changed the effective attitude of God toward human beings from wrath to love, enabling God to do for sinners what otherwise would have been impossible.

Another problem is the impression of coarse literalism sometimes made by repeated references to the blood of Jesus. Blood is indeed a fitting symbol of life itself, and the voluntary shedding of blood a moving metaphor for self-forgetful, self-giving love. Multitudes have been led by concern for the suffering to contribute to a blood bank, or to give transfusions for relatives, friends, or even unknown persons whose lives are endangered. But the language of some hymns distracts attention from the inner meaning of Jesus' offering of self, defeating the purpose of their authors. Terms like "sacred veins," "sprinkled," and "precious stream" may often be used figuratively, but they are offensive to many Christians who are nevertheless deeply moved by the suffering love of God which they find manifested in Jesus' acceptance of the cross.

However, these hymns of penal substitution contain elements of great permanent significance. They make dramatically plain the depths and the extent of human wickedness. They underline the holiness of God who cannot tolerate the pride, self-will, and disobedience of those created in love for communion with God and one another in the actualization of high values. They sense rightly the costliness of the divine mercy and the lengths to which God is willing to go to redeem those alienated by sin, while reflecting vividly the profound gratitude of sensitive souls released from their burden of guilt.

PERSONAL RESPONSE TO DISCLOSURE OF GOD'S SUFFERING LOVE

According to the personal or moral conception of atonement, if we are to be reconciled to God, our sinful wills must be changed. This transformation is accomplished when we are moved by the disclosure of God's self-giving love to repentance and personal commitment. The first two stanzas of a hymn by Peter Abelard, its most famous exponent, state this view clearly:

> Alone thou goest forth, O Lord,
>   in sacrifice to die;
> is this thy sorrow naught to us
>   who pass unheeding by?
>
> Our sins, not thine, thou bearest, Lord;
>   make us thy sorrow feel,
> till through our pity and our shame
>   love answers love's appeal.[30]

An early English expression of this view, intensely personal, is "My song is love unknown," by Samuel Crossman (1624–1683). Of its seven stanzas we quote the first and the last, found in many hymnals.

> My song is love unknown,
>   my Savior's love to me;
> love to the loveless shown,
>   that they might lovely be.
> O who am I, that for my sake
> My Lord should take frail flesh and die?
>
> Here might I stay and sing,
>   no story so divine;
> never was love, dear King,
>   never was grief like thine!
> This is my friend, in whose sweet praise
> I all my days would gladly spend.

One of the most universally beloved hymns on the passion of Christ is "O sacred Head, now wounded," the last section of an anonymous Latin poem from about the eleventh century. Its setting to the tune of PASSION CHORALE has given it special poignancy. Meditation on the undeserved sufferings of Christ evokes a confession of participation in the sin that led, and leads, to his crucifixion, and a fervent prayer for forgiving grace. This culminates in grateful, unreserved commitment:

> What language shall I borrow / to thank thee, dearest Friend,
> for this thy dying sorrow, / thy pity without end?
> O make me thine forever; / and should I fainting be,
> Lord, let me never, never / outlive my love to thee.

Thankful giving of self in response to the divine love manifested in Jesus Christ is also the theme of one of Isaac Watts's best-loved hymns, "When I survey the wondrous cross." Contemplation of the cross leads both to the rejection of previous self-centered values and to unqualified self-dedication:

> Were the whole realm of nature mine,
>   that were a present far too small;
> love so amazing, so divine,
>   demands my soul, my life, my all.

Two twentieth-century hymns merit special attention. Both add a social dimension to the sins that crucify Christ afresh in every generation. In "O crucified Redeemer" Timothy Rees (1874–1939) sees the passion of Christ reenacted wherever "love is outraged," "hope is killed," and human lives are destroyed by bloodshed in war or the bloodless battles that selfish people wage for economic gain. He closes his hymn with the prayer:

> O crucified Redeemer,
>   these are our cries of pain;
> O may they break our selfish hearts,
>   and love come in to reign.[31]

Walter Russell Bowie (1882–1969) opens his Advent hymn "Lord Christ, when first thou cam'st to men" by referring to the men who mocked Jesus with the crown of thorns, but quickly adds:

> And still our wrongs may weave thee now
> new thorns to pierce that steady brow,
>   and robe of sorrow round thee.

Awareness of these wrongs—unfaith, hate, war—move Bowie to ask for "a new advent of the love of Christ" and the peace it promises. He closes with this apostrophe:

> O wounded hands of Jesus, build
>   in us thy new creation;
> our pride is dust, our vaunt is stilled;
>   we wait thy revelation.
> O love that triumphs over loss,
> we bring our hearts before thy cross,
>   to finish thy salvation.[32]

Though Bowie's final stanza speaks of the triumph of love, the hymns just examined tend to overlook the objective victory of God over evil demonstrated in the cross and resurrection. With notable exceptions, their sense of the magnitude of sin and the awesome holiness of God is less keen than that found in hymns illustrative of the other views. However, they recognize the saving significance of the life as well as the death of Jesus. They rightly center attention on the reconciling love of God proclaimed by the gospel. They also make unmistakably clear the need for inner transformation of the sinner if salvation is to become real.

PORTRAYAL OF A NORMATIVE HUMAN LIFE

Many hymns emphasize an aspect of the saving activity of God that deserves more attention—the degree to which the life, teachings, and death of Jesus Christ provide a model of what life can be when empowered by divine grace and informed by the divine will. The Greek fathers found saving value in the knowledge of God's purpose imparted through the exemplary life and sacrificial death of Jesus, and theologians in the Abelardian tradition agree in finding in the gospel narratives a model for human life. Those who are aware of God's forgiving love need guidance on what is involved in a God-centered life. We are saved *to* something as well as *from* something, and what we are saved to is the abundant life promised in John 10:10 and illustrated by the life of Jesus as a whole.

The earliest extant Christian hymn, written probably by Clement of Alexandria about 200, praises the "Shepherd of tender [sometimes translated *eager*] youth, / guiding in love and truth." On the basis of trust in divine strength, the third stanza seeks needed direction:

> Ever be thou our guide,
> our shepherd and our pride,
>   our staff and song;
> Jesus, thou Christ of God,
> by thy perennial Word,
> lead us where thou hast trod,
>   our faith make strong.[33]

A refreshing illustration of the guiding value of the life of Jesus is found in the hymn by Somerset C. Lowry already cited as an example of the substitutionary view of the atonement. The first stanza of "A man there lived in Galilee" closes with these lines:

> A perfect life of perfect deeds
>   once to the world was shown,
> that all mankind might mark his steps
>   and in them plant their own.[34]

Such hymns remind us that those who through Christ are reconciled to God and others find in him trustworthy guidance for living as members of God's family. "Christ also suffered for you, leaving you an example, that you should follow in his steps" (I Peter 2:21).

COMPLEMENTARY TRUTHS

The four interpretations of the saving activity of Jesus Christ differ considerably in details. None of them is sufficient in itself. However, they all express true insights that complement rather than oppose one another, as shown by the presence in some hymns of two or more views that in their historical formulations appear contradictory. If we concentrate on their positive values and avoid their weaknesses, we find that together they comprise an illuminating account. They portray a God who in Christ shows righteous love, condemns sin, and offers forgiving and transforming grace. As human beings respond in gratitude, repentance, faith, and love, they enter the new life of God's daughters and sons. Jesus Christ mediates to sinful, finite men and women the invincible, holy, and sacrificial love of God, thus reconciling them to God, their neighbors, and themselves.

It may be useful to reflect on possible alternative meanings of the language of some of our hymns. To say that Christ died for our sins may mean that he died in our place, paying the price that otherwise would have been exacted of us. But the assertion can also be taken to mean that he died *because* of human sin—the sins of his contemporaries, and by implication our own—thereby making us aware of our iniquity, and by his self-giving, suffering love disclosing God's grace and moving us to repentance.

Martin Luther's Easter hymn "Christ Jesus lay in death's strong bands" declares that Christ died

> . . . for our offenses given;
> but now at God's right hand he stands
> and brings us life from heaven.

These words probably meant for Luther that Christ bore the cost of sin in our stead and destroyed the power of sin and death. However, they may express for other Christians that God as disclosed in Jesus Christ suffers because of our offenses, and by so doing overcomes our sinfulness and opens the way to newness and wholeness of life. Such an interpretation, in the spirit of Isa. 53:4–5, combines elements of truth found in all three of the major atonement theories.

A similar option confronts us if we sing a joyful new hymn by Willard F. Jabusch (b. 1930), "The King of glory comes, the nation rejoices." The third stanza affirms,

> He gave his life for us,
>   the pledge of salvation;
> he took upon himself
>   the sins of the nation.[35]

These lines can be interpreted as substitutionary, yet just as readily they may be taken to mean that the King of glory, by exposing himself to the sins of humanity, demonstrated the devastating results of sin and greed, and at the same time revealed the forgiving mercy of God that accomplishes our reconciliation. Such reinterpretation may enrich the meaning of some of our hymns and extend their usefulness.

7

THE HOLY SPIRIT

Belief in the Holy Spirit has been relatively neglected in the worship and teaching of the church. Apart from the use of the Trinitarian formula in doxologies, benedictions, and other elements in the liturgy, there is little to remind people of this aspect of the faith they presumably profess, or to deepen their understanding of its meaning. Contrast the major emphasis given in most congregations to Advent, Christmas, Lent, and Easter in the church year to the slight attention usually devoted to Pentecost and the season that follows. It is hardly surprising that confusion and ambiguity regarding the Holy Spirit are widespread. We touched briefly on the place of the Spirit in Christian hymnody in Chapter 4,[1] but further exploration is highly desirable.

THE HOLY SPIRIT IN CHRISTIAN TEACHING

Though the biblical writings testify eloquently to the activity of God as Spirit, the ancient creeds have comparatively little to say. The English version of the Apostles' Creed has only one six-word sentence on the Holy Spirit, whereas the Christological article runs to 74 words. In the Nicene Creed as adopted at Constantinople in 381, the long article on Jesus Christ is followed by a much briefer third article affirming belief in "the Holy Spirit, the Lord, the giver of life." The centuries-long controversy that followed—as to whether the Spirit "proceeded" only from the Father or from both the Father and the Son—contributed to the split between the Eastern and Western branches of the church in 1054, but did little to clarify the role of the Spirit in Christian life. In recent years various communions have sought to affirm the significance of the Spirit in contemporary terms.

Keeping in mind the biblical witness, historical declarations, and present-day affirmations and discussions, we can summarize in six propositions the dominant emphases in contemporary belief in the Holy Spirit.

1. The Spirit is the living, indwelling presence of God in the church and the world, God as actively related to and immanent in creation.

2. The Holy Spirit is the Spirit who moved and moves over "the surface of the waters" to create the world (Gen. 1:2), who "descended" on Jesus in his baptism and empowered him throughout his ministry, who at Pentecost initiated the Christian community by transforming fearful disciples into confident witnesses, and who has worked ever since within and outside the church to recreate and renew human life.

3. Hence the Holy Spirit is God continuing the saving action wrought through Jesus Christ, seeking to fulfill God's creative purpose by bringing to reality a new creation.

4. More specifically, the Spirit is:

a. the Life-giver, who seeks constantly to lead persons from fragmentation to inner harmony and fullness of life;

b. the Spirit of truth, who guides persons into deeper understanding of the God disclosed in Jesus Christ, and of God's meaning for their lives (John 14:17; 15:26; 16:13);

c. the Spirit who like fire acts to cleanse, heal, and purify (Acts 2:3–4);

d. the Spirit of power, giving courage, victory over temptation, and strength for service in fulfillment of the divine will (Acts 1:8);

e. the Spirit of love and unity, forming people of faith into a covenant community marked by love to God and one another, solidarity with persons of all races, nationalities, and languages, and responsibility toward the whole created order (Acts 2:1–21, 37–47; 4:31–33; ch. 10).

5. The life of the Spirit is marked by spontaneity, unpredictability, and novelty. Like the wind that "blows where it will" (John 3:8), it cannot be harnessed, controlled, or manipulated for limited human ends.

6. The functions of the Holy Spirit in some ways closely parallel those of the Word incarnated in Jesus Christ. The similarity need not be confusing. Both Word and Spirit are models that help to articulate the Christian experience of God. To say that the Word disclosed in Jesus of Nazareth was active in creation is to affirm the close connection between creation and redemption in the activity of one God. Likewise, when we assert that the Spirit that empowered Jesus is the same Spirit that brought the world into being and continues to work transformingly in the Christian community and the world, we accent both the unity and the rich diversity of the life of God. Truly understood, the terms "Word" and "Spirit" can often be used interchangeably without violence to either. We can say with equivalent meaning

that "the Word became flesh" in Jesus (John 1:14) or that "the Spirit of the Lord . . . anointed" him (Luke 4:18). As G. W. H. Lampe points out, "the Spirit that was in Jesus . . . was the Presence that wrought creatively and redemptively in and through him, the Logos, the Christ."[2] If a choice needed to be made, Spirit would probably be the preferable term, since it suggests more clearly than Word the personal character of the divine, and provides better anchorage for the love, wisdom, power, and righteous purpose that Christian faith finds in God.[3]

THE HOLY SPIRIT IN HYMNODY

Hymns with a central focus on the Holy Spirit are relatively few. A sampling of eight hymnbooks shows from 8 to 23 hymns on the Spirit, with far more that have to do with either God the Father or Christ. The same disparity appears in hymnals arranged according to the church year. Our concern here, however, is not quantitative comparison. We want to know what hymns celebrating the Holy Spirit have to say, and what light they shed on the Christian life. In the main we discover them to be of high quality. They have also been touched less by doctrinal controversy than have our Christological hymns.

Two that come immediately to mind are so well known as to need no more than passing mention: "Spirit of God, descend upon my heart," by George Croly (1780–1860), and "Breathe on me, breath of God," by Edwin Hatch (1835–1889). Both give voice to a fervent desire for that love toward God which marks the life that is wholly centered in and empowered by the Spirit. Both are deeply individualistic, but they manifest neither world denial nor irresponsibility. They are saved from self-centeredness by their concern to love God and what God loves.

The oldest extant hymn centering on the Holy Spirit is the anonymous Latin "Veni Creator Spiritus" from the ninth century, usually set to a plainsong melody. According to John Julian, 35 English translations had been made by 1907. The best known and most widely used is "Come, Holy Ghost, our souls inspire," translated by John Cosin (1594–1672). Initially printed in the Prayer Book for responsive reading, it was first introduced for singing in 1861 by *Hymns Ancient and Modern.* It is still read responsively in the ordination services of various communions; the words of the first two of the four stanzas make plain its appropriateness for this purpose:

> Come, Holy Ghost, our souls inspire
> and lighten with celestial fire;

> thou the anointing Spirit art,
> who dost thy sevenfold gifts impart.
>
> Thy blessed unction from above
> is comfort, life, and fire of love;
> enable with perpetual light
> the dullness of our blinded sight.

Another seventeenth-century translation is that of John Dryden (1631–1700), which begins, "Creator Spirit, by whose aid / the world's foundations first were laid."[4] More accurate than either Cosin's or Dryden's is the translation by Robert Bridges (1844–1930). The flavor of his more contemporary language is happily conveyed in the opening stanza:

> Come, O Creator Spirit, come,
> and make within our hearts thy home;
> to us thy grace celestial give,
> who of thy breathing move and live.[5]

Still more recent is the free translation by John Webster Grant (b. 1919). The first two stanzas provide a good example of the freshness of this version:

> O Holy Spirit, by whose breath
> life rises vibrant out of death,
> come to create, renew, inspire;
> come, kindle in our hearts your fire.
>
> You are the seeker's sure resource,
> of burning love the living source,
> protector in the midst of strife,
> the giver and the Lord of life.[6]

In all of these translations the Holy Spirit is seen as the divine source of creation and new creation; and as the indwelling presence of God bringing life, light, and love, forgiving grace, strength, purity, truth, and inspiration. All close with praise to the Trinity. All refer, like the Latin version, to the sevenfold gifts. What are these gifts of the Spirit?

The reference is to the charisms specified in five passages found in the New Testament letters: Rom. 12:6–8; I Cor. 12:8–10; 12:28; and 14:6; and Eph. 4:11. The Spirit is manifest in diverse ways: wise speech; the expression of knowledge in words; faith; healing; miraculous powers; prophecy; ability to distinguish true from false spirits; ecstatic utterance; and ability to interpret such utterance. Actually, Paul seems to list nine gifts, not seven. But wise speech and the ability to express knowledge in words may be treated as one gift, and the same is true of ecstatic utterance and its interpretation. These are apparently the seven gifts referred to by the ninth-century Latin poet.

Though these words are obviously pertinent to the work of the clergy, in Paul's letters they are addressed to all the Christians in the church at Corinth, and by implication to all Christians at all times. Also, they are examples of the Spirit's gifts, not a complete inventory. The list can be broadened indefinitely to include all our talents, seen as gifts of divine grace to be used in stewardship to the Spirit who is their source.

From the early fifteenth century comes a moving hymn, published in many collections, by the Italian Bianco da Siena (ca. 1367–1434). The felicitous translation by Richard F. Littledale (1833–1890) and the unusual 6.6.11.D. meter of Ralph Vaughan Williams' DOWN AMPNEY give it a wide appeal. The mood of the entire hymn is set by the opening stanza:

> Come down, O love divine,
>   seek thou this soul of mine
> and visit it with thine own ardor glowing;
>   O Comforter, draw near,
>   within my heart appear
> and kindle it, thy holy flame bestowing.

The remaining three stanzas ask light for the earthly path, charity toward others, lowliness of heart, and the unspeakable grace and joy of the life "wherein the Holy Spirit makes his dwelling."

About a century later Martin Luther wrote "Come, Holy Spirit, God and Lord," basing it on a fifteenth-century manuscript that was itself an adaptation of a medieval Latin antiphon. In keeping with the historic functions of the Spirit, the hymn prays for wholeness, for the love and faith needed to unite the church, for guidance to true knowledge of God and freedom from error, and for power to persevere in the Lord's work, whatever trials may come.[7]

In "Holy Spirit, truth divine," included in many standard hymnals, Samuel Longfellow (1819–1892) uses a series of abstract nouns to address the Spirit, but the prayer that follows each is concretely related to the felt needs of the poet and those who join him in song. God is the Spirit of truth, but also of love, power, peace, and right. As truth, the Spirit is petitioned to awaken us and clear our sight; as love, to purge us of self-centeredness; as power, to strengthen us for courageous living; as peace, to calm our turmoil and save us from restless anxiety; as right, to reign over consciences freely committed to the divine purpose.

Hymns on the Holy Spirit written in the twentieth century reflect on the whole a deepened consciousness of the social dimension of life in the Spirit. In "O Spirit of the living God" Henry H. Tweedy (1868–1953) begins with a prayer for the church, but for him the unity portended by Acts 2:2–4 includes a new order of human relations. Thus he asks that the Spirit may inspire the church

> to utter living words
> of truth which all may hear,
> the language all men understand
> when love speaks loud and clear,

paving the way for the coming of "God's glorious commonweal."[8]

John R. Peacey (1896–1971) refers to the Spirit's power that filled the infant church, and asks,

> O Holy Spirit, in the church today,
> no less your power of fellowship display.

Yet the church's passion for unity must extend far beyond its own numbers. So the prayer continues:

> Widen our love, good Spirit, to embrace
> in your strong care the men of every race;
> like wind and fire with life among us move,
> till we are known as Christ's, and Christians prove.[9]

The "explosive years" of recent British hymnody—the decade of the 1970s—have produced a number of first-rate hymns on the Holy Spirit. A look at three of them will provide a fair sample of their message.

Fred Pratt Green prays that he may always treasure three of the Spirit's gifts above all others: love, joy, and peace. Actually these are the first of the nine fruits of the Spirit mentioned by Paul in Gal. 5:22–23. But the difference between gifts and fruits (NEB, harvest) is largely academic. The hymn bears witness that God's love is at the root of every gift, flower, or fruit; that to possess amid evil an indestructible love is joy; and that the Spirit enables us to face the mystery and uncertainty of the future in peace. The closing stanza, still in the first person, changes from singular to plural:

> We go in peace, but made aware
> that in a needy world like this
> our clearest purpose is to share
> love, joy, and peace.[10]

The hymn by Fred Kaan, "We turn to you, O God of every nation," refers specifically to the work of the Holy Spirit only in addressing the "Giver of life and origin of good" in the first stanza, and in

mentioning Pentecost in the final stanza. But it is to God as Spirit,
whose "love is at the heart of all creation," that he turns for healing
of the rifts between people and nations:

> Free every heart from pride and self-reliance,
>   our ways of thought inspire with simple grace;
> break down among us barriers of defiance,
>   speak to the soul of all the human race.

He goes on to pray for wisdom and "the light of love" in all who strive
for right relations, for sensitivity to human needs, and finally for a
sense of the oneness of humanity through the Spirit who dwells in all:

> Unite us all for we are born as brothers;
> defeat our Babel with your Pentecost.[11]

No hymn known to me voices more vividly the excitement and joy
of the Spirit's presence than "There's a spirit in the air," by Brian A.
Wren (b. 1936). Successive stanzas celebrate the action of God in the
breaking of the Communion bread, the feeding of a hungry child, the
struggle to overcome wrong with right, the provision of homes for
the homeless, and changes wrought in human thoughts and ways.
Four of the seven stanzas close with the couplet,

> Praise the love that Christ revealed,
> living, working, in our world.

The other three end with the lines,

> God in Christ has come to stay;
> we can see his power today.[12]

Is there a better delineation of the Holy Spirit than the simple words,
"God in Christ has come to stay"?

Most of the hymns considered in this chapter are prayer poems
addressed to the Spirit of God in whom we live, move, and have our
being. Their petitions are aptly summarized in this prayer by Charles
F. Whiston:

> Come O Holy Spirit,
> come as Holy Fire and burn in us,
> come as Holy Wind and cleanse us within,
> come as Holy Light and lead us in the darkness,
> come as Holy Truth and dispel our ignorance,
> come as Holy Power and enable our weakness,
> come as Holy Life and dwell in us.
> Convict us, convert us, consecrate us
> until we are set free from the service of ourselves
> to be thy servants to the world. . . . Amen.[13]

8

THE CHURCH AND ITS MISSION

The most dramatic manifestation of the activity of the Holy Spirit recorded in the New Testament is that which occurred on the Day of Pentecost in Jerusalem (Acts 2). People of many nations and languages experienced together an "outpouring" of the Spirit which made them vividly aware of their oneness, moved them to repentance, aroused faith in the God disclosed in Jesus Christ, and formed them into a covenant community. Thus the Christian church was born.

It is therefore fitting that in the Apostles' Creed, affirmation of faith in "the holy catholic church" follows immediately that in the Holy Spirit, with one "I believe" serving for both. In the Nicene Creed likewise, the article on the Holy Spirit is followed by the assertion, "We believe in one holy catholic and apostolic church." Recognizing the same relationship, we now follow our study of the Holy Spirit in hymnody with examination of the ways in which hymn writers understand the nature and mission of the church.

There is already a poetic quality in the metaphors used in the New Testament to characterize the church. Most frequently it is referred to as the body of Christ, the people of God, the New Israel, the household of God, a chosen people, a royal priesthood, a holy nation, a temple for the Spirit. We might accurately draw together the rich meanings of these figures if we described the church as the worshiping, witnessing, teaching, serving community of those who have responded in faith to the transforming love of God in Jesus Christ, and who in the power of the Spirit seek to manifest that love and extend its reign.

Now, whether we use the creedal adjectives, the biblical metaphors, or some such summary as that just attempted, we are likely to elicit a strenuous objection: "A beautiful picture, but that's not the church I know. The church as it really exists today is anything but holy. It's divided into hundreds of denominations, and even locally it's often plagued by competing cliques and weakened by individual members who are seemingly unsustained by personal faith, self-centered rather than loving, more interested in exercising power than in witnessing for Christ, and unmoved by the needs of suffering humanity."

So which portrayal of the church is true? The answer, of course, is "Both." The first portrayal is normative, presenting the church as it ought to be, the church God wants. The second is descriptive, listing characteristics that are disturbingly common in the empirical church —although omitting many evidences of far closer approximation to the norm. The church is composed of forgiven sinners who fall short of God's intention for their lives. Moreover, it is a sociological as well as a theological reality, hence exposed to and participant in all of the political, economic, psychological, and social forces that influence the life of any other human institution. As we examine hymns on the church, we shall want to ask whether their authors are singing about the glories of the ideal church or the shortcomings of the actual church, and to what extent they show an awareness of both.

THE NATURE OF THE CHURCH

The ritual provided in *The Worshipbook* (1972) of the United Presbyterian Church for the reception of members from other Christian communions includes this greeting: "Friends: As members of the one, holy, catholic, and apostolic church, you do not come to us as strangers, but as brothers and sisters in the Lord."[1] This use of the four adjectives taken from the Nicene Creed suggests that they are just as pertinent today as they were in the fourth century. We therefore use them as subtopics in discussing what our hymns say about the church.

Unity

Many hymns exhibit a vivid awareness of the genuine community into which those persons are called who recognize "one body and one Spirit, . . . one hope . . . , one Lord, one faith, one baptism, one God and Father of us all" (Eph. 4:4–6).

"Father, we thank you that you planted" is a paraphrase by F. Bland Tucker (b. 1895) of prayers from the Didache, or Teaching of the Twelve Apostles (second century), the earliest known manual of church order. The petition of the second stanza was designed to be used after the Eucharist:

> Watch o'er the church, O Lord, in mercy,
> save it from evil, guard it still;

> perfect it in your love, unite it,
>> cleansed and conformed unto your will.
> As grain, once scattered on the hillsides,
>> was in the broken bread made one,
> so from all lands your church be gathered
>> into your kingdom by your Son.[2]

A distinctive hymn by Cyprian of Carthage (third century), translated by F. L. Battles in 1971, opens each of its three stanzas with the declaration, "The church of Christ is one." Based on Rom. 11:17–21, it compares the church in sequence to the sun, a tree, and a spring. The sun remains "uncleft" even when one or more of its many rays is taken away; though branches broken from a tree cease to grow, the trunk stands firm; though one of the streams that flow from a spring may be choked at its source, the source continues to flow. So the church, though diffused throughout the earth, continues to shine because suffused in the one light of Christ; though the branches of the church are spread around the world, its body remains "whole, unbroken, one"; and though the Wellspring of the church flows outward in many directions, the Head remains always one.[3]

This exalted view of the church is echoed in a much more widely known hymn by Edward H. Plumptre (1821–1891) which begins, "Thy hand, O God, has guided / thy flock from age to age," and closes each stanza with the words, "one church, one faith, one Lord." The hymn recounts how successive generations in the church have proclaimed the goodness of God and bidden men and women to join "the great King's feast." Even when shadows were thick, plenteous grace enabled the witness to continue. In the fourth stanza the possibility is entertained that we might prove faithless and evade the conflict, but the idea is quickly rejected:

> Thy mercy will not fail us,
>> nor leave thy work undone;
> with thy right hand to help us,
>> the victory shall be won.[4]

Brian Wren, in "Lord Christ, the Father's mighty Son," is more realistic about the weaknesses of the church. He laments especially that differences related to the Lord's Supper interfere seriously with the churches' evangelistic task:

> To make us one your prayers were said,
> to make us one you broke the bread
>> for all to receive.
> Its pieces scatter us instead:
>> how can others believe?

The question is answered with a prayer:

> O Christ, forgive us, make us new!
> With love infuse the work we do;
>   your purpose achieve.
> Unite our praise and prayers to you
>   that the world may believe.[5]

Both realistic and hopeful is "Christ is the King! O friends, rejoice," by George K. A. Bell (1883–1958), a leader in the movement that led to the formation of the World Council of Churches in 1948. The first three stanzas summon people to exult in Christ's reign, praise the faithful souls who in ancient times followed Christ and won thousands to Christian discipleship, and summon Christians around the world today to "seek again / the way disciples followed then." The closing stanza is an appeal for unity in loving service:

> Let Love's unconquerable might
> your scattered companies unite
> in service to the Lord of light;
> so shall God's will on earth be done,
> new lamps be lit, new tasks begun,
> and the whole church at last be one.[6]

Holiness

Though the historical church is far from one, it seems even less appropriate to describe the church we know as holy—an adjective ordinarily used to refer to things divine. Reginald Heber in "Holy, holy, holy" declares, "Only thou art holy; / there is none beside thee." What warrant is there, then, for calling the church holy?

Historically, the basic reference of the adjective "holy" has probably been to the ineffable, the unutterable, the awe-inspiring, ordinarily related to the presence of God or the gods. Rudolf Otto in *The Idea of the Holy* describes it as the *mysterium tremendum*—tremendous because it is awesome, uncanny, overpowering, majestic, inexpressible; mysterious because it is "wholly other," yet uniquely fascinating and attractive.[7] However, this understanding of holiness has often been joined, notably in Hebrew-Christian faith, with a strongly ethical element. One definition of holy given by Webster is "infinitely good, perfect, and worthy of homage." In the call of Isaiah (Isa. 6:1–8) the God encountered is superlatively righteous as well as unfathomably mysterious, evoking a sense of the prophet's utter unworthiness, followed by his experience of pardon, cleansing, and commitment.

As a human institution the church cannot be holy as God is holy.

Its holiness is derivative, rooted in the indwelling of the Holy Spirit who called it into being and sustains its life. But because of this relationship the holiness of God offers our best clue to the meaning of holiness as applied to the church. Christians believe that the church and its worship provide special avenues by which we enter the presence of the holy God.

Both mystery and loving concern for people appear in hymnody as elements in the holiness of the church, though both are far removed from divine holiness. The ineffability of God is suggested in the third stanza of John Newton's "Glorious things of thee are spoken":

> Round each habitation hovering,
>> see the cloud and fire appear
> for a glory and a covering
>> showing that the Lord is near.

Hints of the divine mystery are found also in "The church's one foundation." Though Samuel J. Stone (1839–1900) stresses here the unity of the church, he derives it from the church's relation to her Lord: as "his holy bride" she "partakes one holy food" and blesses "one holy name."

Inevitably, the note of mystery is sounded in hymns on the sacraments, as in the verses of Horatius Bonar (1808–1889) which begin:

> Here, O my Lord, I see thee face to face;
>> here would I touch and handle things unseen.

Later the author sings of feasting at "the heavenly table spread for me" in "the hallowed hour of fellowship with thee."

Intimations of the ethical aspect of holiness are found in "One holy church of God appears," by Samuel Longfellow (1819–1892), especially in stanza three:

> The truth is her prophetic gift,
>> the soul, her sacred page;
> and feet on mercy's errands swift
>> do make her pilgrimage.

In the closing stanza the church is urged to "speed" her errand and fulfill her "task sublime":

> With bread of life earth's hunger feed;
>> redeem the evil time![8]

Similar concern for human need as a facet of churchly holiness appears in the prayer of John B. Pollock (1836–1896) which begins, "Jesus, with thy church abide." In one stanza he asks:

> May she guide the poor and blind,
> seek the lost until she find,
> and the broken-hearted bind:
> we beseech thee, hear us.

Finally he prays:

> May she holy triumphs win,
> overthrow the hosts of sin,
> gather all the nations in.[9]

A by-product of the church's relation to the holy God as expressed in hymnody is the durability of the church and its power to overcome opposition. Thus in "O where are kings and empires now" Arthur Cleveland Coxe (1818–1896) contrasts God's holy church with "the kingdoms of the world." Though threatened by earthquakes and tempests, "unshaken as eternal hills, immovable she stands."[10] The same confidence, evoked by the assurance of Matt. 16:18, is voiced by Samuel F. Smith in the hymn that begins,

> Founded on thee, our only Lord,
> on thee, the everlasting Rock,
> thy church shall stand as stands thy word,
> nor fear the storm, nor dread the shock.[11]

Unfortunately, this attitude sometimes blends almost impercepti- bly into triumphalism, a false sense of security, or quietistic content- ment with the ecclesiastical status quo. Thus John Newton, praising the Zion of which glorious things are spoken, goes on to ask:

> On the Rock of Ages founded,
> what can shake thy sure repose?

A related danger is identification of the church with the kingdom of God. The Zion that Newton glorifies is the "city of our God," while for Timothy Dwight (1752–1817) church and kingdom are inter- changeable terms:

> I love thy kingdom, Lord,
> the house of thine abode,
> the church our blest Redeemer saved
> with his own precious blood.

In one hymn Samuel Johnson (1822–1882) ascribes holiness to the church, identifies it with the kingdom, and extols its permanence. The first stanza begins,

> City of God, how broad and far
> outspread thy walls sublime!

The second stanza addresses "one holy church, one army strong." The fourth rejoices in the fact that both singing waves and drifting sands attack the church in vain:

> Unharmed upon the eternal rock
> the eternal city stands.[12]

Christians may rightly regard the church as a chosen instrument of God in the coming of the divine kingdom, but neither the New Testament witness nor a clear-sighted estimate of the church we know offers any convincing justification for equating the two.

Catholicity

In Protestant circles the word *catholic* is widely used as a synonym for *ecumenical*—having to do with the entire inhabited earth. As applied to the church it means universal or worldwide. This interpretation is legitimate and important. However, a further and much deeper meaning is often pointed out by Roman Catholic and Eastern Orthodox theologians.

The term *catholic* is derived from two Greek words, *kata* and *holos*, "according to the whole." With reference to the church, the wholeness refers in part to spatial extension, but even more to organic interrelatedness. According to Yves M.-J. Congar, a catholic church is a living organism whose members are animated and directed by its head, Jesus Christ. Catholicity is that property of the church by which the one (the fullness of the grace of Christ) and the many (the human nature of the church) are harmonized, so that the manifold expressions of the church exist in plenitude, "according to the whole."[13]

Nikos A. Nissiotis states that for Greek Orthodoxy the church is catholic primarily in a qualitative sense. Catholicity connotes fundamentally the wholeness of the salvation effected and offered in Christ and its availability to the entire world. The church is the steward of this wholeness and mediates the fullness of God's truth and grace. In and through its life human beings and the whole world become new creations by the divine action which permeates it.[14]

In both of these interpretations we see the church catholic as a unity-in-diversity, whose members with their varied gifts (see Eph. 4:11–16) are united in a living, interpenetrating communion—a redemptive community in the process of becoming whole and called to bring to others the fullness of life that becomes real when the grace of God flows through all.

The international, multiracial character of the church finds fairly frequent expression in hymnody. Recognition of catholicity as or-

ganic wholeness is less widespread, but it is clearly present in a
number of perceptive lyrics. Sometimes the two ideas are joined.

George W. Briggs (1875–1959) highlights the ecumenical motif in
his "Christ is the world's true light," where Christ shines as the
daystar "of every man and nation." The second stanza opens with the
glad affirmation:

> In Christ all races meet,
>   their ancient feuds forgetting;
> the whole round world complete,
>   from sunrise to its setting.[15]

A similar note is sounded by Roger K. Powell (b. 1914) in the second
stanza of "Lord, we thank thee for our brothers," where he declares,

> God be praised for congregations
>   coming side by side to thee;
> many tongues of many nations
>   sing the greater unity.[16]

In the familiar "In Christ there is no East or West," by John Oxenham (1852–1941), the emphasis on the universality of the church is
so marked that the deeper meaning of catholicity may easily escape
the singer. However, organic oneness is clearly suggested when the
second stanza speaks of the "high communion" of worshipers who
are bound closely together in loving service, and when the final lines
affirm the oneness in Christ of "all Christly souls" around the earth.

The interconnected wholeness of the body of Christ is occasionally
seen to extend beyond the church on earth to "the communion of
saints." Thus Samuel J. Stone in "The church's one foundation"
affirms the earthly church's union with God and her mystic communion "with those whose rest is won." Charles Wesley, sharing this
faith, opens one of his hymns with the invitation:

> Let saints on earth in concert sing
>   with those whose work is done;
> for all the servants of our King
>   in heav'n and earth are one.[17]

Apostolicity

In the history of the church, apostolicity has been interpreted in
three main ways.

1. In Roman Catholic thought it means that the grace of God in
Christ is transmitted through the apostles and their priestly succes-
sors, Christ's human representatives in the work of salvation. The
truth entrusted to the church and the validity of its ministry are

safeguarded by apostolic succession, through ordinations adminis-
tered by priests whose authority has been handed down in unbroken
line from Christ and the apostles whom he chose. The triple power
of teaching, priesthood, and government which the church dis-
charges is the same as that exercised by the Twelve, which proceeded directly from Christ, who is himself prophet, priest, and king.
Churches in the Anglican tradition share this view with respect to
ordination and the sacraments, while modifying it considerably with
regard to teaching and government. In recent Catholic thought,
influenced by the work of theologians like Yves Congar and the
pronouncements of Vatican II, lay persons also have their apostleship, that of mediating life from the body of Christ to the world,
which they are called to turn toward Christ, but it is the clergy who
mediate grace to the faithful.

2. According to the view broadly shared by Eastern Orthodoxy and
Protestant bodies, apostolicity consists in conformity with the faith,
life, and teaching of the apostolic church. In New Testament times
the basic call of God was to repentance, trust, witness, and service
within a fellowship of the transformed. Thus the entire body of believers, called to minister in Christ's name, succeeded to the ministry
of the apostles, and the whole church exercises that ministry today.
It is apostolic when it manifests the ongoing faith and life of the
apostolic church, recreated and renewed in each generation by the
indwelling Spirit of the living God.

3. A third meaning of apostolicity, which is affirmed by churches
holding both of the preceding interpretations, regards it simply as
acceptance of mission. The Greek noun *apostolos* designates a mes-
senger, one sent forth to carry a communication to others. Hence an
apostolic church is one that answers the call to bear witness to the
good news of God's reconciling love disclosed in the coming of Jesus
Christ. It is a community in mission, a body of persons commissioned
and committed to share as widely as possible the abundant life they
have found through Christ.

In recent years this interpretation has been developed in Roman
Catholic stress on the lay apostolate and Protestant emphasis on the
ministry of the laity. Both recognize that the gospel concerns the
whole life of humanity.

The first of the three views of apostolicity just presented is clearly
stated in only one hymn known to me—"Christ is gone up; yet ere
he passed," by John Mason Neale (1818–1866). After declaring that
Christ formed the church to last until his return, the author continues:

> His twelve Apostles first he made
> his ministers of grace;

and they their hands on others laid,
    to fill in turn their place.

So age by age, and year by year,
    his grace was handed on;
and still the holy Church is here,
    although the Lord is gone.[18]

Our hymns come closer to affirming the apostolicity of the church
in the second sense. Though they do not use the word *apostle,* a
number of them do praise the primitive church for its faith, its testimony, its courage, and its prayers. Since the influence of the apostles
was central in the earliest churches, it is safe to regard such hymnic
references as implying apostolic presence and ministry. A good example is the hymn by John R. Peacey (1896–1971) that begins,

Filled with the Spirit's power, with one accord
the infant church confessed its risen Lord.[19]

The same implication may be found in a prayer hymn by William
Harry Turton (1856–1938). Opening with the address, "O thou who
at thy eucharist didst pray," the hymn asks that through the Eucharist and in other ways divisions may be replaced by unity, then in the
closing stanza prays that "wand'rers from thy fold" may be brought

back to the faith which saints believed of old,
    back to the church which still that faith doth keep.[20]

When we turn to apostolicity in the third sense, we find that
hymn writers are quite explicit. Several interpret the commission
of the church as that of spreading light amid darkness. Thus William W. How's familiar "O Word of God incarnate" praises Christ
for the divine gift of the Scriptures, which shine like a lantern
throughout the centuries, and which the church uses to guide men
and women through the shadowy mists. The gift doubtless refers
also to the incarnate Word himself, whom the Scriptures proclaim.
The final stanza is a prayer that the church may be a worthy bearer
of the light.

O make your church, dear Savior,
    a lamp of purest gold,
to bear before the nations
    your true light as of old.

The same motif is prominent in the well-known "O Zion, haste, thy
mission high fulfilling," by Mary A. Thomson (1834–1923). The
church's message is "to tell to all the world that God is light." The
nature of the light becomes clear when the second stanza urges:

> Publish to every people, tongue, and nation
> that God, in whom they live and move, is love.

In "Your love, O God, has all mankind created" (1947, alt. 1972), Albert F. Bayly intercedes for the children of God's worldwide family, who strive for "life and freedom, peace and brotherhood"; confesses that the church has failed to manifest the love of Christ; and prays that it may be moved to bear an effective witness:

> Inspire the church, mid earth's discordant voices,
> to preach the gospel of her Lord above;
> until the day this warring world rejoices
> to hear the mighty harmonies of love.[21]

THE MISSION OF THE CHURCH

As we have seen, a church that is apostolic as well as one, holy, and catholic is a church in mission, sent to manifest the life of God to humanity and to lift the life of humanity to God. It is commissioned to witness to the reconciling, life-transforming love of God revealed in Jesus Christ; to arouse in human beings faith and commitment; and to lead them into righteous, loving relationships with God and other persons of all races and nations. Though the hymns on apostolicity in the third meaning deal broadly with the church's mission, they need to be supplemented by others that reflect more fully what hymn writers conceive that mission to be.

A comparison of the missionary hymns sung forty or fifty years ago with those in standard hymnals and supplements published within the past fifteen years or so discloses some far-reaching changes. During this period dialogue between Christians and adherents of other religions has led to greater mutual appreciation. A new self-consciousness and a heightened sense of the values of their own traditions have emerged among many non-Christians, sometimes producing missionary efforts of their own in nominally Christian lands. Leaders of Christian missionary endeavors have become painfully aware of the linkages between missionary enterprise and Western colonialism and imperialism, political and economic. Widespread revolutionary movements and the demands of the Third World countries for independence have often made missionary activity precarious or impossible. The stark realities of poverty, racism, and oppression have compelled reexamination of the nature and goals of Christian mission and reassessment of what accomplishments may be expected.

Inevitably these developments are reflected in our hymnody. Three in particular should be noted. First, the sharp black-and-white contrast between the darkness of superstition and error of non-Christian religions and the light and truth seen as exclusively Christian possessions has largely disappeared. In the once-popular "From Greenland's icy mountains," Reginald Heber (1783–1826) portrays the people of Greenland, India, and Africa as calling us to deliver "their land from error's chain," and summons churches to take to them the message of salvation:

> Shall we, whose souls are lighted
>   with wisdom from on high,
> shall we to men benighted
>   the lamp of life deny?
> Salvation, O salvation!
>   The joyful sound proclaim,
> till earth's remotest nation
>   has learned Messiah's name.[22]

This hymn appears in relatively few current hymnals, and the original second stanza, which spoke of "the heathen in his blindness" bowing down to wood and stone, has now been deleted from most of them.

Phrases like the following used to appear with a fair amount of frequency in standard hymns: "all the dark places / of earth's needy races"; "thick shadows"; "heathen lands"; "the futile cries . . . of superstition's cruel creed"; "let every idol perish"; "souls in heathen darkness lying / where no light has broken through." Hymns containing such expressions are rarely included in the most recent hymnals.[23]

A second change is a marked decline in optimism regarding attainment of the earlier goal of winning all peoples to Christ. The slogan of the Student Volunteer Movement, "The evangelization of the world in this generation," was echoed in the enthusiastic expectations of some of our hymns. Thus Samuel F. Smith (1808–1895) could write: "The morning light is breaking / the darkness disappears," continuing in the second stanza:

> See all the nations bending
>   before the God we love,
> and thousand hearts ascending
>   in gratitude above;
> while sinners, now confessing,
>   the gospel call obey,
> and seek the Savior's blessing,
>   a nation in a day.[24]

A third important development is a growing awareness that the mission of the church must relate the gospel to the total life of humanity. We cannot effectively present the claim of Christian faith to people today without reference to the economic, political, and social conditions that constantly, and often devastatingly, affect their lives. A message aimed only at saving individual souls is not enough. No missionary effort will win a serious hearing if it does not confront the social forces that unmake souls: the realities of poverty, racism, economic exploitation, and the power structures that bar the path of millions who seek freedom from all forms of inequality and oppression.

Early twentieth-century expressions of this broadened understanding of mission appear in "Heralds of Christ, who bear the King's commands," by Laura S. Copenhaver (1868–1940);[25] "Eternal God, whose power upholds," by Henry H. Tweedy (1868–1953);[26] and "The voice of God is calling," by John Haynes Holmes (1879–1964).[27] Two more recent hymns are representative of current thought.

In "Lord, thy church on earth is seeking" Hugh Sherlock (b. 1905) links the renewal of the church to its willingness to heed the great commission of Matt. 28:19–20, which he broadens to include the admonition, "Serve with love and share my grace." Telling of God's mercy "in all lands and with all races" means responding concretely to the urgent needs of burdened people:

> Freedom give to those in bondage,
>   lift the burdens caused by sin.
> Give new hope, new strength, and courage,
>   grant release from fears within;
> light for darkness, joy for sorrow;
>   love for hatred; peace for strife.
> These and countless blessings follow
>   as the Spirit gives new life.[28]

Fred Pratt Green makes a persuasive plea for Christian responsibility in and for the world by contrasting it with worship that ignores the needs of people outside the church. In "When the church of Jesus / shuts its outer door" he asks that the very prayers we utter while trying to mute the noise outside may make us "ten times more aware" that the world we exclude "is our Christian care."

> If our hearts are lifted / where devotion soars
> high above this hungry / suffering world of ours:
> lest our hymns should drug us / to forget its needs,
> forge our Christian worship / into Christian deeds.

Christians are in the world to demonstrate the self-sacrificial love of Christ. Hence the hymn counters the temptation to salve guilty consciences by gifts of "money, talents, time" with the prayer:

Lord, reprove, inspire us / by the way you give;
teach us, dying Savior, / how true Christians live.[29]

THE SACRAMENTS OF THE CHURCH

Word and Sacrament

Throughout these chapters, hymns have been understood as religious lyrics intended for use in worship. Though worship in the primitive Christian community was an integrated whole, it normally consisted of two phases: the service of the Word; and participation in the Lord's Supper, or Eucharist, at the beginning of which the catechumens, persons receiving instruction in the faith, were dismissed. This distinction between Word and Sacrament has persisted through the centuries. During the Middle Ages attention became increasingly focused on the action of the Mass, with the proclamation of the Word in Scripture and sermon reduced to a minimal role. With the Protestant Reformation, in spite of attempts to restore a balance between the two elements, the situation was often almost reversed; the central emphasis came to be laid on the preaching and interpretation of the gospel, while celebration of the Eucharist became less and less frequent.

Today, under the impact of liturgical studies sponsored by the World Council of Churches and various member communions, Protestants are laying new stress on more frequent and regular observance of the Lord's Supper; while since Vatican II the Roman Catholic Church is according to the sermon and the scholarly study and public and private reading of the Bible an increasingly larger place. On all sides there is recognition that any opposition between Word and Sacrament is false. Rather, they are two ways of presenting and receiving the same reality; hence they belong together, complementing and enriching each other. The Word is an audible Sacrament; the Sacrament, a visible Word.

The hymns examined in these chapters are used chiefly during the service of the Word. But hymns are sung also in preparation for and during the celebration of the Lord's Supper, or Eucharist, which liturgically follows the service of the Word. We therefore need to explore the belief content of representative Communion hymns.

The Eucharist

According to the Anglican Catechism, a sacrament is "an outward and visible sign of an inward and spiritual grace given unto us, ordained by Christ himself; as a means whereby we receive this grace, and a pledge to assure us thereof." In the Lord's Supper, bread and wine representing the body and blood of Christ are consumed by the communicants, signifying the giving and receiving of the forgiving grace of God enacted in the life, death, and resurrection of Jesus Christ. We too easily forget that the Greek word *eucharistia,* formed from the adjective *eu* (good, noble) and the noun *charis* (grace, favor, gratitude), means gratefulness or thanksgiving. Penitence and sorrow for sin are important aspects of the service, but its dominant note should be joy—joyous gratitude for God's self-giving, reconciling love, the restoration of forgiven sinners to communion with the living Christ, and the resultant renewal of community with other human beings. Ironically, the sacrament that should enable us to overcome alienation from God and one another has become one of the most divisive influences in relations between Christians and churches. Two issues basic to the meaning of the Lord's Supper are the nature of the sacrifice of Christ and the manner of the presence of Christ. Convictions regarding both find expression in our hymns.

The Eucharist and Christ's Sacrifice

According to traditional Roman Catholic doctrine, each celebration of the Eucharist is a new offering of Christ "in an unbloody manner." For Eastern Orthodoxy and Anglo-Catholicism it is a "sacramental representation of the once-for-all sacrifice on Calvary and of the perpetual sacrifice that is being offered by our Great High Priest."[30] Protestants are broadly agreed that the sacrament is a reenactment of Christ's self-offering in which he becomes present with redemptive grace to the faith of the church. Roman Catholic thought since Vatican II seems to be moving closer to the Orthodox and Anglo-Catholic view. Following suggestions from Thomas Aquinas and Pope Pius XII, it regards the Eucharist as a re-presentation of the unrepeatable sacrifice on Calvary.

A good statement of the Orthodox and Anglo-Catholic view and the modified Roman Catholic interpretation is the first stanza of a hymn by William H. H. Jervois (1852–1905).

> Wherefore, O Father, we thy humble servants
>   here bring before thee Christ thy well-beloved,
> all-perfect Offering, Sacrifice immortal,
>   spotless Oblation.[31]

Essentially the same conception is expressed in the opening stanza of a hymn by William Bright (1824–1901), though the fact that this hymn appears in some Presbyterian, Baptist, Methodist, and Congre-

gational hymnals as well as Anglican and Catholic books shows that
it permits a broader interpretation:

> And now, O Father, mindful of the love
>   that bought us, once for all, on Calvary's Tree,
> and having with us him that pleads above,
>   we here present, we here spread forth to thee
> that only Offering perfect in thine eyes,
>   the one true, pure, immortal Sacrifice.[32]

A fitting example of the view that sees in the Lord's Supper a
symbolic portrayal of the self-offering of Christ is a very familiar
hymn by Reginald Heber (1783–1826). The first stanza is a metaphorical address to Christ, the second a prayer for the bestowal of grace
through the elements received.

> Bread of the world in mercy broken,
>   wine of the soul in mercy shed,
> by whom the words of life were spoken,
>   and in whose death our sins are dead:
>
> Look on the heart by sorrow broken,
>   look on the tears by sinners shed;
> and be thy feast to us the token
>   that by thy grace our souls are fed.

A similar interpretation is contained in a recent hymn by Bernard
Mischke (b. 1926):

> Cup of blessing that we share,
> does it not his grace declare?
> Is it not the blood of Christ,
> who for us was sacrificed?
> As one body we are fed;
> Christ we share, one cup, one bread.[33]

The Eucharist and Christ's Presence

Another fundamental question regarding the Lord's Supper concerns the relation of the spiritual reality to the material elements.
Practically all Christians agree that somehow Christ is present, but
if we ask *how*, widely divergent answers are given.

The official Roman Catholic position affirms transubstantiation, the
belief that the substance (the underlying reality) of bread and wine
is by the consecration of the priest miraculously changed into the
substance of the body and blood of the risen and glorified Christ,
though the accidents (the sensible appearances perceived by sight,
taste, smell, etc.) remain the same.

According to Lutheran theology, in a conception often somewhat inaccurately called consubstantiation, the substances of bread and wine are unchanged, but to them are added the substances of the body and blood of Christ, truly present "in, with, and under" the physical realities.

In the thought of John Calvin (1509–1564) the bread and wine are signs of a present reality that cannot be seen or rationally comprehended, but that is connected to the form of the physical elements. The material symbols not only represent the body and blood of Christ to us, but also *present* them to us when we receive them in faith. Thus the Reformed churches teach that the body and blood of Christ are truly present to the faith of the receiver.

Ulrich Zwingli (1484–1531) shifted attention from the elements to the believers who partake of them. He regarded the Eucharist mainly as a commemoration or a memorial, involving, however, a present re-creation and not merely a remembrance of the past. In this act Christ is truly present in the recipients rather than in the bread and wine they receive. Zwinglian influence is apparent in many Protestants today, who often combine receptionism with Calvinistic tendencies.

We cannot expect theories like these to be neatly or precisely expressed in hymns. Authors do not consciously set out to write hymns that state specific views on the manner of Christ's presence. Yet inevitably the devotional language they use reflects their understanding, or that of their tradition, of what the Lord's Supper means.

The Roman Catholic doctrine of transubstantiation is obvious in the second stanza of the hymn by Thomas Aquinas, "Of the glorious Body telling":

> Word made flesh, by word he maketh
>   very bread his flesh to be;
> man in wine Christ's Blood partaketh;
>   and if senses fail to see,
> faith alone the true heart waketh
>   to behold the mystery.[34]

The Lutheran view is apparent in "Lord Jesus Christ, we humbly pray," by Henry E. Jacobs (1844–1932), who prays:

> Beneath these forms of bread and wine
> enrich us with thy grace divine.

In the third stanza he adds:

> All that thou art we here receive,
> and all we are to thee we give.[35]

John E. Bowers (b. 1923) concurs. In a hymn on the nativity of Christ, " 'Glory to God!' all heav'n with joy is ringing," he connects the manger with the table:

> Though now no crib or cradle is concealing
> Jesus our Lord in that far-distant shrine,
> Christ at each eucharist is still revealing
> his very self in forms of bread and wine.[36]

An unmistakably Zwinglian view is stated in a hymn by James Montgomery (1771–1854), "According to thy gracious word." Each of the first three stanzas closes with a promise to remember Jesus— his covenant, his suffering, his love. In the final stanza, like the dying thief, the author prays that Jesus, when the kingdom comes, will remember him.

Most Communion hymns weave together varied interpretations, as their authors seek to express the rich meanings the sacrament holds for them. Thus a hymn by Thomas Aquinas, "Thee we adore, O hidden Savior, thee," contains a stanza that might have been written by either Zwingli or Calvin:

> O blest Memorial of our dying Lord,
> who living Bread to men doth here afford!
> O may our souls forever feed on thee,
> and thou, O Christ, forever precious be.[37]

Points of contact with all three of the great Reformers can be detected in a new hymn by Colin P. Thompson (b. 1945):

> Christian people, raise your song,
>   chase away all grieving;
> sing your joy and be made strong,
>   our Lord's life receiving;
> nature's gifts of wheat and vine
>   now are set before us:
> as we offer bread and wine
>   Christ comes to restore us.[38]

Other Important Emphases

Along with the historical areas of doctrinal diversity regarding sacrifice and presence, hymns on the Lord's Supper give voice to a number of positive affirmations in which there is considerable agreement.

1. *Thanksgiving,* the basic meaning of the word *Eucharist.* It is expressed or implied in some of the hymns that stress sacrifice and presence, but also appears in many others. A hymn by Louis F.

Benson (1855–1930), "For the bread, which thou hast broken," gives thanks alike for the broken bread, the poured wine, and the spoken words.[39] G. A. Tomlinson (b. 1906), in "O holy Father, God most dear," closes his first stanza with the couplet,

> For bread set forth, for wine outpoured
> we bless thee, all-creating Lord;

then goes on in gratitude for the deeper meaning of the elements:

> O Christ, who at the supper-board
> took bread and wine and spoke the word,
> and in that solemn paschal meal
> gave Flesh and Blood our wound to heal;
> for man redeemed, for life restored,
> we bless thee, all-creating Word.[40]

2. *Confession.* Often sensitivity to divine grace and favor springs from either an awareness of unworthiness or a consciousness of sin forgiven. Hence hymns on the Lord's Supper, like the ritual for the sacrament, sometimes sound the note of confession. This note, heard in Heber's "Bread of the world in mercy broken," is audible also in the opening lines of a recent hymn by Muus Jacobse (b. 1909):

> We who once were dead
> now live, fully knowing
> Jesus is our head.
> Life is overflowing
> when he breaks the bread.

The same theme appears in the next stanza:

> We were lost in night,
> but you sought and found us.[41]

Significantly, the confession of sin implicit in these lines is closely linked with gratitude for life restored. This is true also of most eucharistic liturgies, though stress on confession in relation to thanks for forgiveness is stronger in our rituals than in our hymns. There are many hymns on the suffering and death of Jesus and our complicity in attitudes and deeds like those which crucified him, but few of these are in the context of the Lord's Supper. Many on the Eucharist express celebration, thanksgiving, praise, and rejoicing, but only a few concentrate on bewailing the sin from which faith affirms we are redeemed and renewed by the self-giving love of Christ.

3. *Communion.* Many hymns on the Lord's Supper stress its role in making real the divine presence, thus facilitating communion between God and those who in faith receive the bread and wine. A

considerable number extend this communion to include that of the human participants with one another. "Come, risen Lord, and deign to be our guest," by George W. Briggs (1875–1959), prays that those who bear one name and break "one bread of life" may truly comprise a united church. To J. A. Cramer (1723–1788) this community of Christians points the way to a still broader fellowship. In "Let all who share one bread and cup," a translation from the German by Fred Kaan, he admonishes us to remember

> the oneness of that host of countless number
> of those who are, as children of one Father,
>   part of each other.[42]

In "Broken bread and outpoured wine" Scott McCormick, Jr. (b. 1929), relates this oneness specifically to our racial and national divisions:

> Black and white, mankind at odds,
>   a world divided we:
> let's take again the gift of Christ
>   to make us whole and free!
> His one death is ours to share;
>   his righteousness also.
> O strengthen, God, this meal to mean
>   our being one in him.[43]

4. *Dedication.* For many hymn writers, as for Christians in general, the Eucharist involves dedication. The divine self-giving prompts human recipients to respond gratefully with the offering of their lives —a personal offering that becomes in turn the channel of a new gift of God's grace. In "Dear Lord, to you again our gifts we bring" H. C. A. Gaunt (b. 1902) traces the way in which our imperfect gifts of bread and wine, the fruits of our toil, are blessed and enriched and returned to us in lives renewed, to be used by God in the healing of human ills.

> Our lips receive your wine, our hands your bread;
>   you give us back the selves we offered you,
>   won by the Cross, by Calvary made new,
> a heart enriched, a life raised from the dead.
>   Grant us to take and guard your treasure well,
>   that we in you, and you in us may dwell.[44]

An ancient hymn from the Liturgy of Malabar, ascribed to Ephraim the Syrian (ca. 306–373), makes the eucharistic dedication quite concrete by offering specific parts of the body that took part in

the sacrament: hands, ears, tongues, eyes, and feet. The first stanza
is representative:

> Strengthen for service, Lord, the hands
> that holy things have taken;
> and let the ears that heard your Word
> to falsehood never waken.[45]

Several hymns remind us that the Spirit of God, incarnated in Jesus
Christ and symbolized in his Supper, also seeks embodiment in the
whole of our common life. There too we are assured of God's presence and power. Thus on Corpus Christi Day in Roman Catholic
lands the church takes the Mass to the marketplaces and crossroads
of villages and towns to manifest the presence of Christ where people
live, work, and play. But all Christians in all lands on all days can
enact the life of God in their ordinary occupations.

Illustrative of this understanding is a new hymn by Omer Westendorf (b. 1916, alt.), set to the Welsh tune THE ASH GROVE. As worshipers leave the Eucharist they sing:

> Sent forth by God's blessing, our true faith confessing,
> the people of God from his dwelling take leave.
> The supper is ended. Oh, now be extended
> the fruits of this service in all who believe.
> The seed of his teaching, receptive souls reaching,
> shall blossom in action for God and for all.
> His grace did invite us, his love shall unite us
> to work for God's kingdom and answer his call.[46]

5. *Hope.* The Lord's Supper also points toward the future in hope
and expectation. Rooted in the institution of the Eucharist is the deep
faith of the primitive church that the self-sacrificial love represented
in the simple meal, as in the life and death of Jesus as a whole, will
be ultimately fulfilled in the coming of God's righteous rule (see I
Cor. 11:25–26; Luke 22:16–18).

This eschatological hope is voiced in several hymns already
quoted, sometimes with vivid imagery. Louis Benson closes his "For
the bread, which thou hast broken" with the prayer,

> In the world where thou dost send us
> let thy kingdom come, O Lord.

Thomas Aquinas writes of "the hope and peace which from thy
presence flow," and envisages the time when he will gaze on Christ's
unveiled face, "the vision of thy glory and thy grace."

Joel W. Lundeen (b. 1918) relates this ultimate hope to the quality of Christian living that prepares for its fulfillment. In "Now we join in celebration" he prays to him through whom we are reconciled to God and one another:

> Give us grace to live for others,
> serving all, both friends and strangers,
> seeking justice, love, and mercy
> till you come in final glory.[47]

Although we have distinguished five main meanings in the hymns cited, we usually find two or more overlapping themes in the same lyric. Two hymns are particularly striking in this respect because they summarize eloquently so much of what the Eucharist means for Christian faith.

A very recent hymn by Brian Wren provides such a summary, while also sounding the note of joy that is basic.

> I come with joy to meet my Lord,
> forgiven, loved, and free,
> in awe and wonder to recall
> his life laid down for me.

To the confession and thanksgiving apparent in these lines he adds his discovery "in Christ's communion bread" of the "true community of love" with "Christians far and near." Symbolically, in the third stanza the *I* changes to *us:*

> As Christ breaks bread for men to share
> each proud division ends.
> That love that made us, makes us one,
> and strangers now are friends.

Then, in the joy of this new community, rooted in the presence of Christ, we offer our lives in his service:

> Together met, together bound,
> we'll go our different ways,
> and as his people in the world
> we'll live and speak his praise.[48]

The only motif not clearly present is that of hope.

All five themes are voiced with moving simplicity in the black spiritual "Let us break bread together," which invites us successively to break bread, drink wine, and praise God "together on our knees." The three brief stanzas express both communion and thanksgiving, while the refrain gives voice to confession and hope:

> When I fall on my knees, with my face to the rising sun,
> O Lord, have mercy on me.

Every line of the song breathes the spirit of personal dedication to the God whose love is freely given.

THE RENEWAL OF THE CHURCH

A high-water mark in Christian history was the Second Vatican Council (1962–1965), called by Pope John XXIII primarily as a means for spiritual renewal. Building on work begun in previous decades, its documents and deliberations have had profound effects in virtually every area of church life—biblical studies, worship, lay rights and responsibilities, ecumenical relations, and social outreach. The urge to renewal in Protestant bodies, though not so massively organized, has also been strong in recent years, as churches explore how to make a more effective witness in the complex world of today.

The felt need for spiritual deepening, an intelligent, caring response to human pain, and concrete Christian action for just and peaceful human relations has produced a number of exciting hymns that deal specifically with the renewal of the church.

Fred Kaan focuses attention on the church's internal inertia, which he sees as hampering its constructive influence in society.

> O God of the eternal now, why is your church so slow?
> What is it that prevents us all in grace and faith to grow?
>
> If, Lord, it is our love of ease by which we thwart your plan,
> then call us out, unsettle us, and lead us by the hand.

He then asks for willingness to take risks and move with courage into the future:

> Give us the heart of Abraham, for changes make us bold;
> and bless us only so that we in turn may bless the world.[49]

Fred Pratt Green is convinced that the church moved by the Spirit of God can be reborn.

> The Church of Christ, in every age
> beset by change, but Spirit-led,
> must claim and test its heritage
> and keep on rising from the dead.

Concerned especially for the victimized poor "across the world" and "across the street," people "who never live before they die," he calls for a servant church and a caring church

> that longs to be
> a partner in Christ's sacrifice,
> and clothed in Christ's humanity.

The task of the church is clear:

> We have no mission but to serve
>   in full obedience to our Lord;
> to care for all, without reserve,
>   and spread his liberating Word.[50]

A hymn by Kenneth L. Cober (b. 1902) is happily linked with the old English melody ALL IS WELL. It opens with a prayer:

> Renew thy church, her ministries restore:
>   both to serve and adore.
> Make her again as salt throughout the land,
>   and as light from a stand.
> 'Mid somber shadows of the night,
> where greed and hatred spread their blight,
>   O send us forth with power endued.
>   Help us, Lord, be renewed.

The following stanzas ask for the church a living knowledge of the written word of God and the Word manifest in Christ, the presence and guidance of God in prayer, and a heightened capacity to love. The closing lines are a fitting summary:

> As thou hast loved and given thy life,
>   to end hostility and strife,
>   O share thy grace from heaven above.
>   Teach us, Lord, how to love.[51]

9

THE CHRISTIAN LIFE

In the preceding chapter we spoke of the church as the community of persons who have responded trustfully to the transforming love of God disclosed in Jesus Christ, and who in the power of the Spirit endeavor to manifest that love and widen its reign. Christians, then, are those who compose the community of faith. They are persons who answer God's gracious address to them by trustful commitment to God's purpose, willingness to be guided and empowered by God's Spirit, love toward God and those God loves, and concern for the whole of God's creation. Released from the self-centeredness of sin, they are freed for the dynamic relationship of harmony with God and their neighbors that the New Testament calls salvation.

Especially clear in portraying the Christian life as a response in faith to God's reconciling love is the anonymous hymn (ca. 1878) that opens with the lines:

> I sought the Lord, and afterward I knew
> he moved my soul to seek him, seeking me;
> it was not I that found, O Savior true;
> no, I was found of thee.

The author goes on to interpret the whole of his present life as reply to the prior action of God:

> I find, I walk, I love, but oh, the whole
> of love is but my answer, Lord, to thee!
> For thou wert long beforehand with my soul;
> always thou lovedst me.[1]

What, then, are the marks of the life that flows from this response? More particularly, how do our hymn writers interpret them? Appearing in typical hymns are several interlocking motifs.

FAITH IN GOD

Unquestionably an active faith is a basic element in Christian living. Yet in hymns as elsewhere the word has varied meanings, two of which especially should be pointed out.

Faith may refer to intellectual belief, assent to a statement or a set of propositions. Thus the historic creeds are affirmations of faith, and members of the United Church of Christ join in a "Statement of Faith." Faith as acceptance of a body of belief is ordinarily uppermost when we speak of "the Christian faith," as it is in Faber's familiar refrain, "Faith of our fathers, holy faith, / we will be true to thee till death."

Faith may also mean primarily trust in, or confident reliance on, its object, as in Hebrews 11 and in Paul's declaration that we are "justified by faith quite apart from success in keeping the law" (Rom. 3:28). Trust is also central in Ray Palmer's "My faith looks up to thee," as in a hymn of Luther as paraphrased by F. L. and M. D. Battles in 1965:

> A Christian must by faith be filled,
>   and be made rich, like Christ, his head;
> by faith, his righteousness and life,
>   he is to Christ's great bounty led.

The fundamental importance of such faith is apparent when we realize that from it "flow forth both love and joy," which in turn evoke concern to serve others.[2]

When the authors of hymns sing of faith they usually have in mind trust in God or in Jesus Christ for salvation, or commitment of their lives to God in the assurance that when they are in God's keeping all is well. Within this basic attitude, however, wide differences are evident. In songs like Louise M. R. Stead's " 'Tis so sweet to trust in Jesus,"[3] faith is saccharine, shallow, and excessively sentimental. The central thrust of Faber's "There's a wideness in God's mercy" is a joyous assertion of the breadth and height of the love of God. But when the author claims that if our love were only simple enough to take God at his word, "our lives would be all sunshine, / in the sweetness of our Lord," he overlooks both the deeper dimension of faith and the rugged demands that reality often makes upon it.

In some other hymns faith becomes passive resignation to what is deemed to be the divine will, often with the implied assumption that whatever happens is willed by God. Thus in "My Jesus, as thou wilt!" Benjamin Schmolck (1672–1737) writes:

> Each changing future scene I gladly trust with thee.
> Straight to my home above I travel calmly on,
> and sing, in life or death, "My Lord, thy will be done."[4]

In view of the numerous events that cannot soundly be regarded as purposed by a Christlike God, such songs make it easy for alert, critical minds to dismiss religion as an opiate.

Sometimes faith is embraced as an escape from the burdens of life. John Powell, S.J., writes of "a peace of soul approach to religion. It makes of God a gigantic Bayer Aspirin. . . . Take God three times a day and you won't feel any pain." This attitude surfaces in a disturbing number of hymns.

Adam Drese (1620–1701) prays simply, "Jesus, call thou me from the world to thee."[5] Others contrast more specifically the earthly wilderness of trouble, sin, and sorrow with the peace and solace of God's care. In "Peace, perfect peace" Edward H. Bickersteth (1825–1906) assures believers, "On Jesus' bosom naught but calm is found."[6]

Two other hymns employ the metaphor of leaning to express confidence that security and inner peace are the lot of the individual who trusts in God. Both have the appeal of tunes that sing themselves, easily distracting attention from their self-centered content. Civilla D. Martin (1869–1948) admonishes the believer:

> Be not dismayed whate'er betide,
> God will take care of you.

God's care, she asserts, is so unlimited that "nothing you ask will be denied."[7]

In like fashion, in "What a fellowship, what a joy divine," Elisha A. Hoffman exclaims,

> What have I to dread, what have I to fear,
> leaning on the everlasting arms?

The refrain reiterates that with this protection the Christian is "safe and secure from all alarms."[8]

There is a place for hymns of comfort and spiritual strength when we are buffeted by adversity, but not for those which invite us to seek inner peace while blotting out the needs of other human beings and the tasks God may have for us. Tranquillity is in some circumstances a Christian virtue, but it may also cover a sinful evasion of responsibility. Hymns of the kind just cited are, as Evelyn Underhill declares, close to psychological sin,

stressing as they do a childish weakness and love of shelter and petting, a neurotic shrinking from full human life, a morbid preoccupation with failure and guilt. Such hymns make devitalizing suggestions, adverse to the health and energy of the spiritual life, and are all the more powerful because they are sung collectively and in rhythm, and are cast in an emotional mold.[9]

Happily, hymns that deal with faith in terms of childish sentimentalism, passive resignation, or self-centered escapism are outnumbered by those that move on a much deeper level. Hymns that paraphrase or are based on Psalm 23 (22 in Greek and Latin texts) provide good examples of this dimension. Like the Shepherd Psalm itself they are cast in the first person singular, but they do not evade reality or gloss over responsibility. The quiet trust they voice applies not only to periods of rest and restoration by still waters but also to times when believers must walk actively in paths of righteousness. Trust in God guards them ultimately against fear of evil, but they do not claim that God's care grants them immunity from the circumstances that arouse fear.

In the books consulted I have found 15 hymns that paraphrase this psalm, and an additional one that is strongly influenced by it. Most of them are in rhymed verse; two ignore meter and are set to plainsong melodies; one is a round. The most widely known are "The King of love my Shepherd is," by Henry W. Baker (1821–1877), which appears in at least 29 of the hymnbooks studied; "The Lord's my Shepherd, I'll not want," from the Scottish Psalter of 1650 (26 hymnbooks); and "In heavenly love abiding," by Anna L. Waring (1823–1910), found in 22 hymnals. Appearing in only 10 hymnbooks but frequently sung in "My Shepherd will supply my need," by Isaac Watts.[10] Among 11 versions that appear in from one to seven hymnals is "The Lord is my pacesetter; I shall not rush," strikingly new in its application of the psalm to the pressure and speed of our technological age.[11]

Some of the noblest hymnic expressions of faith are selections from the poetry of Alfred, Lord Tennyson (1809–1892), and John Greenleaf Whittier (1807–1892). Found in a number of books are hymns comprising four to six stanzas of the eleven-stanza Prologue to Tennyson's *In Memoriam*. The opening lines sound the theme of the whole:

> Strong Son of God, immortal Love,
>   whom we, that have not seen thy face,
>   by faith, and faith alone, embrace,
> believing where we cannot prove;
>
> . . . .
> Thou wilt not leave us in the dust;
>   thou madest man, he knows not why;
>   he thinks he was not made to die;
> and thou hast made him: thou art just.

Later stanzas reiterate the inadequacy of "our little systems," "broken lights" of God. Yet Tennyson is not content to place knowledge and faith in opposition to one another. Harmony of the two is needed for a healthy spiritual life:

> Let knowledge grow from more to more,
>   but more of reverence in us dwell;
>   that mind and soul, according well,
>   may make one music as before,
>
> but vaster. . . . [12]

Whittier's "Dear Lord and Father of mankind" is included in many collections. Less well known are three hymns of faith comprising various selections from his poem "The Eternal Goodness."[13] In these two facets of trust in God are dominant. One is the assurance of the divine goodness and God's sustaining power amid the struggles and pains of life here and now:

> Within the maddening maze of things,
>   when tossed by storm and flood,
>   to one fixed trust my spirit clings;
>   I know that God is good.

In spite of our human weakness,

> the bruised reed he will not break
> but strengthen and sustain.

The other facet is faith that our future is in the hands of God. Hence we can believe that no real harm can come to us as we await "the muffled oar." Though "the silent sea" is vast and unknown, we "cannot drift beyond his love and care."

For Donald W. Hughes (1911–1967) faith gives stability amid the unsettling changes of history:

> Beyond the mist and doubt
> of this uncertain day,
> I trust in thine eternal name,
> beyond all changes still the same,
> and in that name I pray.

Such trust also brings deep serenity in spite of the turbulence of events, and "I am not afraid." Hughes does not denigrate science, but recognizes its limitations in relation to our ultimate questions, and rejoices in the answer of faith-supported love:

> For science's remotest probe
> feels but the fringes of thy robe:
> love looks upon thy face.[14]

PRAYER

If faith is to live and grow, it must be nourished by a personal relationship with God—a relationship that cannot reach its highest levels without regular prayer. Hence hymns on prayer, and especially hymns that are prayers, have a prominent place in most collections. As the familiar lines of James Montgomery declare, prayer need not always be verbal: "Prayer is the soul's sincere desire, / uttered or unexpressed." Yet most hymns verbalize either the need of prayer or some aspect of the life of prayer. All of the principal forms of communion with God are represented.

"Lord, as I wake I turn to you," by Brian Foley (b. 1919), based on Psalm 5, combines praise, thanksgiving, petition, and commitment:

> Your loving gift of grace to me,
>   those favors I could never earn,
> call for my thanks in praise and prayer,
>   call me to love you in return.
>
> Lord, make my life a life of love,
>   keep me from sin in all I do;
> Lord, make your law my only law,
>   your will my will, for love of you.[15]

The first two stanzas of Fred Pratt Green's "For the fruits of his creation" thank God for the human labor and the silent processes of growth that produce food, as well as for the divinely willed concern to share it with the hungry. The hymn then celebrates the spiritual fruits of God's creativity:

> For the harvests of his Spirit,
>   thanks be to God;
> for the good all men inherit,
>   thanks be to God;
> for the wonders that astound us,
> for the truths that still confound us,
> most of all, that love has found us,
>   thanks be to God.[16]

Donald Hughes's "Creator of the earth and skies / to whom all truth and power belong" is centrally a prayer of penitence:

> We have not known you: to the skies
>   our monuments of folly soar,
> and all our self-wrought miseries
>   have made us trust ourselves the more.

> We have not loved you: far and wide
>   the wreckage of our hatred spreads,
> and evils wrought by human pride
>   recoil on unrepentant heads.

Hence we are led to confess our "foolish confidence" and "pride of knowledge" and ask for divine grace, that God's "quickening word" may "turn our darkness into day."[17]

In "Forgive our sins as we forgive," Rosamond E. Herklots (b. 1905) perceives that our prayers for pardon are hollow unless accompanied by willingness to forgive others:

> How can your pardon reach and bless
>   the unforgiving heart
> that broods on wrongs, and will not let
>   old bitterness depart?

Yet in the light of the cross our own need is exposed:

> How small the debts men owe to us,
>   how great our debt to you!

This awareness moves us to pray:

> Lord, cleanse the depths within our souls
>   and bid resentment cease;
> then reconciled to God and man,
>   our lives will spread your peace.[18]

The black spiritual, "Lord, I want to be a Christian in my heart," expresses fittingly the aspiration of those who are reconciled. Implicitly it asks God to help the singer to become truly Christian, more loving, more holy, and like Jesus.[19]

A notable hymn of dedication by Howell Elvet Lewis (1860–1953) addresses the "Lord of light, whose name shines brighter" than all the heavenly bodies, and continues with the prayer:

> Deign to make us your co-workers
>   in the kingdom of your grace.

In succeeding stanzas the author asks that God's will may be furthered by human toil and courage, humility in struggle and suffering, the prayers of the faithful, and the reconciling love disclosed in the cross. He prays also that our growing knowledge may be kept subject to the divine purpose, and that our zeal may be hallowed by divine charity. A refrain paraphrases the petition of the Lord's Prayer that God's will be done on earth as in heaven.[20]

THE PRACTICE OF THE DIVINE PRESENCE

Blending almost indistinguishably with prayer as conscious communion with God is life in the attitude of prayer, the practice of the divine presence in a continuing spirit of praise, gratitude, and commitment. Thus a hymn fashioned from Psalm 34 in Tate and Brady's *New Version of the Psalms of David* (1696) begins:

> Through all the changing scenes of life,
>   in trouble and in joy,
> the praises of my God shall still
>   my heart and tongue employ.

Several hymns shift the focus from the whole course of human life to the days of every week. The model for this more specific application is found in the words of Richard of Chichester (1197–1253) which have been popularized in the recent musical *Godspell.*

> Day by day,
> dear Lord, of thee three things I pray:
>   to see thee more clearly,
>   love thee more dearly,
>   follow thee more nearly,
> day by day.[21]

The same theme is sounded by George Herbert (1593–1633) in his "King of glory, King of peace, / I will love thee":

> Seven whole days, not one in seven, / I will praise thee;
> in my heart, though not in heaven, / I can raise thee.
>
> Small it is, in this poor sort / to enroll thee;
> e'en eternity's too short / to extol thee.[22]

Still further specification of this attitude occurs in several hymns that trace the divine presence through the course of each individual day. In "Father, in the dawning light," a paraphrase of a Filipino poem by Nellie Reyes, Daniel T. Niles voices his need for God and his sense of fulfillment in God, not only at dawn but "in the noonday heat" and "when it's evening time, / and the twilight falls."[23]

The example *par excellence* of this emphasis is "Lord of all hopefulness, Lord of all joy," by Jan Struther (1901–1953), which prays in the opening stanza,

> Be there at our waking, and give us, we pray,
> your bliss in our hearts, Lord, at the break of the day.

The remaining stanzas, addressed respectively to the Lord of all eagerness and faith, of all kindliness and grace, and of all gentleness and calm, ask:

> Be there at our labours, and give us, we pray,
> your strength in our hearts, at the noon of the day. . . .

> Be there at our homing, and give us, we pray,
> your love in our hearts, Lord at the eve of the day. . . .

> Be there at our sleeping, and give us we pray,
> your peace in our hearts, Lord, at the end of the day.[24]

One of Fred Kaan's most recent hymns, which he captions "celebration, everywhere, any time" (1975), gathers up colorfully the Christian insight that the whole of life, not merely special hours, days, or seasons, is the proper sphere for praising and serving God. It is set to a sprightly tune by Doreen Potter.

> Christ is crucified today, / Christmas is tomorrow.
> Lent will fall in summertime, / Easter is to follow.

> Christ is here and everywhere, / one with all his people,
> but we mark his whereabouts / with our Sunday steeples.

> Christ is Lord—we fence him out / from routine and Monday;
> tie him down to holiness, / feasting, fasting, Sunday.

> Lord, forgive our formal ways / and our special seasons;
> free us from the faith that stills, / stifles or imprisons.

> Make us whole and bind in one / reason and emotion,
> let our life-style manifest / day-to-day devotion.

> Give us grace to seize and use / every situation,
> any time for worship, love, / blessing, celebration![25]

SOCIAL CONCERN

Integral to a fully Christian life—not merely a desirable addition —is serious and continuing concern for just relations in human society. Responsibility to and for the neighbor is an intrinsic aspect of our whole Judeo-Christian heritage, from the Cain-Abel story in Genesis 4 through the giving of the Ten Commandments on Sinai (Ex. 20:1–17; Deut. 5:1–27), the writings of the Hebrew prophets, the teachings of Jesus, the two "great commandments" to love God and neighbor (Deut. 6:5; Lev. 19:18; Mark 12:33; Luke 10:27; Rom. 13:8–9; Gal. 5:14; James 2:8), and the radical implications of the events surrounding the founding of the Christian church (Acts 2:44–47; 4:32–35; ch. 10). Christian social responsibility is recognized by most contemporary hymnals, though in some instances it is largely overlooked. Taken as a whole, hymns exhibit three main attitudes toward the Christian's relation to society.

Self-centered Individualism

A view that surfaces fairly frequently in hymns of the eighteenth and nineteenth centuries sees the Christian life as a journey toward heaven through many dangers and trials, in which God can be counted on to keep us pure and bring us safely home. Ethical relationships on the way seem to be important only as they advance the individual believer toward the destination. In "Children of the heavenly King, / as we journey let us sing" John Cennick (1718–1755) emphasizes the joy rather than the hardship of the pilgrimage. We are "sons of light," and "Zion's city is in sight." We can go on "undismayed" for

> we are traveling home to God,
>   in the way our fathers trod;
> they are happy now, and we
>   soon their happiness shall see.[26]

Other hymns of this type stress the harsh ordeals the Christian must often endure, and call for courageous struggle, with the assurance that divine help is available. Thus George Heath (1750–1822) admonishes:

> My soul, be on thy guard;
>   ten thousand foes arise;
> the hosts of sin are pressing hard
>   to draw thee from the skies.

The battle will continue until death, but by God's aid the soul can anticipate being crowned with victory and reaching its eternal abode.[27]

The promise of a safe haven is central in "Peace, perfect peace, in this dark world of sin," by Edward H. Bickersteth. Though we may be pressed "by thronging duties" and beset by "sorrows surging round," internal calm and safety are ours if we keep close to Jesus. In a glaring mixed metaphor the writer assures us that "the blood of Jesus whispers peace within." Moreover, "earth's struggles soon shall cease, / and Jesus calls us to heaven's perfect peace."[28]

To question the otherworldliness of hymns like these is in no sense to exclude the truth or worth of belief in life after death. Christian faith sees earthly life in an eternal context and quite consistently looks forward in hope to enlarging opportunities for creative growth beyond the grave. But it also regards the here and now with all seriousness.

Nor do questions about purely private religion imply indifference toward individual religious experience. What is questioned is the extreme concern for personal salvation that allows no room for serious regard for other persons or for attention to the social situations that undermine their well-being.

Faith that encourages a divine-human encounter must accord to "I" and "my" hymns a rightful place. They need not be exclusively self-centered, but rather may record the deepest spiritual experiences of the individual—his or her defeats, victories, aspirations, needs, moods, and discoveries. When they do this, they may provide a constructive vehicle of expression for the similar thoughts and feelings of other persons. There is nothing about Washington Gladden's "O Master, let me walk with thee," George Matheson's "O Love that will not let me go," or Isaac Watts's "When I survey the wondrous cross" that cannot be shared by all Christians; such hymns are therefore quite appropriate for congregational use.

The situation is quite different, however, with Watts's "When I can read my title clear / to mansions in the skies." Louis F. Benson observes that "the complacent selfishness" of this song "has driven it from the hymnals."[29] Similar concern may lead us to avoid using some hymns still printed in various hymnbooks. In a forthright address some years ago Paul Scherer declared that instead of singing "Blessed assurance, Jesus is mine," we should exult in the assurance, "I am his." He then added his judgment that we sing more Christian heresy in our hymns than all the church councils have ever condemned!

When in doubt about the appropriateness for corporate worship of a particular hymn, a sound guideline is to ask: Is it sufficiently universal in its account of personal experiences that its use of words like *I, me,* and *my* can be in singing translated in effect to *we, us,* and *our,* so that a body of worshipers can voice through them their common experience? Sometimes an otherwise good hymn can be saved by the omission of an offending stanza, especially when the deleted lines can be replaced by words harmonious with Christian faith. This has been done with salutary effect in the version of Elizabeth C. Clephane's "Beneath the cross of Jesus" in the Presbyterian *Worshipbook.* The third stanza, in which the author is "content to let the world go by," has been replaced by one written by Dalton E. McDonald and Donald D. Kettring, which gives a

constructive focus to "the wonders of redeeming love" emphasized
by the hymn:

> "Take up your cross," said Jesus,
>   "and follow after me."
> I take your cross to learn your will,
>   whate'er the cost may be;
> we share the vision of a world
>   which puts an end to strife,
> and work that all mankind shall know
>   your way, your truth, your life.

Active Love for Others

Among the many hymns that convey the ethical dimension of
Christian faith, some concentrate attention on relations between
individuals. Charles Wesley's "A charge to keep I have" links concern for his ultimate destiny with his vocation to fulfill the divine will
now. He is charged to glorify God and fit his "never-dying soul" for
the sky, but also

> to serve the present age,
>   my calling to fulfill;
> O may it all my powers engage
>   to do my Master's will![30]

That the accent on neighbor love is not confined to modern hymnody is shown clearly by a ninth-century Latin hymn recently made
available in English:

> Where charity and love prevail,
>   there God is ever found;
> brought here together by Christ's love,
>   by love are we thus bound.
>
> Forgive we now each other's faults
>   as we our faults confess;
> and let us love each other well
>   in Christian holiness.[31]

Frequently this note is sounded with special clarity in hymns of
concern for those who suffer. Thus in "Lord Christ, who on thy heart
didst bear," Henry Arnold Thomas (1848–1924) declares that the
happiness we as Christians ask and the service we crave is

> that we may care, as thou hast cared,
>   for sick and lame, for deaf and blind,

and freely share, as thou hast shared,
in all the sorrows of mankind.[32]

This theme appears particularly in a number of recent hymns based on Jesus' parable of the sheep and the goats (Matt. 25:31–46).[33]

In many hymns the appeal to love others is broadened to include all of our relations to them. In "We find thee, Lord," Giles Ambrose (b. 1912) declares that we discover God in the needs of other human beings, so that when we respond in words and deeds of love "we serve the man for Others." What we do for their sake we render to the God who is "incarnate in our neighbor."[34]

Kurt Rommel relates this incarnation to God's self-embodiment in human life in the coming of Jesus Christ. In a German hymn, "Wer kann mir sagen, wo Jesus Christus geboren ist?" (1967), translated by Emily Chisholm in 1973, Rommel asks where and when Jesus Christ is born, and replies: wherever and whenever

men are beginning to live as brothers,
and aim at winning a new world for others.

These queries lead to a third, with its fitting response:

O who can tell me why Jesus Christ is born today?
Christ is born today that men should *begin*
to live as brothers, and aim at winning
a new world for others—
Christ is born for *this*. [35]

The recently popular hymn "We are one in the Spirit," by Peter Scholtes (b. 1928), roots radical concern for others in our ultimate oneness as children of one God. Because of this, we will respect one another's worth and share our work and our lives. Then people will "know we are Christians by our love."[36]

In several hymns love toward the individual neighbor merges with responsibility for social change. Those in whom Christ is present are involved in manifold group relationships that help or hinder their growth as persons, and "winning a new world for others" requires resolute action for justice and peace.

Responsibility for Social Justice

Since the mid-nineteenth century, hymns have manifested a slowly increasing concern for social justice and world peace. The familiar "God the omnipotent!" a conflation of hymns by Henry F. Chorley and John Ellerton, written respectively in 1842 and 1870, closes each stanza with a prayer for peace. Ebenezer Elliott's "When

wilt thou save the people?," concerned with the salvation of persons
"from vice, oppression, and despair," appeared in 1850.[37] James Russell Lowell's "Once to every man and nation" (1845) is part of a poem
written to arouse action to end slavery. Whittier's "O brother man,
fold to thy heart thy brother," which envisages the fall of all shackles
and the end of "wild war music," is a selection from a fifteen-stanza
poem based on James 1:27, published in 1850. "Eternal Ruler of the
ceaseless round," written by John W. Chadwick (1840–1904) at the
height of the Civil War, addresses God as "Guide of the nations" from
night into day:

> We would be one in hatred of all wrong,
>   one in the love of all things sweet and fair.[38]

However, it is only in the twentieth century that songs relating
Christian faith to the ills of society have emerged as a major type of
hymnody, and only in the middle and later decades of this century
have they appeared in any considerable number in hymnbooks. Significantly, the *Lutheran Book of Worship* (1978) contains twenty-six
hymns in the section entitled "Society"; and twenty of these were
written since 1900. Other books manifest the same trend. From
these rather rich offerings we select a few examples.

The central motif of all these songs is stated eloquently by Gilbert
K. Chesterton (1874–1936) in his only hymn, written in 1906, which
begins:

> O God of earth and altar,
>   bow down and hear our cry;
> our earthly rulers falter,
>   our people drift and die;
> the walls of gold entomb us;
>   the swords of scorn divide;
> take not thy thunder from us,
>   but take away our pride.

The hymn goes on to pray for deliverance from terror, lies, shallow
remedies, dishonorable deeds, and indifference. The final stanza
prays that all persons may be united by the judging and saving action
of God.

"The love of God is broad like beach and meadow," is a striking
translation (1972) by Fred Kaan of a Swedish hymn by Anders Frostenson (1968). It sees our strife as a violation of faith in the universal
love of God which Christians profess. The answer lies in the free
response of men and women to that love, yet they misuse the freedom they long for:

> But there are walls that keep us all divided;
>   we fence each other in with hate and war.
> Fear is the bricks-and-mortar of our prison,
>   our pride of self the prison coat we wear.

The fourth stanza pleads for both judgment and compassion, and then repeats the same two lines that close the other three:

> The love of God is broad like beach and meadow,
>   wide as the wind, and an eternal home.[39]

A powerful expression of the commitment to end war is the hymn by William W. Reid, Jr. (1958, alt. 1972), the central thrust of which is found in the opening stanzas:

> O God of every nation, / of every race and land,
> redeem the whole creation / with your almighty hand;
> where hate and fear divide us / and bitter threats are hurled,
> in love and mercy guide us / and heal our strife-torn world.
>
> From search for wealth and power / and scorn of truth and right,
> from trust in bombs that shower / destruction through the night,
> from pride of race and station / and blindness to your way,
> deliver every nation, / eternal God, we pray.[40]

A Christian conscience regarding race relations, largely quiescent from the Civil War to the mid-twentieth century, has awakened in hymnody as in other aspects of Christian life and thought. In "From the shores of many nations," James H. Hargett (b. 1930) traces the deliverance of black people from legal slavery, then confesses:

> In the heart of this our nation,
>   there are those in bondage still;
> bound in seething ghetto places
>   captives of a ruthless will.
> Bring the power of grace and judgment;
>   from death's grip may life unfurl;
> liberating resurrection,
>   serving, shaping God's new world.[41]

Richard G. Jones (b. 1926) states simply a major theological foundation for commitment to racial equality and unsegregated opportunity for all people:

> The God who rules this earth
>   gave life to every race;
> he chose its day of birth,
>   the color of its face;

>so none may claim superior grade
>within the family he's made.

However, in the sin that infects us all we have corrupted brotherhood, spreading racial pride, strife, and fear. But in Christ our divisions are bridged and we recognize our oneness:

>He comes with unrestricted grace
>to heal the hearts of every race.[42]

Ever since Frank Mason North's "Where cross the crowded ways of life" (1903)—probably the first hymn with primary reference to the modern city—hymnists have occasionally sought to relate the gospel to the strident competition, the depersonalization, and the poverty, as well as the values, of urban life today. Paradoxically, Erik Routley (b. 1917) has given us one of the most sensitive of these hymns, though he reports that he usually finds hymns about social justice "boring and superfluous" and prefers hymns on the glory of God, the beauty of Christ, and the delights of heaven![43] In "All who love and serve your city" (1966) he calls on city dwellers, amid their "daily stress," their cries "for peace and justice," their "loss and sorrow," their "wasted work and wasted play," and their pained awareness of the retreat of "honor, peace, and love," to "seek the Lord, who is your life." There is in these stanzas, however, no offer of easy solutions, and no appeal for radical change, but a reminder that life entails hard effort. "All days are days of judgment," and the Lord is present even with those who spurn him, "offering peace and Calvary's hill." The hymn closes on a positive note:

>Risen Lord! shall yet the city
>be the city of despair?
>Come today, our Judge, our Glory;
>be its name, "The Lord is there!"[44]

North's hymn is as realistic as Routley's regarding the wretchedness and greed of the city, but in praying for the healing presence of Christ it expects city dwellers to respond by following his path of love, leading ultimately to the city of God. Probably "The Lord is there!" implies for Routley hope and strength for remedial action in God's name. But this is not explicit, and his words say nothing about a coming city of God. Yet his address to the "risen Lord" suggests that "Calvary's hill" is the way to an Easter victory. Such similarities-in-difference may accurately symbolize the different moods and expectations of Christians between 1903 and 1966!

The burden of Fred Kaan's "Sing we of the modern city" (1968) is the depersonalization of urban life. The city is the scene of both "joy and stress," but its outstanding mark is its millions of nameless people living in endless rows of houses "in their urban wilderness." Yet amid its hectic speed and changing trends and crazes, Christ is present.

> God is not remote in heaven,
>   but on earth to share our shame,
> changing graph and mass and numbers
>   into persons with a name.
> Christ has shown, beyond statistics,
>   human life with glory crowned,
> by his timeless presence proving
>   people matter, people count.[45]

Recent awareness of ecological problems and the energy crisis has stimulated hymns on Christian responsibility for preservation of our natural resources. Representative of these is a song by Fred Pratt Green which begins, "God in his love for us lent us this planet, . . . cradle of life and the home of our race," and gives thanks. There follows acknowledgment that for countless years we have ruined harvests by war; now we pollute land, water, and air; destroy irreplaceable beauty; and recklessly despoil resources needed by later generations, "selling the future for present rewards." The hymn closes with a prayer for deliverance from our folly:

> Earth is the Lord's; it is ours to enjoy it,
>   ours, as his stewards, to farm and defend.
> Now from pollution, disease, and damnation,
>   good Lord, deliver us, world without end.[46]

A fitting summary of the solemn responsibility of all who love God and neighbor is the hymn by Ian Ferguson (b. 1921), dated 1967, "Am I my brother's keeper?" The first two stanzas depict vividly the lame excuse of Cain after murdering Abel and the hand-washing rationalization of Pilate when he delivered Jesus to be crucified. The third stanza states the Christian imperative:

> As long as people hunger, / as long as people thirst,
> and ignorance and illness / and warfare do their worst,
> as long as there's injustice / in any of God's lands,
> I am my brother's keeper, / I dare not wash my hands.[47]

STRUGGLE AND JOY

The "joy and stress" observed by Kaan in the modern city also characterize present-day life as a whole, and Christian life as well. Hymnists have not overlooked either, or the subtle way in which they are connected.

From "Christian! dost thou see them," written by Andrew of Crete (ca. 660–732) to twentieth-century hymns like Charles A. Tindley's "When the storms of life are raging" (1905), Christians have been summoned to confront with courage the "powers of darkness" without and within. Almost at random we think of John Bunyan's "He who would valiant be," from the seventeenth century; Philip Doddridge's "Awake, my soul, stretch every nerve," from the eighteenth century; and of nineteenth-century hymns like William H. Bathurst's "O for a faith that will not shrink," J. S. B. Monsell's "Fight the good fight," and Ernest Shurtleff's "Lead on, O King eternal."

Other hymns speak eloquently of the tribulation and weariness to be expected on our pilgrimage are John M. Neale's "Art thou weary, art thou languid," James Montgomery's "In the hour of trial," Bernhardt S. Ingemann's "Through the night of doubt and sorrow," and George Heath's "My soul, be on thy guard."

Quite naturally, hymns of conflict often use military imagery. We think readily of some that have gained popularity partly because of rousing tunes fitted to their content: Reginald Heber's "The Son of God goes forth to war," George Duffield's "Stand up, stand up for Jesus," Sabine Baring-Gould's "Onward, Christian Soldiers," Charles Wesley's "Soldiers of Christ, arise," Isaac Watts's "Am I a soldier of the cross," and George T. Coster's "March on, O soul, with strength." Searching questions raised by alert Christian consciences have led to declining use of such songs in Christian worship.

Since hymns of struggle normally affirm the presence and power of God amid hardship, they point toward numerous others that emphasize the joy of the Christian life. Frequently sung are Francis of Assisi's "All creatures of our God and King," John Milton's "Let us with a gladsome mind," Charles Wesley's "Rejoice, the Lord is King!," Edward H. Plumptre's "Rejoice, ye pure in heart," Christian Henry Bateman's "Come, Christians, join to sing," and Henry van Dyke's "Joyful, joyful, we adore thee." To those should be added most of our Christmas and Easter carols and hymns. Rejoicing is also central in many of the songs of praise and celebration, with their frequent alleluias, which mark the worship of the charismatic movement, various intentional communities, and many youth groups today.

Among the newer songs that have won a place in some of the standard hymnals and supplements is "Lord of the Dance," by Sydney Carter (b. 1915), which carries on the tradition of the English carol "Tomorrow shall be my dancing day." In the carol the Son of God declares that the purpose of his incarnation is "to call my true love [humanity] to my dance." The metaphor expresses the joy and the love of Christian life and is consistent with the New Testament portrayal of Jesus. The song is no shallow appeal to make merry and forget the travail of life. "It's hard to dance with the devil on your back." But its central message is the glad tidings that God wills good for creation, and that we are invited to join happily in fulfilling God's loving purpose:

> They cut me down and I leap up high—
> I am the life that'll never, never die;
> I'll live in you if you'll live in me—
> I am the Lord of the Dance, said he.[48]

Many other hymns that emphasize joy contain strong intimations of hardship, while many whose major note is struggle point in faith toward victory. Black spirituals like "There is a balm in Gilead" and freedom songs like "We shall overcome" provide ready examples. It remains cause for amazement to many outside the black experience how slaves could sing, "Nobody knows the trouble I've seen," then add without hesitation the apparently irrational conclusion, "Glory, hallelujah!"

Few lyrics illustrate the paradox more impressively than the hymn by Nick Hodson (b. 1941) that begins:

> It's a long, hard journey, and the road keeps turning
>   and we just keep traveling on;
> the signs aren't clear enough, the ends aren't near enough,
>   and half our time is gone.

Yet amid our troubles the Lord keeps guiding us "as long as we're trav'ling his road." The closing stanzas sum up lucidly the spirit in which we are called to live the Christian life:

> Well, he never told us that the road before us
>   would be smooth or simple or clear.
> But he set us singing and our hopes keep springing
>   and we're raised from hating and fear.
>
> Well, the road is ours with its rocks and flowers
>   and mica gleams in the stone.
> Well, there's joy awaiting in the celebrating
>   that we're never walking alone.[49]

10

CONSUMMATION

From New Testament times onward, Christian faith has always included reference to God's intent for the future. The Apostles' Creed speaks of the communion of saints, the resurrection of the body, and the life everlasting. The Nicene Creed looks for "the resurrection of the dead, and the life of the world to come." Many later affirmations of faith add, as do the New Testament writings, the expectation of the divine kingdom—the consummation of God's righteous rule.

Assertions concerning the meaning of faith for the human future appear also throughout the history of Christian hymnody. Hymns on providence, for example, sing of God's guidance in our pilgrimage toward the unknown, while those on the Lord's Supper include the dimension of hope. Hymns on the Christian life voice trust that divine mercy underlies both life and death, and speak of the coming of God's kingdom of justice and peace. In examining representative hymns on the future we shall consider, in order, belief in everlasting life and the expectation of the consummation of history in the kingdom of God.

LIFE ETERNAL

Two main types of hymns express belief in life after physical death: those which disparage earthly existence and long for heaven; and those which view eternal life as continuation and fulfillment of life in the present world.

Longing for Heaven

A poem of 2,966 lines by Bernard of Cluny (ca. 1145) draws a sharp contrast between the corruption of medieval society and the blessedness of heaven. From the translation of 96 lines by John M. Neale in

160

1851 have come four hymns still in use, the best known of which is "Jerusalem the golden, / with milk and honey blest." These stanzas largely omit Bernard's negative view of earthly life, singing rather of "the dear land of rest" where, "clad in robes of white," we shall be released from care and enjoy the fruits of triumph over evil. Therefore, we sing exultantly:

> O sweet and blessed country, / the home of God's elect!
> O sweet and blessed country / that eager hearts expect!

This quatrain appears also in another selection from Bernard's poem, "For thee, O dear, dear country," which likewise emphasizes the glories of heaven.[1] Two other hymns from the same source preserve the contrast of the original: "The world is very evil; / the times are waxing late";[2] and "Brief life is here our portion." The latter presents a series of vivid antitheses: brief sorrow and care—life tearless and unending; short toil—eternal rest; grief—unutterable pleasure; night —light; storm—calm; battle—crown; shadows—morning.[3]

Reminiscent of Bernard is a sixteenth-century English poem of 104 lines by an author known only as F. B. P., possibly a Roman Catholic priest sentenced to death in London about 1593. From these have been formed the hymn that begins:

> Jerusalem, my happy home,
>   would God I were in thee!
> Would God my woes were at an end,
>   thy joys that I might see![4]

We can readily understand how a man under sentence of death in a time of religious persecution could write such words and mean them, but they can hardly be sung sincerely by more than a very few worshipers in an average congregation today.

Somewhat more joyous in both words and music is "Ten thousand times ten thousand," by Henry Alford (1810–1871). It pictures the fight of "the ransomed saints" with death and sin, and portrays them as exiles longing for home. But the emphasis is on their victory and the welcome that awaits them on "Canaan's happy shore":

> O day, for which creation
>   and all its tribes were made;
> O joy, for all its former woes
>   a thousandfold repaid.[5]

"Jesus, still lead on," recast by the Moravian Christian Gregor in 1778 from two hymns by Nicolaus Ludwig von Zinzendorf and translated by Jane L. Borthwick in 1846, is content to picture heaven simply as "our Father's land," a "bright shore / where we weep no more." The author notes the dreariness, temptations, and dangers of our present existence, but he accepts the need for our earthly journey, and prays for strength to make it in faith and hope. The spirit of the hymn is summed up well in the opening stanza:

> Jesus, still lead on, / till our rest be won;
> and, although the way be cheerless,
> we will follow, calm and fearless;
> guide us by your hand / to our Father's land.[6]

A considerable number of hymns focused on the peace and happiness of the life to come appeared in the nineteenth century—songs like Frederick W. Faber's "O Paradise, O Paradise, / who doth not crave for rest?";[7] Ellen H. Gates's "I will sing you a song of that beautiful land";[8] Wilhelm A. Wexels' "Oh, happy day when we shall stand";[9] and "The Homeland, O the Homeland!," probably by Hugh R. Haweis, with its lines, "I'm sighing for that country, / my heart is aching here."[10] Sandra S. Sizer has found 96 hymns on heaven, "an enormous proportion," among the 739 in *Gospel Hymns Nos. 1–6 Complete* (1895), edited by Ira D. Sankey, James McGranahan, and George C. Stebbins.[11] However, relatively few hymns of this type are to be found in present-day hymnals. Interest in their message seems to have declined in the early decades of the twentieth century. Nevertheless, belief in eternal life as sequel and fulfillment of life here and now continues to be affirmed in hymns both new and old.

Fulfillment

Few hymns are more positive regarding the worth of earthly life than the universally loved "All creatures of our God and King," by Francis of Assisi (1182–1226). In seven stanzas he calls on "all things," the forces of nature and plants and animals no less than human beings, to praise their Creator with repeated alleluias. In this context he includes one stanza, unfortunately omitted in most current hymnals, which asks death to join the chorus, and in so doing affirms death, not as an enemy, but as the consummation of life:

> And thou, most kind and gentle death,
> waiting to hush our latest breath,
>   O praise him, alleluia!
> Thou leadest home the child of God,
> and Christ the Lord the way hath trod;
>   O praise him, O praise him,
>   alleluia, alleluia, alleluia![12]

This hymn may serve as a prototype for many others that in different ways voice faith in human life beyond death without denigrating the years of our earthly existence. Thus Harriet Beecher Stowe (1812–1896) in her "Still, still with thee, when purple morning breaketh" regards her sense of the presence of God in the quiet of each earthly morning as a promise and foretaste of a more wonderful communion:

> So shall it be at last, in that bright morning,
>   when the soul waketh, and the shadows flee;
> O in that hour, fairer than daylight dawning,
>   shall rise the glorious thought, I am with thee.

Concentrated much more than Stowe's verses on the end of earthly life is Henry F. Lyte's ever-popular "Abide with me; fast falls the eventide." Written probably in 1847 when the author's health was failing, and less than three months before he died, it stresses the growing dimness of earth's joys and the swift ebbing of life's little day. Yet Lyte says nothing to deprecate the worth of his fifty-four years on earth, and he remains sufficiently alert to the concerns of this present life to feel "the tempter's power" and to seek the grace of one who is both "guide and stay." In these days when increasing numbers of the elderly are in our congregations, and when all worshipers face the threat of nuclear devastation, hymns that relate time and eternity have their rightful place.

Few hymns combine realism and faith regarding life and death so well as does a new one (1975) by Fred Kaan that begins:

> Today I live, but once shall come my death;
>   one day shall still my laughter and my crying,
> bring to a halt my heartbeat and my breath:
>   Lord, give me faith for living and for dying.

Not knowing when or where he will die, he asks the Lord to save him from depression and morbid fears, and to help him so to live that, freed from regrets over the past, he can commit his spirit into God's hands. He then turns to present responsibilities:

> Meanwhile, I live and move and I am glad,
>   enjoy this life and all its interweaving;
> each given day, as I take up the thread,
>   let love suggest my mode, my mood of living.[13]

Though the hymns just cited are deeply personal, using singular pronouns, they are not self-centered. The affirmations and aspirations they express may be shared by all people of faith. This inclusiveness is quite explicit in a number of hymns that celebrate the "com-

munion of saints," the unity of the Christian community on earth
with the larger company of those who have entered the heavenly
kingdom. For example, Charles Wesley's "Come, let us join our
friends above" includes the invitation:

> Let saints on earth in concert sing
> with those to glory gone;
> for all the servants of our King
> in earth and heaven are one.[14]

Faith in the reality of the transtemporal community emerges
clearly in the hymn by William W. How (1823–1897) that begins:

> For all the saints, who from their labors rest,
> who thee by faith before the world confessed,
> thy name, O Jesus, be forever blest. Alleluia!

The original poem of eleven stanzas praises God in successive stanzas
for apostles, evangelists, and martyrs, but includes all "who nobly
fought of old," the "blest communion, fellowship divine." Awareness
of unity with them imparts strength to those who struggle here, who
may joyously anticipate joining the larger fellowship:

> And when the strife is fierce, the warfare long,
> steals on the ear the distant triumph song,
> and hearts are brave again, and arms are strong. Alleluia!

Christ's Victory and Ours

In the thought of Paul the apostle, faith in the imperishability of
the human "spiritual body" is linked inseparably to faith in the resurrection of Jesus Christ. By vanquishing death Christ has removed its
sting: "God be praised, he gives us the victory through our Lord Jesus
Christ" (I Cor. 15:54–57). The same connection is made by many of
our hymns, especially those celebrating Easter. The following passages are representative:

From the Greek "Come, you faithful, raise the strain," the first of
eight odes comprising the "Golden Canon," by John of Damascus (d.
ca. 754), translated by J. M. Neale in 1859, and slightly altered:

> 'Tis the spring of souls today;
> Christ has burst his prison.

From "The day of resurrection," another ode from the "Golden
Canon":

> From death to life eternal,
> from earth up to the sky,

> our Christ has brought us over
> with hymns of victory.

From the anonymous Latin hymn, "The strife is o'er, the battle done":

> Lord, by the stripes which wounded thee,
> from death's dread sting thy servants free,
> that we may live, and sing to thee,
>   "Alleluia!"

From Charles Wesley's "Christ the Lord is risen today":

> Soar we now where Christ has led,
> following our exalted Head;
> made like him, like him we rise;
> ours the cross, the grave, the skies.

From "Thine is the glory, risen, conquering Son," by Edmond Louis Budry (1854–1932), translated from the French by Richard Birch Hoyle (1875–1939) and set to the tune of "See, the conquering hero comes," from Handel's *Judas Maccabaeus:*

> Make us more than conquerors, through thy deathless love;
> bring us safe through Jordan, to thy home above.

A lucid contemporary summary of the meaning of Christ's resurrection for the human hope for life eternal is George Wallace Briggs's "Now is eternal life / if risen with Christ we stand." The second stanza proclaims:

> For God, the living God,
> stooped down to man's estate;
> by death destroying death
> Christ opened wide life's gate.
> He lives, who died; he reigns on high;
> who live in him shall never die.[15]

The songs that I have called hymns of fulfillment affirm faith in the future life but say little about its nature. Largely missing from them are fanciful descriptions of the glories of heaven. They speak more —though only briefly—of victory over temptation and sin, becoming like Christ, peace and rest, and above all of being at home in the presence of God. Influenced by traditional views like those found in Augustine and Thomas Aquinas, they seem to envisage a blessedness complete and final rather than the new opportunity for creative growth surmised by many twentieth-century theologians. However, references to Christlikeness, life reborn, and the spring of souls suggest faith in a quality of life that is dynamically perfectible rather than statically perfect. Further, expectation of a new life in the presence of the eternal Spirit opens the way to pursuit and actualization of the values God cherishes. Finite minds incapable of penetrating the unknown may fittingly look for fulfillment in communion with God, and dispense with details.

THE KINGDOM OF GOD

As Christians have looked toward the future in hope, they have linked expectation of eternal life together with faith in the coming kingdom of God. Both have to do with fulfillment of the divine purpose for human life and history. Thus the Statement of Faith of the United Church of Christ declares that God "promises to all who trust him . . . eternal life in his kingdom which has no end."

Jesus began his ministry with the proclamation: "The time has come; the kingdom of God is upon you; repent, and believe the Gospel" (Mark 1:15). The phrase "the kingdom of God" or an equivalent occurs 99 times in the Synoptic Gospels. The petition "Your kingdom come" follows naturally from the hallowing of God's name in the prayer Jesus taught his disciples.

What does the petition mean when it constitutes the motif of the hymns used in Christian worship? Here some confusion easily arises because the word *kingdom* is used both in hymnody and in the New Testament to designate three conceptions of divine rule: (1) Frequently it refers to the kingdom of God announced by Jesus. (2) Sometimes it applies to the triumphant reign of Christ connoted by New Testament accounts of the ascension (Luke 24:51; Acts 1:9–11). (3) In still other instances the kingdom is related to the return of Christ in judgment to establish the divine reign which will last forever (Matt. 24:3–31; 25:31–46; Mark 13:1–27; Acts 1:11; Rev., chs. 1–22).

The kingdom in the second sense is, for Christians, already real. Hymns like "Crown him with many crowns" and "Look, ye saints, the sight is glorious" picture Christ as even now King of kings. Yet the divine power and love still wait to be acknowledged and made regnant in human society. Hence we are concerned here chiefly with the first and third meanings—a future rule to be consummated in a community devoted to fulfillment of the divine will. Two different images are involved: the kingdom of God and the return of Christ.

"Your Kingdom Come"

Predictably, hymnists deal with some of the same questions as those raised by New Testament scholars. What is the nature of the kingdom? Does it result from divine or human action? When will it be realized?

THE NATURE OF THE KINGDOM

For our hymnists, as for other interpreters, the term *kingdom* in relation to God is qualitative rather than geographical. Primarily it designates the rule or reign of God, not the place or territory where God is in charge. What kind of world can we expect when God's rule is complete?

In "Thy kingdom come, O God, / thy rule, O Christ, begin," Lewis Hensley (1824–1905) interprets the coming to mean the breaking of "the tyrannies of sin." He then provides further content in the form of questions:

> Where is thy reign of peace, / and purity and love?
> When shall all hatred cease, / as in the realms above?
>
> When comes the promised time / that war shall be no more,
> and lust, oppression, crime / shall flee thy face before?[16]

In " 'Thy kingdom come,' on bended knee" Frederick L. Hosmer (1840–1929) looks for

> the day in whose clear-shining light
>   all wrong shall stand revealed,
> when justice shall be clothed with might,
>   and every hurt be healed;
> when knowledge, hand in hand with peace,
>   shall walk the earth abroad—
> the day of perfect righteousness,
>   the promised day of God.[17]

For George Wallace Briggs in "Christ is the world's true light," the kingdom means the reign of Christ the Prince of Peace.

> New life, new hope awakes
>   where'er men own his sway:
> freedom her bondage breaks,
>   and night is turned to day.

"In Christ" all races and nations forsake their feuds and fears, and substitute ploughshares and pruning hooks for swords and spears.

DIVINE OR HUMAN AGENCY?

Mirrored in our hymnody is the long-standing view that only God can actualize the kingdom, since human beings are too weak and especially too sinful for so great a task. It would therefore be presumptuous to expect it to be accomplished by human effort. Such a faith seems to be implicit in John Milton's "The Lord will come and not be slow, / his footsteps cannot err." Righteousness will be God's "royal harbinger," and truth will blossom on the earth, but these will be divine gifts: "justice, from her heavenly bower," will "look down on mortal men." So the poet prays,

> Rise, God, judge thou the earth in might,
>   this wicked earth redress;
> for thou art he who shall by right
>   the nations all possess.

When this occurs, the nations will glorify their Maker by whose strong hand great wonders are done:

> Thou in thy everlasting seat
> remainest God alone.[18]

Among more recent hymns, the opening address of "God the omnipotent! King, who ordainest" reflects the assumption of later stanzas that God alone can give peace in our time. Other hymns agree in giving priority to divine action, but they also assume the need of a positive human response to God's gift of the kingdom. Without denying that divine grace is the *sine qua non*, they expect human beings to offer themselves as instruments through which God's will is done.

Such is the expectation of "Father eternal, Ruler of creation," by Laurence Housman (1865–1959), which sees the kingdom as the culmination of God's creative action, "which moved ere form was made." The hymn is basically a prayer of confession of human failures and a plea for help:

> Races and peoples, lo, we stand divided,
>   and, sharing not our griefs, no joy can share;
> by wars and tumults love is mocked, derided,
>   his conquering cross no kingdom wills to bear.

Envious, fearful, and jealous, the nations build "proud towers which shall not reach to heaven." Hence we pray:

> How shall we love you, holy, hidden Being,
>   if we love not the world which you have made?
> O give us brother-love for better seeing

> your Word made flesh, and in a manger laid:
> Your kingdom come, O Lord, your will be done.[19]

The hymn is God-centered throughout, but its confession of pride, lovelessness, and greed implies that we could and should have acted differently; while the prayers for "brother-love" and the realization of God's rule assume human responsibility for the changes God seeks. To pray "your will be done" includes the choice and intention to do what God wills.

Of special interest is the hymn by Walter Russell Bowie (1882–1969), "O holy city, seen of John," because it combines the apocalyptic vision of Revelation 21, which pictures the new Jerusalem "coming down out of heaven from God," with the prayer:

> Give us, O God, the strength to build
> the city that has stood
> too long a dream, whose laws are love,
> whose ways are brotherhood,
> and where the sun that shines becomes
> God's grace for human good.[20]

For Robert B. Y. Scott (b. 1899) in "O day of God, draw nigh," the coming of the kingdom entails divine judgment and power, but also human faith and obedience:

> Bring to our troubled minds,
> uncertain and afraid,
> the quiet of a steadfast faith,
> calm of a call obeyed.

The hymn continues with prayers for justice and peace, but assumes the need for human cooperation:

> Bring justice to our land,
> that all may dwell secure,
> and finely build for days to come
> foundations that endure.[21]

When Will It Come?

When some Pharisees asked Jesus when the kingdom was coming, he replied, "The kingdom of God is in the midst of you" (Luke 17:21, RSV). Yet he also asked his followers to pray for its coming. This paradox appears in the answers given by hymn writers to the Pharisees' question. They agree that in the coming of Jesus the foundations of the kingdom have been laid, but that its full attainment remains in the future. In the main they expect it to come gradually rather than suddenly. They leave open the question of whether to expect its fulfillment within or beyond history, and they offer no schedule of dates, but in faith they hope and pray that in significant respects the kingdom will advance as God's will is done on earth.

Two widely known hymns express clearly the belief that the kingdom is both present and future. James Montgomery's "Hail to the Lord's anointed" is an Advent hymn in two senses. The opening of one stanza celebrates the beginning of Jesus' "reign on earth":

> He comes to break oppression,
>   to set the captive free,
> to take away transgression,
>   and rule in equity.

After further descriptions of the righteousness, peace, and love to be actualized in Jesus' ministry, the hymn connects the adoration of the Magi with the praise to be elicited from all people as God's rule advances:

> To him shall prayer unceasing
>   and daily vows ascend;
> his kingdom still increasing,
>   a kingdom without end.

The same note is heard in an unexpected place—the closing stanza of a beautiful evening hymn by John Ellerton, "The day you gave us, Lord, is ended." In a mood of quiet thanksgiving the hymn traces the creative work of God as dawn, daylight, and darkness follow each other in land after land around the earth, while prayers of the faithful rise hour by hour in ceaseless praise. These accompaniments of the eastward movement of the earth become for Ellerton a symbol of both the constancy and the growth of the rule of God:

> So be it, Lord; your throne shall never,
>   like earth's proud empires, pass away;
> your kingdom stands, and grows forever,
>   till all your creatures own your sway.

More confident than most later hymnists about the coming of the kingdom in its fullness is Arthur C. Ainger (1841–1919), who wrote in 1894:

> God is working his purpose out
>   as year succeeds to year;
> God is working his purpose out,
>   and the time is drawing near.

Worshipers are called to proclaim everywhere the gospel of Christ's truth and to strive to free those captive to sorrow and sin. The closing stanza reminds us that

> all we can do is nothing worth
> unless God blesses the deed.

Nevertheless, the time is surely coming "when the earth shall be filled with the glory of God / as the waters cover the sea." Writing in 1945, Albert F. Bayly conveys a similar message:

> Rejoice, O people, in the mounting years,
>   wherein God's mighty purposes unfold;
> from age to age his righteous reign appears,
>   from land to land the love of Christ is told.

Prophets, saints, martyrs, and eager hearts in later years have proclaimed and demonstrated the message of deliverance. We must admit that today "low lies man's pride and human wisdom dies." Yet we can still rejoice, for

> . . . on the cross God's love reveals its power,
>   and from his waiting church new hopes arise.[22]

Ruth Duck's "Lead on, O cloud of Presence" (1974) stresses movement toward the kingdom. Patterned after "Lead on, O King eternal" and like the earlier hymn set to LANCASHIRE, it replaces royal and military language with the exodus imagery of a journey toward promised freedom. Though the way is perilous, "the journey is our home," and we travel by God's light. Those who start may not reach the destination, but

> we pray our sons and daughters / may live to see that land
> where justice rules with mercy / and love is law's demand.[23]

"Come, Lord Jesus"

The New Testament evidences a widespread expectation in the primitive church of the return of Christ at the end of the age, an event that would consummate the victory of God over evil and usher in the Lord's everlasting kingdom. The most influential expression of this eschatological hope is the book of Revelation, probably written about A.D. 95 during the persecutions of Domitian. In fanciful apocalyptic imagery it seeks to comfort suffering Christians by assuring them that the might of Rome ("Babylon" in the book) will be overthrown by the "King of kings and Lord of lords" (Rev. 11:15; 17:14; 19:16), who will gather the faithful into the New Jerusalem which will endure forever. Many hymns reflect this tradition, in effect giving voice to the prayer of Rev. 22:20: "Come, Lord Jesus!"

A major theme of these writers is that Christ will return in judgment, separating the sheep from the goats, welcoming the redeemed into eternal blessedness and effecting the final rejection of the wicked. Thus a twelfth-century poem by Bernard of Cluny begins:

> The clouds of judgment gather; / the time is growing late
> be sober and be watchful; / our judge is at the gate:
> the judge who comes in mercy, / the judge who comes in might
> to put an end to evil / and diadem the right.[24]

Six centuries later Charles Coffin begins his hymn "The advent of our God" by welcoming the birth of Christ "to make us free." Then he proclaims,

> As judge, on clouds of light,
> he soon will come again,
> his scattered people to unite
> with them in heaven to reign.

The faithful are urged to prepare for the great event:

> Let this old Adam day by day
> God's image still put on.[25]

Some hymns on the return of Christ display the individualistic self-centeredness that we noted above in some lyric interpretations of life after death. Thus Gloria and William J. Gaither in "The market place is empty" (1970) describe the cessation of all earthly life when Christ comes again, adding to each stanza the refrain:

> O the King is coming, the King is coming!
> Praise God, he's coming for me! me![26]

Such expressions may reflect simply the deeply personal nature of religious faith. Yet most hymns that deal with Christ's return manage to preserve the personal element while using plural pronouns and adjectives. In the hymn already cited, Bernard of Cluny sings of "the peace of all the faithful, / the calm of all the blest." In "Oh, happy day when we shall stand," Wilhelm A. Wexels declares that "all peoples at the Lord's right hand / shall find their names engraved."[27] Similarly, Charles Wesley in his familiar "Rejoice, the Lord is King!" affirms that the Lord will take his servants "to their eternal home"; and Laurentius Laurenti (1660–1722) begins his hymn on Christ's coming again with the call, "Rejoice, all ye believers," and closes it with the prayer that we may see "the day of earth's redemption that brings us home to Thee."[28]

To the questions, Who will bring to pass the reign of Christ? and, When will it occur? the answers are not hard to find. To Christ alone belongs the decision as to when to return in glory, and his power alone will consummate the new age. Such a momentous event lies completely beyond the capacity of human beings to accomplish. The bridegroom invites us to the wedding feast; we can only accept the invitation and prepare for the great occasion by keeping our lamps ready.

Likewise, no human being knows the day or the hour when Christ will come again (see Matt. 24:42; Rev. 1:7). All we can know is that he will come suddenly, without warning, not as the culmination of a long process in which God's will is increasingly attained. However, most hymn writers who deal with the return expect or hope that it will occur soon. An anonymous Greek hymn translated by John Brownlie (1859–1925) begins, "The King shall come when morning dawns / and light triumphant breaks." Brighter even than the resurrection morn will be that fair morning "when Christ our King in beauty comes, / and we his face shall see." So the faithful eagerly await him and pray, "Come quickly, King of kings!"[29]

According to these authors, the realm soon to begin is a heavenly one. They expect the end of earthly existence and the establishment of a posthistorical, transtemporal kingdom. This expectation appears unmistakably in a stirring German hymn by Philipp Nicolai (1556–1608), translated by Catherine Winkworth (1827–1878), "Wake, awake! for night is flying." It is based on Jesus' parable of the wise virgins preparing to meet the heavenly bridegroom (Matt. 25:1–13). After alerting the virgins, the watchmen announce to Zion the coming of "her Friend from heaven" adorned with truth and grace. The hymn then pictures the supreme happiness of those who enter the festal hall singing:

> Now let all the heavens adore you,
> and saints and angels sing before you.
> The harps and cymbals all unite.
> Of one pearl each shining portal,
> where, dwelling with the choir immortal
> we gather round your dazzling light.[30]

What we have in these hymns is a valiant attempt to describe what defies description—the consummation of all things in the eternal felicity of those who will inhabit the city of God. The life envisioned is the "eternal repose" pictured by Augustine at the close of *The City of God.*

Differences and Agreements

We have discovered in our hymnody two very different interpretations of the kingdom. One stresses fulfillment of the divine will in the movement toward justice and peace in human society; the other, the return of Christ in judgment and the entrance of the faithful into eternal joy. One envisages a long, slow process of realization; the other, a sudden and complete victory of God over all evil. One recognizes the need for a free human response to the primary action of God; the other regards the accomplishment as the work of God alone. One sees God's rule as occurring whenever the divine will is done on earth, while expecting its posthistorical extension; the other locates the reign of Christ in a heavenly order that begins when history ends.

Nevertheless, the contrast should not be exaggerated. The central emphases of the two views highlight equally important aspects of authentic Christian faith. The gospel does affirm the positive possibilities of life in this world and the need to struggle now for divine ends. It also insists that we see present life in an eternal perspective —an outlook that imparts ultimate significance to our earthly pilgrimage. Moreover, the two interpretations exhibit a number of common elements.

Both assert the reality of divine judgment, present and future.

Both believe in the ultimate victory of the divine purpose.

Both trust above all the saving, renewing action of God in Jesus Christ.

Both assign an active role to humanity: men and women must either labor to advance the rule of God or at least prepare for it by right living now.

For both, the ultimate goal is a society, not a loose collection of individuals. In view of what we now know of the cosmos, a physical return of Christ "in the clouds of the air" to take the redeemed with him to a physical heaven is incredible. But discard of this notion of a "second coming" does not affect the basic meaning of Christian hope, which the two interpretations share: that God's purpose in creation will be consummated—that the Spirit who wrought in Jesus Christ is the ultimate power in the world, and is even now leading humanity toward ultimate realization of the beloved community God seeks.

PART THREE
SPECIAL TOPICS

11

GOSPEL HYMNS

The term "gospel hymn" came into use in the middle and late nineteenth century to describe the songs which, because of their folk-like tunes and popular appeal, contributed powerfully to the success of the mass evangelistic movements in England and America. Apparently applied first to a hymnbook compiled by Edward Mote in 1836, the rubric appeared in the titles of all six of the collections assembled by Ira D. Sankey and his colleagues from 1875 to 1895.[1]

The word *gospel* (Anglo-Saxon *godspell*), a translation of the Greek *euangelion* and the Latin *evangelium*, means "good tale" or "good tidings." In Christian usage, therefore, the gospel is the good news of the salvation offered to human beings by the action of God in Jesus Christ. Any hymn that proclaims this good news might be properly called a gospel hymn. Because of the revivalistic associations of the term, it came to be applied more specifically to hymns designed to move people to Christian discipleship. Gradually the meaning was broadened to include songs expressing the desire of believers for a deeper personal relationship to Christ.

TRADITIONAL GOSPEL HYMNS

In the United States, revivals began in upstate New York in the 1820s, led by Charles Grandison Finney. A major revival occurred in 1857–58 following a financial panic. However, mass evangelism reached its greatest popularity in the Moody-Sankey revivals of the last three decades of the century. The final collection of the hymns used in these meetings, *Gospel Hymns Nos. 1–6 Complete*, includes 739 numbers, of which "over 125" are described by the editors as "standard hymns and tunes of the church." Sankey's collections sold over 50 million copies. Almost incredibly, it is estimated that more than 1,500 hymnbooks of the "gospel" type were published before 1900.

Even as mass evangelism has continued down to the present, with such leaders as Billy Sunday, Gipsy Smith, and Billy Graham, so the writing, publication, and use of gospel hymns has gone forward throughout the twentieth century. Musicians like Charles M. Alexander, Homer A. Rodeheaver, and Charles H. Gabriel were especially influential in the early decades. Many hymns from the Sankey collections have retained their popularity. We shall utilize in this chapter two main sources: (1) those hymns from the approximately 614 gospel songs in Sankey's 1895 collection which are also to be found in selected denominational and independent hymnals today—omitting those which seem to qualify as "standard church hymns" included by Sankey; (2) twentieth-century hymns of the gospel type which appear in the same books. A reliable indication of the continuing attraction of the former is provided by the numbers that appear in the latest editions of the following hymnbooks: in *Hymns for the Living Church* (1974), 65; *The Baptist Hymnal* (1975), 56; *Hymns for the Family of God* (1976), 51; *The Mennonite Hymnal* (1969), 41; the United Methodist *Book of Hymns* (1964), 34; the *Pilgrim Hymnal* (1958), 11; *Hymns II* (Inter-Varsity, 1976), 11.

Characteristics

In general the gospel hymns are marked by plain, unadorned, readily understandable words, with much use of metaphors drawn from ordinary life. Frequently these appear in contrasting pairs, such as: tempest—harbor; bondage—release; hunger—manna; wounds—healing. Most of the hymns are expressions of deep religious feelings, both negative and positive, enabling them to win a ready response from people who themselves feel intensely their own needs and hopes. The repetition of ideas and phrases found often in successive stanzas of one hymn is accentuated by the use of refrains that summarize the thought and make it easily remembered. As pointed out by Sandra S. Sizer, forms of address vary from statements, affirmations, or stories, with no audience specified; to exhortations to sinners ("come to Jesus!") or Christians ("have faith!" "work!"); to praise, thanksgiving, or supplication.[2] The music is characterized by a flowing rhythm and a simplicity in both tunes and harmonizations that make the songs easily singable. The tunes of the refrains often essentially repeat those of the stanzas, and comparison of the melodies of different hymns discloses enough similarity to enable Erik Routley to say that "all the tunes are virtually the same tune."[3]

Seven main themes occur in the gospel hymns.

1. Their central emphasis is the reality of personal salvation through Jesus Christ. This comes to expression in a variety of ways.

a. Frequently it takes the form of joyous gratitude for what Jesus has done, as when Francis H. Rowley exults, "I will sing the wondrous story / of the Christ who died for me,"[4] or when Philip P. Bliss sings:

"Man of Sorrows," what a name / for the Son of God who came ruined sinners to reclaim! / Hallelujah! what a Savior![5]

b. Sometimes the hymn is a prayer for help, either in beginning the Christian life or in surmounting its difficulties. Thus Fanny J. Crosby pleads in "Jesus, keep me near the cross":

> Near the cross! O Lamb of God,
> bring its scenes before me;
> help me walk from day to day
> with its shadows o'er me.[6]

c. Still other hymns centered in Jesus involve life commitment. Widely known is Charlotte Elliott's "Just as I am, without one plea." Also illustrative of this motif is William T. Sleeper's "Out of my bondage, sorrow, and night, / Jesus, I come, Jesus, I come."[7]

d. Many gospel hymns are exhortations to sinners to accept the saving benefits of Jesus' death. Thus John H. Stockton's "Come, every soul by sin oppressed, / there's mercy with the Lord" urges an immediate response:

> For Jesus shed his precious blood,
> rich blessings to bestow;
> plunge now into the crimson flood
> that washes white as snow.[8]

e. With very few exceptions the gospel hymns reflect a penal, substitutionary view of the atonement, with frequent references to the efficacy of the shed blood of Christ. Thus Elisha A. Hoffman rejoices:

> Christ has for sin atonement made,
> what a wonderful Savior!
> We are redeemed! The price is paid!
> What a wonderful Savior![9]

The second stanza goes on to praise Christ for "the cleansing blood" "that reconciled my soul to God," again inserting the exclamation in the second and fourth lines.

2. Repeatedly affirmed is the intimate relationship between the redeemed sinner and the Savior. For James G. Small, Jesus is a dear friend:

> I've found a Friend, O such a Friend!
> He loved me ere I knew him;

> he drew me with the cords of love,
>   and thus he bound me to him.[10]

In a much more recent song, "Jesus my Lord will love me forever" (1943), Norman J. Clayton rejoices:

> Now I belong to Jesus, / Jesus belongs to me,
> not for the years of time alone, / but for eternity.[11]

3. Another recurring theme is the helplessness and complete dependence of the recipient of salvation. Often the sinner appears as the victim of uncontrollable forces—not the rebel portrayed in many of the hymns of Isaac Watts. A hymn of Joseph Hart opens with the invitation:

> Come, ye sinners, poor and needy,
>   weak and wounded, sick and sore;
> Jesus ready stands to save you,
>   full of pity, love, and power.[12]

The appropriate response is voiced by William McDonald:

> I am coming to the cross;
>   I am poor and weak and blind.[13]

Similarly, Elvina M. Hall confesses:

> I hear the Savior say, / "Thy strength indeed is small,
> child of weakness, watch and pray, / find in me thine all in all."

Aware that only his power can change her "leper's spots" and melt her "heart of stone," she surrenders to his saving grace, declaring in the refrain:

> Jesus paid it all, / all to him I owe;
> sin had left a crimson stain, / he washed it white as snow.[14]

4. Repeatedly the gospel hymns stress the experience of rest and security available to those who trust in Jesus. William O. Cushing speaks of hiding amid life's tempests in the shelter of the Rock:

> O safe to the Rock that is higher than I,
>   my soul in its conflicts and sorrows would fly;
> so sinful, so weary, thine, thine I would be;
>   thou blest Rock of Ages, I'm hiding in thee.[15]

Twenty years later (1896) the same author shifts the metaphor to one used by Jesus when he wept over Jerusalem (Matt. 23:37):

> Under his wings I am safely abiding,
>   though the night deepens and tempests are wild,

> still I can trust him; I know he will keep me;
> he has redeemed me, and I am his child.

The refrain concludes:

> Under his wings my soul shall abide,
> safely abide forever.[16]

5. However, the gospel hymns do not invariably portray the Christian life as passive. A number of them summon the believer to strive for Christlikeness of character. Sabine Baring-Gould's "Onward, Christian soldiers" and George Duffield, Jr.'s "Stand up, stand up for Jesus" are calls to courageous struggle in the cause of Christ. Christians are urged to tread "where the saints have trod" and press forward until the victor's crown is won.

Frances R. Havergal is more concrete. Her "Truehearted, wholehearted" pledges "valiant endeavor and loving obedience."[17] The multitudes who join her in singing "Take my life, and let it be / consecrated, Lord, to thee" dedicate all their powers unreservedly to the service of God.

Other hymns voice the desire for growth and increased dedication. For Johnson Oatman, Jr., this means "pressing on the upward way" where he gains new heights "every day." He wants "to live above the world," away from doubts, fears, and "Satan's darts." So he prays to be lifted up to the higher ground of "heaven's table land."[18] Much closer to Havergal's ethical concern is the aspiration of Charles H. Gabriel. In "More like the Master I would ever be," he asks for "more zeal to labor, more courage to be true," more of the Master's "love to others," and "more earnest effort to bring his kingdom in."[19]

6. Unmistakable is the strongly individualistic character of the gospel hymns. The pronouns *we, us,* and *our* appear occasionally, but they are greatly outnumbered by *I, me,* and *my*. This circumstance reflects accurately the intensely personal nature of the faith embodied in the hymns. When the first-person plural pronoun is used, it ordinarily refers to the community of the saved. Concern for those outside this community is expressed mainly in evangelistic appeals to them to accept the salvation freely available in Christ, leading to their reception into the circle of the blessed. The outreach involved when the second-person pronoun is used is typically of this kind. Thus S. O'Malley Clough begins one hymn, "I have a Savior, he's pleading in glory," goes on to tell of the tender, watchful care this relationship involves, and concludes the stanza with the appeal, "But O, that my Savior were your Savior too!"[20] Thus the salvation offered is as individual as that already cherished by the witness.

The persons who respond are not encouraged to work responsibly in the world to diminish conflict or advance justice; rather they are welcomed into a group in which Christ protects them from the world while they with one another deepen their own experience of the love of God. In "Lord Jesus Christ, we seek thy face," Alexander Stewart voices thanks for Christ's cleansing and sanctifying work, then continues:

> Shut in with thee, far, far above
>   the restless world that wars below,
> we seek to learn and prove thy love,
>   thy wisdom and thy grace to know.[21]

7. Many of the gospel hymns emphasize that heaven is the destination of the believer. When Lelia N. Morris prays, "Nearer, still nearer, close to thy heart / draw me, my Savior, so precious thou art," she has in mind a present experience that is completed in heaven:

> Nearer, still nearer, while life shall last,
> till safe in glory my anchor is cast;
> thro' endless ages, ever to be
> nearer, my Savior, still nearer to thee.[22]

A fascinating example of this expectation is Isaac Watts's "Come, ye that love the Lord," because of the way in which Robert Lowry has changed the original into a typical gospel hymn. In several "standard" church hymnals the words are set to ST. THOMAS or another tune equally sedate.[23] However, in *Gospel Hymns* Lowry has contributed his own tune (MARCHING TO ZION), inserted repeats of the third and fourth lines of each stanza, and added a refrain, transforming the song into a jubilant, rollicking affirmation of life on the way to heaven. The fourth stanza affirms:

> We're marching thro' Emmanuel's ground [repeat],
>   to fairer worlds on high [repeat].

Then comes the refrain, which has already been sung three times:

> We're marching to Zion, / beautiful, beautiful Zion;
> We're marching upward to Zion, / the beautiful city of God.[24]

An Appraisal

Without question the gospel hymns have contributed immeasurably to the sense of personal dignity and worth in innumerable thousands of people reached in the peak periods of mass evangelism. They combined with the messages of the preachers to bring hope and faith to multitudes who felt buffeted and short-changed by an indifferent or hostile world. For such people, to be able to sing to a lilting melody, along with hundreds of other enthusiastic men and women, "I'm a child of the King," "Jesus died for me," or "My name's written there," was in effect an assurance that the supreme power in the universe cared for them as individuals. No doubt these songs continue to perform this function today for many lonely, perplexed, economically marginal victims of the depersonalization of mechanized, computerized society.

Probably hymns of the gospel type have also helped to make Christian faith personally appealing for many who are not moved by the more dignified, restrained, objective music heard in the majority of mainstream churches. Psychologically, aesthetically, and culturally, these people can readily identify with the uncomplicated thought and warm feeling of gospel music, while remaining untouched by hymns of greater theological depth and superior musical quality.

The need for a religion of the heart as well as the head cannot be denied. The most impeccable theology may fail to touch people at the point of their greatest need. There is likewise no place for an elitist Christianity that looks down on those whose educational and cultural opportunities have been limited. Yet a superficial evangelism in either preaching or music is not likely to bring genuine newness or wholeness of life to many persons in our day, even though crowds may respond with their presence and their money. People of all educational levels are familiar with and constantly make use of new and sophisticated developments in science and technology that have produced radical changes in areas like communications, travel, medicine, and recreation. Why should we uncritically accept as adequate for the church today a type of hymnody that appealed to part of the population—but by no means all—seventy-five to one hundred years ago? The repetition ad infinitum of stock phrases that have lost much of their meaning, set to tunes of ephemeral worth, cannot convey effectively to people in our time the fullness, truth, and transforming power of the gospel of Christ.

The average church needs in its hymnic repertoire songs suited to the ongoing worship and life of the congregation and capable of aiding their growth toward Christian maturity. Even Ira Sankey never favored the exclusive use of gospel songs. He intended them primarily for specifically evangelistic meetings. In order to meet the spiritual needs of all its people, the church may wish to make judicious use of some of these.

On the whole, the gospel hymns reflect a defective understanding of the Christian faith. In their almost exclusive focus on redemption they largely overlook the creative and sustaining activity of God. Their Christology deifies Jesus, disregarding the human aspect of the person of Christ that is guarded by the classic creeds, and assuming in effect a unitarianism of the Son. Their uncritical espousal of a penal, substitutionary conception of the atonement misses much of the deep meaning of Jesus Christ for human salvation. They offer an abstract view of sin and guilt that often overlooks the dynamic particularity of the attitudes and acts in which human beings center their lives in self instead of God. With their stress on rest, security, trophies, thrones, crowns, and the like they make the Christian life deceptively easy, frequently passing over the struggles and hard choices involved in genuine Christian discipleship.[25]

An important positive value in the gospel hymns is the testimony they offer to the validity of personal Christian experience. Most of them bear witness to a reality that the authors themselves have encountered. Whether the authors refer to the Lord Jesus, God, Christ, or the Savior, they seem to be telling of one whom they have met in a firsthand encounter. This kind of awareness is a precious ingredient of authentic Christian faith. Unfortunately, this experiential quality is sometimes accompanied by an extreme individualism that is not so praiseworthy. The private relation of the individual to Jesus or God may be so emphasized and savored that the sense of responsibility toward other human beings is dimmed or lost. Few indeed of the gospel hymns manifest concern for persons suffering from unjust social conditions or oppressed by those who exercise power over them.

Yet sweeping judgments must be avoided. On the one hand, large numbers of professing Christians who have not been noticeably influenced by gospel songs are just as lacking in real social concern as those who contentedly sing of being saved by the blood. On the other hand, among those who in worship make considerable use of gospel songs, or materials embodying a similar theology, are some who are sharply critical of many features of the social order and firmly committed to radical change.

Walter Rauschenbusch (1861–1918), the great pioneer of the social gospel in America, was himself identified with gospel hymnody during his pastorate (1886–1891) of the Second German Baptist Church in a depressed area of New York City. He joined Ira D. Sankey in compiling and editing *Evangeliums-Lieder,*[26] a hymnbook for German-speaking people that contained 196 songs from *Gospel Hymns Nos. 1–5.* Rauschenbusch himself translated 82 of them. Rauschenbusch had a sincere evangelistic interest in winning men and women to a "new birth" in Christ. He believed no less firmly in the need for social salvation, and as a Christian he supported a socialist program aimed at securing equality of human rights and a democratic distribution of economic power. Apparently he felt no incongruity in his twofold reading of the gospel. He could hardly have found his social interpretation of the gospel in the gospel songs. But given his commitment to social change, grounded in his study of the New Testament and the prophets and his firsthand contact with human distress, he apparently derived from these hymns nourishment for a personal faith that strengthened his social witness.

Linked to the extreme individualism of the gospel hymns is their almost exclusively otherworldly understanding of Christian hope. Concentrating on the joys of the life to come, they ignore the positive values attainable here and now and the responsibility Christians have for realizing them. Songs that merely point people to the skies play directly into the hands of the Marxist claim that religion is only an opiate. It is one thing to remind suffering, dispirited persons of their eternal destiny; it is quite another to neglect mentioning the possibilities open to them, however limited, for a fuller life in this world.

BLACK GOSPEL HYMNODY

No account of gospel hymnody would be adequate if it omitted the black gospel music that has emerged in America since the time of the Great Depression. Black gospel has of course been influenced by "white gospel," but it must be understood primarily as the most recent phase in the development of the religious music tradition distinctive of the black experience of deprivation and oppression.

In *"Somebody's Calling My Name,"* Wyatt Tee Walker has traced that development through five main stages: (1) slave utterances (moans, chants, cries for deliverance); (2) spirituals (faith-songs, sorrow-songs, plantation hymns); (3) meter music (Watts, Charles Wesley, Sankey, and others); (4) hymns of "improvisation" (Euro-American hymns with "beat"); and (5) gospel music (music of hard times, cross-fertilized with secular music).[27] During this process black people were inevitably influenced in several ways by the surrounding white culture. They made their own certain basic elements of Euro-American Christian theology. They modified some hymn structures, and by improvisation recreated some hymns according to the needs of black performance practice. They also utilized, while Africanizing, the Western tonal system. The result was the crystallization of a newly developing hymn form.

The roots of black gospel hymnody are in the black spirituals, and like them it mirrors the life of the folk whose experience produced it. However, in contrast to the anonymity of the spirituals, the gospel tunes and lyrics are the work of known authors and composers.

What Is Black Gospel?

According to Thomas A. Dorsey, often called the "father of gospel music," black gospel means "a message of good tidings expounded by one who has walked the path of trouble and hard times."[28] As Walker has shown, it has been influenced also by the promise of better things that accompanied the black migration to the industrial North during and after World War II, by the Supreme Court decision of 1954 which struck down segregation in public education, and by the hope generated by the nonviolent protest led by Martin Luther King, Jr., and the resulting civil rights legislation. But formidable barriers to the full equality of blacks and other minorities remain in both North and South, and in some respects they are more massive than before. This fact continues to be reflected in black gospel music and the way it is sung. These songs express on the one hand the alienation, pain, and distress felt by black people in a predominantly white society; and on the other the self-respect, awareness of personal worth, and hope of deliverance that they derive from their Christian faith.

The most distinctive musical characteristics of black gospel music are traceable to its African folk heritage. Pearl Williams-Jones has listed fifteen "African related traits" present in black gospel techniques, forms, and performances, including dynamic rhythm, improvisation, repetition, percussive playing, antiphonal response and communal participation, handclapping and foot-patting, shouting, dancing, and oral transmission.[29] However, she points out that such Africanisms have become assimilated into and changed by the Afro-American style; "swing," for example, is an adaptation which has produced a rhythm quite distinguishable from that of African drumming.

Two features of this gospel music merit special emphasis here. One is the freedom and spontaneity of its performance, opening up almost unlimited possibilities for improvisation, ornamentation, and changes in melody or rhythm. Thus no printing of music or text can transmit the full flavor of black gospel; it must be experienced.

The other especially noteworthy feature is congregational participation. Black gospel has been widely sung in concert halls by soloists, quartets, and choirs. But it remains a product of the black church, and it is in church worship that its full meaning is disclosed. Even when it is performed in congregations by choirs, soloists, or small ensembles, the people take part by humming, swaying, clapping, foot-stomping, and shouting. Frequently the rendition is antiphonal, between the song leader or preacher and the congregation, and the emotion generated is often electric in its power. At peak moments an entire congregation may be moved without signal to join a soloist in singing words that voice their deepest feelings.

What Do the Texts Say?

Though the black gospel songs rely on an idiom that is more oral than written, they do use words, and the words are important. They are sung with fervor because they express the good news which speaks to the condition of the singers. Their basic message can be summarized under five headings.

1. Our trust is in God. Many of the songs bear personal witness to the reality of God's supportive care in the past, and on this basis pray for his help in present and future trials. In "Yes, God is real" Kenneth Morris (b. 1916) refers to the doubt, scorn, and rejection he sometimes encounters, yet affirms:

> There are some things I may not know;
> there are some places I can't go,
> but I am sure of this one thing,
> that God is real, for I can feel him deep within.

The refrain reiterates and broadens the assurance of the three stanzas:

> Yes, God is real, real in my soul.
> Yes, God is real for he has washed and made me whole;
> his love for me is like pure gold.
> Yes, God is real, for I can feel him in my soul.[30]

In the same mood Robert Fryson declares that "God is." Repeatedly the choir sings "God is . . . ," and the soloist responds with phrases like "my protection," "my life in darkness," "my joy in times of sorrow," "my all in all." These stanzas are followed by a series of declarations responding to the soloist's assertions. "God is":

> He moves all pain, misery, and strife. . . .
> He promised to meet me and never to leave me.
> He never, never comes short of his words. . . .
> I got to fast and pray,
> stay in the narrow way, . . .
> live my life clean every day. . . .
> I want to go with him when he comes back;
> I've come too far and I'll never turn back.
> God is . . . my all and all.[31]

Curtis Burrell (1978) declares in spite of much adversity, "I don't feel no ways tired." He testifies that though he has been sick, lonely, and troubled, God has sustained him. He has journeyed too long to give up now: "I don't believe that God would bring me this far just to leave me."[32]

Such trust in God is a central emphasis in two songs by Thomas A.

Dorsey. In one of these, "like a ship that's toss'd and driven," he finds
himself battered by raging storms, but takes comfort in the faith that
"the Lord will make a way somehow." He confronts evil and misunderstanding on every hand, and finds no consolation in complaining
friends. Yet repeatedly he tells his heart to be patient, because God
will help bear his burdens:

> When the load bears down so heavy
>   the weight is shown upon my brow,
> there's a sweet relief in knowing
>   O, the Lord will make a way somehow.[33]

The other song by Dorsey is the moving "Take my hand, precious
Lord," written a week after the deaths of his wife and his only child.
It epitomizes both anguish and quiet faith.

> Precious Lord, take my hand, lead me on, help me stand;
>   I am tired, I am weak, I am worn;
> thru the storm, thru the night, lead me on to the light.
>   Take my hand, precious Lord, lead me home.
>
> . . . .
>
> When the darkness appears and the night draws near
>   and the day is past and gone,
> at the river I stand; guide my feet, hold my hand.
>   Take my hand, precious Lord, lead me home.[34]

2. Jesus can be counted on to save and guide us. In one song by
Clinton Utterbach, after all of God's efforts to win his people's obedience are rebuffed, leaving them "wretched and lost," the Lord de-
cides on a plan to cleanse the sinful children and make them whole.
The chorus sings: "I'll send my Son so that all might be saved."[35]

In "Old Ship of Zion" Thomas A. Dorsey pictures himself "lost in
sin and sorrow / on an isle in life's dark sea," when he sees a ship in
the distance. As it draws near, the captain beckons and calls out,

> "I have come, my friend, to save you,
>   step on board and follow me."

The chorus identifies the craft as "the old ship of Zion," and urges
time after time: "All of my Father's children, get on board." The
marooned sailor hesitates because of the wild waves, but gains courage when the captain calms the sea and promises (in the chorus,
repeatedly), "There's no danger in the water." Finally he accepts.

> Then I stepp'd aboard the vessel.
>   Thro' the straits and thro' the gorge,
> Many years it sailed the waters,
>   many souls have made the voyage.

> Then I recognized the captain,
>   it was Jesus in command.
> 'Tis the old ship of Zion,
>   and it's bound for Canaan land.

The chorus declares over and over:

> She has landed many thousands . . . ;
> get on board;
> get on board, all of God's children, get on board.[36]

A song by Sam Cook uses an infrequent metaphor, portraying Jesus as a fence, indeed a moving fence that protects the wayfarer on his journey! It begins with a prayer that Jesus will guide the traveler's footsteps and protect him every day as he walks the narrow way. The chorus breathes confidence that the prayer will be answered:

> Jesus, be a fence all around me. . . .
> Oh, I know you can and I know you will.[37]

3. Though we can always count on God's help, we must do our part in life's struggle. Doris Akers refuses to evade responsibility:

> Lord, don't move that mountain,
>   but give me strength to climb it.
> Please don't move that stumbling block,
>   but lead me, Lord, around it.

These lines are the refrain of a 1958 song in which the author expects her way to be difficult, prays for her foes, and asks for aid in her strivings.[38]

The same attitude appears in a song by Jessy Dixon, "The failure's not in God; it's in me, it's in me." Instead of blaming God, she confesses that she hasn't done all that she should; she has "not earned all of his good." The failure is hers, not God's.[39]

In "Trees" (1979), Margaret Pleasant Douroux (b. 1941) uses a series of simple comparisons based on Judg. 9:8–15 to express her will to fulfill her own role in life.

> Trees don't want to be mountains,
>   they just praise the Lord.

Mountains, rivers, oceans, and the heavenly bodies likewise are not envious, but happy to be what they are. So:

> If I want to be a servant of
>   the man who made the trees,
> I've got to live the life He
>   wants me to live.[40]

4. Our goal in life should be a right relationship with God, not prestige or possessions. In "Give me a clean heart" (1970) Margaret Pleasant Douroux refuses to ask "for the riches of the land" or "for high men to know my name." Instead she prays simply:

> Give me a clean heart, so I may serve thee.
> Lord, fix my heart, so that I may be used by thee.[41]

In "Lord, touch me" (1955) Martha Eason Banks voices in prayer a similar view of what really matters. Though many people seek monetary wealth or earthly power, she asks only for guidance to follow God's way:

> Teach me to love and teach me to pray;
> grant me a light to shine day by day.

The granting of this prayer will be for her joy unending and unsurpassed.[42]

Kenneth Morris is content because he finds happiness in Christ. In "Christ is all" (1946) he declares:

> I don't possess houses or lands, fine
>   clothes or jewelry.
> Sorrows and cares in this old world
>   my lot seems to be;
> but I have a Christ who paid the price
>   way back on Calv'ry,
> and Christ is all, all and all this world to me.

Two other stanzas extend the rejected values to power and position, while finding in Christ "my sight, my guiding light thru pathless seas." The refrain underlines the commitment: "Christ is all, he's everything to me."[43]

5. Though our lives here are full of trouble, in faith we can look forward to eternal joy with God. Many of the black gospel songs are oriented toward heaven. At heart, however, they represent much more than traditional religious escapism. Coming out of a heritage that over many years has involved constant affronts to self-respect and threats to security and life itself, these authors are realistic about both life and death. Tony Heilbut mentions that during the 1950s Dorothy Love and June Cheeks never forgot "conditions back home"—lynchings, bombed schools, segregated facilities. Black gospel singing is therefore often marked by urgency, emotional and spiritual intensity, and fervent cries, and much of it recognizes the imminent danger of death. "We're here today and gone today." "Death may soon disrobe all of what we now possess." Rock and soul music may sing of disappointed love, but they dodge the deeper

issues. "Gospel is simply the only music sung by people in terrible conditions *about* those conditions, in an attempt to get out of them."[44]

Against this backdrop we can better understand the thoughts and feelings of songs like Lucy Campbell's "Just to behold his face," Albert E. Brumley's "I'll fly away," and others. In "How I got over" (1951) Clara Ward imaginatively projects herself into the future, looks back, wonders how she has reached the land of promise, and rejoices that she will see Jesus who made her free. In deep gratitude she cries that she's going to sing and shout in the heavenly Jerusalem:

> Well, I'm goin' to join the heavenly choir,
> goin' to sing and never get tired.[45]

In this spirit Walter Hawkins announces that he's "Goin' up yonder" (1976):

> I can take the pain, / the heartaches they bring;
> the comfort's there in knowing / I'll soon be gone.
> As God gives me grace, / I'll run this race,
> until I see my Savior / face to face.
>   [with many repetitions]
> I'm goin' up yonder / to be with my Lord.[46]

One of the most vivid expressions of this response to long-endured anguish is "Soon and very soon, / we are going to see the King," by Andraé Crouch (b. 1947). There'll be "no more crying there," and "no more dying there," for we are going to see the King. Each stanza leads into a series of hallelujahs, followed by the extended affirmation:

> Should there be any rivers we must cross,
> should there be any mountains we must climb,
> God will supply all the strength that we need,
> give us the grace 'til we reach the other side. . . .
> Yes, there are some of us who have laid down our lives,
> but we shall all live again on the other side.[47]

Black Gospel and Social Change

The texts of black gospel music are so intimately related to its distinctive style and to the unique experience of those who write and perform it that cogent evaluation of the words alone seems well-nigh impossible. Moreover, it would be presumptuous of a white observer, however understanding, to attempt to pass objective judgment on the beliefs of worshipers who because of their very blackness have endured throughout their lives restrictions, frustrations, injustices, and dangers that powerfully affect their religious convictions, but that he cannot possibly perceive as they experience them.

For these reasons I shall limit my comments to one problem only, although it touches several facets of the faith of black Christians. Three of the most competent interpreters of black gospel—Wyatt Walker, Pearl Williams-Jones, and Tony Heilbut—regard it as both an expression of the longing for freedom from oppression and a contribution to the struggle for liberation. Clearly this music has been profoundly influenced by the suffering and privation of black people. Is it also helping to bring about the changes needed if liberation is to occur? It is difficult to read the black gospel songs or hear them sung without wondering how this influence has been exerted.

Walker shows convincingly that black sacred music as a whole has significantly strengthened efforts to improve the lot of black people. Such influence is manifest in the black spirituals and the central role played by freedom songs during the civil rights movement of the 1950s and '60s. Many of the spirituals voiced yearnings for freedom from servitude. Today protest songs performed by talented groups like Sweet Honey in the Rock are closely linked to the struggle of minorities for justice.[48]

In contrast, typical black gospel lyrics seem at first sight to have little to do with changing social conditions to win justice for the disadvantaged in this world. Seldom do the words point singers or hearers toward a witness for social, economic, or political equality. Nevertheless, there may be operative here what Pearl Williams-Jones calls the characteristic West African avoidance of the "inelegance" of direct statement. This appears in the blues, which are typically symbolic and circuitous. Black protest, says Williams-Jones, "is as often unspoken and implied as it is overtly expressed." Gospel music is a form of protest music, replacing Euro-American hymns, anthems, plainchants, and psalms with lyrics based on Western theological teachings interpreted to fit the black experience.[49]

Lawrence Levine, commenting on the contemporary applicability of the spirituals, observes that twentieth-century blacks, like their slave ancestors, have found strength in applying to themselves the words of Samson: "If I had my way, O Lordy, Lordy, . . . I would tear this building down." They continued to prize religion "for the justice it brought to a world that lacked it. . . . In freedom as in slavery, the Devil—over whom blacks generally triumphed in their songs—often looked suspiciously like a surrogate for the white man." In Levine's view the gospel songs, like the spirituals, are basically "songs of hope and affirmation."[50] Such judgments suggest that beneath the surface may be present considerably more concern for social change than a literal interpretation would perceive.

Many blacks—like many whites—have little understanding of social structures and little power to change them. In spite of great gains, large numbers of black people still feel helpless and inadequate against the callous indifference and hostility they confront daily. Yet this situation does not justify despair. When gospel singers affirm heaven as their destination they are asserting that no human power can define the limits of their existence. God alone is the ultimate authority.

Mattie Johnson, a gospel singer with Stars of Faith in Washington, D.C., reports what she sensed in one congregation before her group sang: "I felt troubles. I felt a little turbulence. They needed something to soothe them, to smooth them, something to think on to forget the troubles."[51] This remark reminds us immediately of Karl Marx's view of religion as "the opium of the people." Yet we may easily overlook the fact that Marx regarded it as necessary opium under the circumstances. He wrote: "Religious distress is at the same time the *expression* of real distress and the *protest* against real distress. It is the sigh of the oppressed creature, the heart of a heartless world." Hence Marx's attack was directed less against the "illusions of religion" than against the "condition which needs illusions."[52] I disagree sharply with Marx's dismissal of religion as illusion and his opinion that when economic oppression is removed religion will die, but his perceptive analysis sheds light on the black gospel songs about "goin' up yonder." The longing, generated in part by deep distress, may be in itself a protest against it, whether or not that protest is literally verbalized.

If we look carefully at the black gospel texts, read between the lines, and really feel the emotion expressed in the singing, we can discover four positive ways in which these songs help blacks to deal with the injustices that afflict them.

1. Gospel singing provides a way to vent the worry, fear, and tension of everyday life. Some of the anxiety derives from the constant need for black people to live simultaneously in two competing worlds—trying to find and preserve their own identity as Afro-Americans while meeting the often abrasive demands of the dominant white culture. Sometimes the problem is both emotional and physical, such as how to endure bus rides of an hour or longer twice a day to reach domestic jobs in the suburbs, along with the demeaning treatment often received from affluent white employers. Thomas Morgan reports that request calls from such people often jam the telephone lines of two full-time gospel radio stations in Washington, D.C.[53]

Mattie Johnson knows she is singing to people with marital problems, parents of children who are sick or in trouble with the law, or impoverished tenants who can't pay the rent. Sometimes she finds that simply screaming the name of Jesus gives them the release they need! Just as "Steal away" often had a double meaning for slaves, offering them spiritual refreshment and inviting them to a secret meeting to consider their grievances, so a gospel song may relieve pressure and renew strength for battles still to be fought.

2. The black gospel songs deepen the sense of personal dignity, worth, and self-respect of those who sing and hear them. James H. Cone's comment on the blues is at least equally applicable to the gospel lyrics: they "affirm the somebodiness of black people."[54] To the individual facing barriers erected by an uncaring white majority or beaten down by uncontrollable circumstances they bring the good news that he or she is ultimately not at the mercy of indifferent or hostile powers, but the object of God's love personalized in Jesus. It is God who is in charge, not self-seeking, deceitful men. The Pilot cares enough to rescue the stranded wanderer and take him home on the good ship of Zion. Black gospel lyrics assure distraught people that they belong to God, who can be trusted to bring them safely through all their troubles. Tony Heilbut writes: "Gospel singers are experts in all the ugliest sides of American life. But they always stand tall and walk upright: 'We're marching to Zion' on a 'Highway to Heaven,' which takes all the best of them, those who don't sell out, through hell."[55]

3. Gospel singing strengthens the black community's awareness of its unity and cultural identity, helping to counteract the influences that pull its members in different directions. The act of singing together, partially in response to problems that are shared as well as individual, deepens perception of common needs and goals and the basic oneness of the group. Thus Wyatt Walker affirms, "The creation of Gospel music is a social statement that in the face of America's rejection, Black folks made a conscious decision to be themselves."[56] Religious music that really blends their African heritage with their present character as members of American society helps them to actualize a unity that transcends hyphenation. This should help to break down barriers and facilitate movement toward equality and justice.

4. The black gospel songs are an important source of emotional support and spiritual power for persons committed to social change. Such persons bring to their worship a concern rooted in their own experience of hardship, their biblical insights, their personal thought and prayer, and understanding gained from discussion with others. Though the songs may not focus directly on the changes sought, they may reinforce convictions reached on other grounds, strengthen community awareness, and deepen the consciousness of the worshipers that God is with them in their struggle. Songs like "Precious

Lord" strengthened the resolve of Martin Luther King, Jr., even though Dorsey's lyric says not a word about jobs, education, housing, or desegregation.

No one knows what proportion of people who sing black gospel are active in civil rights organizations. Nor do we know how many white Christians who sing "Where cross the crowded ways" are personally involved in a caring ministry to those "in haunts of wretchedness and need." But in both cases Christians who seek fullness of life for all God's children can find spiritual power through opening their hearts in worship to the God who wants all to be free.

12

FOLK HYMNODY

The past two decades have witnessed dramatic changes in popular music. In the 1960s the impact of the Beatles on rock music, together with their experimentation with new forms and arrangements and their simple and appealing lyrics, aroused excitement and emulation around the world. In America during the same period Bob Dylan, following the tradition of Woody Guthrie, brought to popular music an inventiveness that won a wide and enthusiastic response. His adoption in 1965 of electronically amplified instruments and many rock and roll rhythms produced what came to be known as folk rock. His songs "The Times They Are A-Changin' " and "Blowin' in the Wind" became rallying cries for the civil rights movement.

Broadly parallel to developments like these in secular music, and partly influenced by them, has been the appearance of a variety of religiously oriented works that respond to the feeling and thinking, the fears and hopes and questions of people in a time of great ferment and uncertainty. Dramatic productions like *Jesus Christ Superstar, Godspell,* and Leonard Bernstein's *Mass* come readily to mind, along with song performances like the Hawkins Singers' "O Happy Day" and Judy Collins' "Amazing Grace." One manifestation of this tendency has been the emergence of a new folk hymnody.

Many Christians have revolted against, or in any case are unhappy with, what they regard as the formal language, the pious assurances, and the outworn clichés of numerous hymns from earlier centuries. They want instead songs that state how they really feel now, including the questions they ask. They want their worship enriched by lyrics that ring true to contemporary experience. We have already looked at some of the hymns that reflect this concern, songs by such writers as Fred Pratt Green, Brian Wren, Richard G. Jones, Herbert F. Brokering, Catherine Cameron, and Fred Kaan. Most of these preserve the form of earlier hymns but use fresh language and relate faith to present-day life and culture. Others, however, seek further innovation, and experiment with new forms, as we have noted in

Sydney Carter's "Lord of the Dance" and Richard G. Jones's "God who created this garden of earth." Songs like these, though written by known authors, can perhaps not inaccurately be called folk hymns.

INNOVATIVE HYMNS IN FOLK IDIOMS

Among contemporary hymns it is not easy to distinguish precisely between those with a folk or "pop" idiom and those which are closer to older forms. Some might be classified either way, and differently by different interpreters. However, certain broad characteristics of folk hymns can be listed. I suggest seven.

1. They grow out of the day-by-day lives of ordinary people and portray the bearing of the gospel on their needs and aspirations. Thus they often reflect the ethnic and cultural peculiarities of a particular folk.

2. Rooted in an oral tradition, they tend to be informal, conversational, and somewhat repetitive in style, corresponding closely to indigenous speech patterns, with relatively little attention to form or beauty.

3. Historically, both words and music are anonymous. However, in recent years a number of known authors and composers have sought to produce hymns in folk style, and frequently texts and melodies are by the same person—a combination that rarely occurs in "mainstream" church music.

4. The language is simple, direct, down-to-earth; the music singable and lively, within the range of the normal voice, and uncomplicated in melody and rhythm.

5. Folk hymns often involve protest—against the abstraction, superficiality, and conventionality of much traditional religion, as well as features of contemporary society such as materialism, trust in armaments, and indifference to poverty and hunger.

6. The singing is frequently action-oriented, kinetic, dramatic, pointed toward change in attitudes and life-styles—a feature accented by the use of a portable instrument for accompaniment. The guitar fittingly symbolizes the demand of folk hymnody and protest songs for individual and social change and movement toward more just human relations. Many contemporary folk hymns are printed with music only for the melody line, with guitar chords.

7. Folk hymnody is innovative and experimental, unbound by traditional forms, and open to new ways of singing the good news to people living today.

Religious folk songs with characteristics like these are by no means a new phenomenon. To place the present discussion in its appropriate historical setting, we cite two southern Appalachian carols from earlier years. Both marvel at the love of God given so freely for the salvation of unworthy sinners. The earlier one, published first in *Southern Harmony* in 1835, begins:

> What wondrous love is this, oh my soul, oh my soul!
> what wondrous love is this, oh my soul!
> What wondrous love is this
> that caused the Lord of bliss
> to bear the dreadful curse for my soul, for my soul,
> to bear the dreadful curse for my soul?[1]

In Murphy, North Carolina, in 1933, John Jacob Niles heard the young daughter of some traveling evangelists singing:

> I wonder as I wander, out under the sky,
> how Jesus my Savior did come for to die.

The singer voices amazement at the lowly birth of one who was the King, yet cared enough to act in sacrificial love for the sake of perverse sinners on earth.[2]

Such mountain carols offer no sophisticated theology, but the poetic simplicity of the words and the haunting beauty of the music are vehicles for expressing a central question and suggesting an answer that goes to the heart of Christian faith.

The past quarter century has produced a profusion of religious songs manifesting some or all of the characteristics listed above. Many are exceedingly shallow in content; others convey a Christian message in a form that enables them to speak to the condition of numerous people today, especially youth.[3]

Coming to expression in the folk hymns are three main themes: joyful praise and thanksgiving, assurance of God's presence in difficulties, and the ethical implications of the gospel.

1. *Joyful Praise and Thanksgiving.* This is one of the most frequent emphases of the songs by Richard K. Avery and Donald S. Marsh. One of their best statements of it, sung to a calypso rhythm, begins with the jubilant refrain which also follows each stanza:

> Ev'ry morning is Easter morning from now on!
> Ev'ry day's Resurrection day,
> the past is over and gone!

The stanzas rejoice in the meaning of the Easter victory for typical aspects of human life. For example:

> Goodbye guilt, goodbye fear, good riddance!
> Hello Lord, hello sun!

> I am one of the Easter people!
> My new life has begun![4]

Puerto Rican Christians have contributed a song stimulated by the book of Revelation and Isaiah 45–46, "Alabaré a mi Señor" (I will praise my Lord):

> John saw the number of all those redeemed,
>   and all were singing praises to the Lord.
> Thousands were praying, ten thousands rejoicing,
>   and all were singing praises to the Lord.

In the second stanza earthly worshipers join the acclaim:

> There is no God as great as you, O Lord;
>   there is none, there is none.

God's "mighty wonders," including the moving of mountains, are accomplished not with an army or weapons, "but by the Holy Spirit's power." The third stanza goes on to declare that "Puerto Rico shall be saved" by the Spirit's power, and a note suggests that it may be sung several times, using the names of different countries, cities, or other communities.[5]

2. *Divine Presence in Difficulties.* A touching folk hymn now widely sung begins:

> Jesus walked this lonesome valley;
>   he had to walk it by himself.
> O, nobody else could walk it for him;
>   he had to walk it by himself.

In the succeeding stanzas the opening line becomes first "We must walk this lonesome valley," then "You must go and stand your trial." There is no verbal assurance of divine help—a circumstance no doubt accentuated by the isolation of those who struggled for existence in the remote valleys of the southern Appalachians. But the implication is nonetheless there: we are not really alone, since Jesus also faced trials that he could not evade. He emerged victorious, and so can we.[6]

The assurance is much more direct in another song:

> Peace, troubled soul, thou needst not fear
> (Jesus says he will be with you to the end).

In all four stanzas, reflecting the experience of those who need mercy and strength for right living, the parenthetical promise is inserted after each new line. The refrain combines assurance with joyous praise.[7]

A work song from Ghana translated by Tom Colvin (b. 1925), "Christ the worker," portrays Christ as a "skillful craftsman" and yokemaker whose yokes lighten human labor. However, it relates the divine aid personified in Jesus to all the burdens borne by human beings:

> You who labor, you who labor,
> listen to his call;
> he will make that heavy burden light. . . .
>
> Christ the worker, Christ the worker,
> God in man,—
> teach us how to do all work for God.[8]

An American folk hymn promises the divine presence equally in times of grief, temptation, and doubt. Successive stanzas ask, "Is there anybody here like Mary a-weeping, . . . Peter a-sinking, . . . Thomas a-doubting?" Such persons are assured that Jesus will draw near if they but call on him. The refrain exults in the good news and gives glory to God.[9]

3. *Ethical Implications of the Gospel.* Many contemporary folk hymns focus attention on the practical meaning of faith in God for a wide variety of human relationships. Some are vigorous in protest against indifference in church and society. With Luke 10:36–37 and Matt. 25:31–46 as his foundation, Sydney Carter asks:

> When I needed a neighbor, were you there, were you there?
> When I needed a neighbor, were you there?
> *And the creed and the color and the name won't matter.*
> *Were you there?*

Succeeding stanzas press the question with regard to the hungry, thirsty, cold, and naked, and to those needing shelter and healing, closing with the affirmation:

> Wherever you travel, I'll be there, I'll be there;
> wherever you travel, I'll be there.
> *And the creed and the color and the name won't matter.*
> *I'll be there.*[10]

Carter sometimes uses humor and irony to expose the weaknesses of conventional Christianity. His "No use knocking on the window" depicts a modern innkeeper who turns away a would-be lodger on a rainy Christmas Day. Not content with reporting that all the beds are booked, the owner defends the "Christian men and women" with whom he identifies himself. "We're keeping what we've got, sir," and are "always willing, never able."[11]

Likewise critical of smug, self-centered religion is a hymn for which David S. Goodall (b. 1922) wrote both words and music. The opening stanza is an accurate sample of the whole.

> When the pious prayers we make
>   are a wall of pride,
> lest the faithful few awake
>   to the world outside;
> when a man won't mix with a race
>   which he disapproves,
> only God descends to make clean the face
>   of the world he loves.[12]

Other current songs are more positive in their appeal for Christian social concern. A good example is "When God almighty came to be one of us," by Michael E. Hewlett (b. 1916). Addressing in order common people like midwives, carpenters, and shepherds; rulers, public servants, and officers of the law; ancient astrologers and sophisticated scientists, he calls on them all to sing and dance to the glory of God who in Christ has come to live among us. Why? Because "God in his mercy uses the commonplace," "God in his purpose uses the governments," "God uses knowledge, God uses ignorance," and has need of all of these. The closing stanza, calling on all creation to join in the song, is a fitting summary:

> Sing, all creation, made for his purposes,
>   called by his providence to live and move;
> none is unwanted, none insignificant,
>   Love needs a universe of folk to love:
> young men and maidens, old men and children,
>   black ones and colored ones and white ones too.
> God in his coming, and to eternity,
>   God took upon himself the need of you.[13]

Avery and Marsh sound much the same note with respect to relations between the sexes:

> Male and female, God created:
> man and woman, by God's love.
> Boy and girl, girl and boy . . .
> Single or together, equal and sharing,
> boldly declaring, This is who we are.

The next stanzas rejoice that both are made by God "free to choose our work and way," "diff'rent but united, praising each other." The final stanza expands the celebration of diversified interdependence to take in international and racial relations. The refrain celebrates the truth implicit in all four stanzas: "We are all the children of God! Hallelujah!"[14]

In " 'Moses, I know you're the man,' / the Lord said," Estelle White (b. 1925), a former Carmelite nun, reminds us that the people of God from Moses on have always been a pilgrim people, God's "traveling, wandering race." The second stanza makes plain that they must be ever ready for changes and new beginnings:

> "Don't get too set in your ways,"
> the Lord said.
> "Each step is only a phase."[15]

In this survey we have omitted many songs that are doctrinally superficial or questionable and aesthetically crude—unworthy for use in Christian worship. However, the folk hymns just cited exemplify a considerable number that are for the most part Scripturally based and consistent with historic Christian teaching. Indeed, they sometimes uncover and emphasize truths that have often been bypassed by professing Christians and churches. Their free, informal style, their sensitivity to the realities of life today, and their closeness to the feelings of ordinary people enable them to touch many persons who remain unmoved by more traditional hymns.

Naturally the question arises as to whether their quality equips them to endure. No doubt many will disappear within a few years. However, some have already won their way into standard hymnals, as have songs from the folk cultures of earlier periods. Probably others will be similarly recognized.

Yet whether a folk hymn survives or not is perhaps not the main question. If it is really reaching people in these changing, threatening times with the assurance and challenge of Christian faith and helping them to become aware of the love and power of God, it should be welcomed and used. Just as Christian truth must be reinterpreted for every generation, so songs are needed through which people can sing their faith in their present setting. Even those which are soon cast aside and replaced will have done their work. In the meantime other hymns of noble beauty, truth, and power will continue to span the centuries.

SONGS OF CELEBRATION

Among contemporary folk hymns are many geared to the needs of a variety of local church groups and intentional communities actively committed to personal and church renewal, often in connection with some phase of the charismatic movement. For example, *Sound of Living Waters* aims to present "fresh sounds reflecting the cascade of joyous praise, of awesome wonder, of sincerity and hope, which accompany the Holy Spirit's renewal in the church today." The writers and arrangers of these lyrics, reacting against the dreary solemnity they find in much traditional church music, explore new and unconventional ways of glorifying God. The resulting songs may be aptly named songs of celebration, since in gratitude and joy they focus on what God has done and is doing for the transformation and fulfillment of human lives.

The recent multiplication of celebrative songs has been so great and their quality so uneven that selection of characteristic samples is extremely difficult. Representative, I believe, are the songbooks that, though widely used elsewhere, have been found helpful in the worship of two Christian communities with somewhat similar goals, the Sojourners Fellowship in Washington, D.C., and the Community of Celebration in Woodland Park, Colorado.[16] These collections are *Sound of Living Waters* (1974), *Fresh Sounds* (1976), *Cry Hosanna* (1980), and the several editions of *Songs of Praise* (1975–1980).[17]

Sojourners Fellowship is a community of radically biblical evangelicals committed to rebuilding the church and calling it to become an effective agent of social change. Centered in Christian faith nurtured by regular worship, members seek to be instruments of the transforming power of God in the whole of human life. As Jim Wallis puts it, "The healing, justice, and peace that God wants for the world begins with the love and unity shared by those who have been made a new family in Christ."[18] Christ's healing work, adds Bob Sabath, "begins with our own hates, fears, hurts, and broken pasts, but continues with healing among the races and between nations, between male and female, rich and poor."[19] The desire to share Christ's reconciling mission in the world leads to peacemaking, opposition to preparation for nuclear war, identification with the poor and oppressed, and full sharing of economic resources within the community. Located in a congested inner-city section of the nation's capital, Sojourners operates a day care center for children of working parents, publishes a monthly magazine, and seeks in a variety of ways to fulfill its objectives.

The Community of Celebration in Woodland Park, Colorado, has roots in the charismatic renewal movement in the Episcopal Church. It has been markedly influenced by the charismatic ministries of Graham Pulkingham in Houston, Texas, and Millport, Isle of Cumbrae, Scotland. It is officially sanctioned by the Episcopal Church and uses facilities provided by the church, but carries on an ecumenical ministry. It is dedicated to "spreading a vision of the corporate renewal of the structures and ministries of the church."[20] Natural

families and a few single persons have joined to form a community
of households in which income and tasks are distributed according
to need. They seek to reach out—to "opt into life" in the world—
through the Fisherfolk, a traveling team of about ten persons who
visit churches and communities across the country, using music,
dance, and drama to advance the vision of the community. Participants believe that they cannot experience and mediate the power of
God as a servant people in the world unless they experience it in
their worship with one another. From this center they are struggling
with the broad issues of Christian discipleship in today's complex
society.

Sojourners and the Community of Celebration use similar worship
resources, including the three songbooks co-compiled or edited by
Betty Pulkingham. Five major emphases are apparent in these collections.

1. *Joyful Praise.* The dominant feature of songs of celebration is
praise. Many begin or end with some form of "Alleluia" or "Hallelujah." The Topical Index of *Cry Hosanna* lists 57 entries of a total
of 142 under Praise and Thanksgiving—far more than under any
other heading.

Charles Christmas urges,

> Give thanks to our God, and let him be praised
> with sanctified hearts and hands that are raised.[21]

A song by John B. Foley, S.J., sounds the same note in the first-
person singular. Based on Psalm 16, it opens with the refrain, "For
you are my God; you alone are my joy. / Defend me, O Lord." The
first two stanzas thank God for faithful comrades and a goodly heritage. The next two rejoice in the security to be found in God's guiding presence.[22]

In "How beautiful the morning and the day," Owen Barker rejoices in the bounteous blessings "of peace and joy and rapture" that
cause his spirit to sing "to him who is the glory of the day." He then
goes on to recite more specific occasions for thanksgiving:

> How merciful the workings of his grace,
> arousing faith and action my soul would never face
> without his matchless mercy and his grace.
>
> How barren was my life before he came,
> supplying love and healing; I live now to acclaim
> the majesty and wonder of his name.[23]

Selected passages from Joel 2 and 3 are the basis for a song by
Priscilla Wright that rejoices over the fruits of fig trees, vineyards,
and wheat fields, but even more because of spiritual blessings.

> My people shall know that I am the Lord;
>   their shame I have taken away.
> My Spirit will lead them together again,
>   my Spirit will show them the way.
>
> My children shall dwell in a body of love;
>   a light to the world they will be.
> Life shall come forth from the Father above;
>   my body will set mankind free.[24]

A song by Jan Harrington combines the rejoicing of Hab. 3:17–18 with the trust expressed in the King James translation of Job 13:15:

> I will rejoice in the Lord alway. . . .
> Though the fig trees are barren and the cattle all die,
> and the crops have failed and the fields empty lie;
> and though he slay me, even though he slay me,
> yet I'll rejoice in the Lord alway.[25]

This use of repetition occurs frequently. In "The joy of the Lord is my strength," by Alliene G. Vale, the first stanza is simply this line multiplied by four. The refrain consists of three lines with the words "Aha, ha ha ha ha ha ha ha ha ha" and a fourth that repeats the opening statement.[26]

An anonymous song begins "Thank you, thank you, Jesus," completing the first stanza with eight more "thank you's" and the addition, "in my heart."[27] "Sing to the Lord," a song with words and music by Donald Fishel, traces the action of God from Creation through the Fall, the liberation of the Hebrews from bondage under Moses, the coming of Jesus, the call of Peter, and the invitation to sinners today to accept salvation. An introduction urges the worshipers eight times to "sing to the Lord a new song," and the refrain repeats the same call four times more.[28]

2. *The Centrality of Jesus.* Though these songs presuppose a Trinitarian view of God, they specify Jesus as the object of celebration more frequently than God, Father, Christ, or Holy Spirit. Typical is the anonymous witness:

> Jesus Christ is alive today.
>   I/we know it's true.
> Sov'reign of the universe,
>   I/we give him homage due.[29]

Most of the writers seem to agree with this interpretation. Jesus *is* God, not our supreme revelation of God; Jesus and God are interchangeable terms.

Sometimes differing conceptions appear within one song. Thus in

"Jesus is Lord! Creation's voice proclaims it," David J. Mansell affirms that by Jesus' power "each tree and flower was planned and made," but later attributes to the Holy Spirit the works that demonstrate the Lordship of Jesus.[30] However, in celebrating Jesus as Lord and King these authors are not concerned with critical Christological questions. For them the important thing is to rejoice in what Jesus has done, primarily for human salvation.

"Oh, the blood of Jesus," an anonymous song, exults repetitiously that Jesus' blood "washes white as snow," that the word of Jesus "cleanses white as snow," and that "the love of Jesus . . . makes his body whole."[31]

Another anonymous lyric, which begins by declaring, "The fullness of the Godhead bodily dwelleth with my Lord," adds that "we are complete in him." It then goes on to state that "it's not by words of righteousness but by his grace alone, / that we are complete in him"; and draws the comfortable conclusion:

> There's nothing that I can do
> for Jesus did it all [three times]
> and we are complete in him.[32]

Naturally, some of the celebrative songs are addressed to Jesus. One unknown writer declares:

> Jesus, you're a wonder, [three times]
> Jesus, you're a wonder to my soul.
> Glory, hallelujah! [three times]
> you're a wonder to my soul.[33]

Such confessions lead to personal commitment, as when one writer testifies:

> I want to live for Jesus ev'ry day.
> I want to live for Jesus come what may.
> Take the world and all its pleasure,
> I've got a more enduring treasure.
> I want to live for Jesus ev'ry day.[34]

Quite consistently, the next step is telling others about Jesus and inviting them to yield their lives to him. One song promises:

> Here comes Jesus, see him walking on the water.
> He'll lift you up and he'll help you to stand.
> Here comes Jesus, he's the master of the waves that roll.
> Here comes Jesus, he'll make you whole.[35]

Helen H. Lemmel is more directive, urging:

Turn your eyes upon Jesus,
look full in his wonderful face.

From the perspective thus gained, we are assured earthly values will lose their appeal.[36]

3. *The Activity of the Holy Spirit.* As the subtitle of one collection indicates, many of the celebrative lyrics are "songs of the Spirit." The relation between Jesus and the Holy Spirit is not always clear, but in the main the Spirit carries forward the saving work begun in the earthly life of Jesus. In "Wind, wind, blow on me," by Jane and Betsy Clowe, Jesus promises the coming of the Spirit, who at Pentecost came to the church in his name. Jesus Christ also sends the Holy Spirit today. The fourth stanza is a prayer:

Set us free to love our brothers;
set us free to live for others,
that the world the Son might see
and Jesus' name exalted be.[37]

A song by Tedd Smith identifies the presence of the Spirit with that of Jesus:

There's a quiet understanding when we're gathered in the Spirit.
There's a love we feel in Jesus, there's a manna that he feeds us.
It's a promise that he gives us when we gather in his name.

The song goes on to thank Jesus for the love, understanding, guidance, and oneness that he brings.[38]

A song by Carey Landry begins with the refrain: "The Spirit is a-movin' all over, all over this land." As the Spirit comes, doors open, fires burn in his people, we are called to serve, the world is renewed as we recreate it in love and joy, walls fall down as divisions are healed, and people are empowered to spread the Spirit's fire in all humanity.[39]

Inspired by such events, Christians are called to open their lives to the Spirit's power. Daniel Iverson has provided both words and music for a familiar song:

Spirit of the living God, fall afresh on me.
Spirit of the living God, fall afresh on me.
Melt me, mold me, fill me, use me.
Spirit of the living God, fall afresh on me.[40]

4. *The Celebrating Community.* Fittingly, songs of celebration often rejoice in the oneness experienced by the gathered community. A song of the Fisherfolk that begins, "We really want to thank

you, Lord," voices thanks for the incomparable richness of the life
Christ shared, then for the life of the resulting fellowship:

> We thank you, Lord, for our life together,
> to live and move in the love of Christ,
> the tenderness which sets us free
> to serve you with our lives.[41]

At a special gathering of the Community of Celebration in November 1979, this hymn was felt to capture the essence of the community:

God is our Father, for he has made us his own,
made Jesus our brother, and hand in hand we grow together as one.
Sing praise to the Lord with tambourine.
Sing praise to the Lord with clapping hands.
Sing praise to the Lord with dancing feet.
Sing praise to the Lord with our voice.

These words are followed by a refrain consisting wholly of "la, la, la, . . ." sung to the music of the opening lines.[42]

A song by Patrick Appleford, "O Lord, all the world belongs to you," envisages the extension of this oneness to the whole of humanity, but recognizes that this can occur only as the world is turned upside down.

> The world lives divided and apart;
> you draw men together and we start
> in your body to see that in fellowship we
> can be turning the world upside down.

Men and women must learn that true greatness comes not from amassing possessions or exercising authority, but in servanthood. Such transformation and renewal can be furthered by a Spirit-filled church which God calls "to be turning the world upside down."[43]

5. *Outreach in Christian Love.* Each member of the celebrating community is called to Christian concern for others. Some songs express this through Scriptural admonitions: "Seek ye first"; "A new commandment I give unto you"; "Be like your Father"; or "Won't you come?" (based on Luke 14:16–24).[44] In others, singers ask the help of Jesus or the Spirit as they seek to fulfill their responsibilities to all of God's children. For example, Tom Colvin, with his friends in Ghana, moved by the humble act of Jesus in washing his disciples' feet, prays in an opening refrain:

> Jesu, Jesu, fill us with your love,
> show us how to serve the neighbors we have from you.

Who are the neighbors we should love and serve?

> Neighbors are rich folk and poor;
> neighbors are black, brown, and white;
> neighbors are nearby and far away.[45]

Another song, "Look around you, can you see?," by Jodi Page Clark, portrays the Lord as calling on his followers to look around at the grief, violence, and hardness that trouble people today, and admonishing them:

> "Walk among them, I'll go with you.
> Reach out to them with my hands.
> Suffer with me, and together
> we will serve them, help them stand."

These words elicit the affirmative response:

> Forgive us, Father, hear our prayer.
> We would walk with you anywhere,
> through your suff'ring, with forgiveness,
> take your life into the world.

The refrain pleads simply, "Kyrie eleison, Christe eleison."[46]

The refrain of a song by Sandy Hardyman (1978) prays, "Lord, give us your Spirit that is love." The three stanzas make the prayer quite concrete:

> Where children cry let us wipe their tears away,
> and where children fall let us raise them to their feet.
>
> Where there is pain let us be your healing hands,
> and where there is grief let us comfort with your love.
>
> Where people hate let us dwell among them with love,
> and where people fight let us bind their deepest wounds.[47]

One of the best expressions of Christian outreach is the much-loved prayer of St. Francis, "Lord, make me an instrument of thy peace," adapted and set to a flowing melody by Sebastian Temple arranged by Betty Pulkingham:

> Make me a channel of your peace.
> Where there is hatred let me bring your love;
> where there is injury, your pardon, Lord;
> and where there's doubt, true faith in you.

In the second stanza those who are channels of God's peace ask that they may replace despair with hope, darkness with light, and sadness with joy. The third affirms three basic truths of the gospel:

> It is in pardoning that we are pardoned,
> in giving to all men that we receive,
> and in dying that we're born to eternal life.

The refrain prays for the self-forgetfulness that enables us to be channels of peace:

> Oh master, grant that I may never seek
> so much to be consoled as to console;
> to be understood as to understand;
> to be loved, as to love with all my soul.[48]

Some brief comments about these songs as a whole are in order. Whenever Christians respond to new stirrings of the Spirit, and especially when they relate these to new cultural and social situations, it is inevitable that they should seek new forms of expression in worship and song. The very newness of both cause and effect also makes for unevenness of quality in the songs produced.

One significant contribution of the series *Sound of Living Waters,* *Fresh Sounds,* and *Cry Hosanna* is their inclusion of new versions of many of the psalms. These reflect authentically the praise and faith of the originals and preserve the solid worship values of the Hebrew poetry, enhancing them for present-day use by attractive and imaginative musical settings by Mimi Farra, Betty Pulkingham, and others.

Otherwise, these songs seldom measure up in substance or poetic merit to the typical church hymnody which those who prefer them often decry. Their authors would no doubt reply—and rightly—that sincerity of thought and depth of feeling are more important than neatness of form or even beauty of language. Yet there are contemporary hymn writers who manage to combine fresh ideas, variety of expression, and openness to the Spirit's leading with felicitous poetry. One wonders how the monotony involved in the sheer repetitiveness of some of the songs can support the excitement and freshness of genuine celebration.

Robert H. Mitchell rightly cautions that often celebration is sought as a feeling or mood to be induced for its own sake, instead of springing from an inner attitude of genuine worship.[49] This tendency is indicated by the directions for singing frequently printed above songs in folk hymnals—"briskly," "with joyful dignity," "quietly," "boldly," "with pulsating rhythm," "gently."

Taken alone, these songs would not provide a balanced diet for Christian worship. The compilers seem to recognize this by their inclusion of some time-honored hymns and their provision of contemporary musical settings and descants for a few traditional lyrics. The worship of communities of celebration has been enriched by the use of well-chosen songs from many lands. It could be further enhanced by greater utilization of the central heritage of Christian song, and especially of the newer hymns which in fresh language relate Christian faith to today's world.

The theology of the songs of celebration is disappointing. Their innovative language and music are out of harmony with the traditionalism of the beliefs they express. Do we really reach people where they are today if we use current folk idioms and musical forms to convey theological concepts inherited unchanged from previous centuries, unaffected by new understandings of the universe and of human nature? This incongruity appears especially in Christological passages.

One song has God saying to his Son, "My people need to be redeemed." So Jesus "took up his cross and went to die for you and me."[50] Here we have not only a naive concept of the relation of Jesus to God but also a suggestion of the substitutionary understanding of the atonement that appears in many of the songs. The assumption of another song that "Jesus did it all," hence that "we are complete in him,"[51] runs counter to the dynamic view of human personality widely held by thoughtful Christians today and assumed by members of Sojourners when they accept responsibility for changes in human relations. Other songs that address "Sweet Jesus"[52] or begin with the greeting, "Good morning, Jesus, good morning, Love; / I know you come from heaven above,"[53] display a sentimentalism out of accord with the rugged strength of the Christ portrayed in the Gospels.

In my exploration of celebration songs my first impression was that they manifested accurately the fervor and excitement of charismatic Christians, but contained little to support the commitment to change social values and structures that marks members of many intentional communities.[54] However, the second part of this impression underwent a distinct revision as the study proceeded, especially through greater familiarity with *Cry Hosanna*. This collection, along with some entries in its two predecessors, provides a helpful basis for Christian social outreach, in three ways.

First, many of the songs nourish positive feelings of community solidarity, and should therefore motivate members to work for the objectives that brought them together.

Secondly, within such communities these songs are used by persons who bring to their worship a radically prophetic faith derived from study of the Bible, sensitivity to human injustice, and active involvement in movements aimed at change. Songs that heighten in such persons an awareness of the power and love of God can strengthen their commitment and energize their efforts, whether or not the texts specifically refer to the needs felt or the goals sought.

Finally, a considerable number of celebration songs explicitly relate the life of the Spirit to the suffering of human beings. Christians are portrayed as freed from self-love that they may in turn act in love to free others from captivity. They are summoned to serve their neighbors, and neighbors are defined as people of all races, nations, and economic levels. They respond to God's saving action by repentance for self-centeredness and by dedication to the task of taking Christ's life into the world. The Christian community, created and empowered by God's Spirit, is called to be a light to the world and an agent of God in setting humanity free.

Songs like these do not deal specifically with the issues of war and peace, race relations, economic injustice, or environmental pollution.[55] Nevertheless, they present an interpretation of Christian faith and life that recognizes salvation as both individual and social, and some of them relate social outreach integrally to concern for the spiritual renewal of individual Christians and the church. This kind of synthesis is urgently needed today.

13

INCLUSIVE LANGUAGE

In recent years perceptive Christian women, with much male support, have participated actively in the movement demanding equal rights and opportunities for women in all areas of society. Astute interpreters of Christian faith like Letty M. Russell, Virginia Ramey Mollenkott, Rosemary Radford Ruether, and Leonard Swidler have written illuminatingly on the biblical and theological grounds for removing sex-related restrictions and asserting the full equality of women in the churches and elsewhere. Indeed, Christians especially should be concerned to affirm the dignity and rights of women. The universality of the gospel itself undermines all justification for the dominance of any group. The apostle Paul makes plain that baptism frees us from all false divisions to appreciation of our true unity: "All baptized in Christ, you have all clothed yourselves in Christ, and there are no more distinctions between Jew and Greek, slave and free, male and female, but all of you are one in Christ Jesus" (Gal. 3:27–28, Jerusalem Bible).

This radically egalitarian position is winning increasing acceptance within the churches. Barriers to the full exercise of leadership responsibilities by women are being removed at all levels. Inevitably this concern involves attention to the language of worship, which historically has been male-oriented. The Education and Ministry unit of the National Council of Churches has recently acted to provide an inclusive-language translation of the ecumenical lectionary that will seek to avoid generic words like *man* which exclude or imply a secondary status for women. Similar sensitivity has emerged regarding the extent of sexist language in our hymns.

THE PROBLEM OF SEXIST LANGUAGE

Sensitivity to masculine-dominated language in hymns is a recent development. The Introduction of *The Hymnal 1940 Companion,* describing one of the finest twentieth-century collections, provides unwittingly a vivid illustration of how easily we can be exclusive even while trying to be inclusive. Citing inclusiveness and universality as marks of the hymnbook, the editors mention race, nationality, religion, and learning as influences which sometimes separate "men." This omission of the barrier of sex and the assumption that women are represented by men reflect accurately the attitudes typical of the period—attitudes that are still widely held.

Growing numbers of Christians, especially in America, are distressed by passages in hymns that use male images to refer to God, female terms to characterize entities such as nature or the church, and masculine nouns and pronouns to designate women as well as men. Yet at the same time many church members, including women, ask in effect, "Why all the fuss? Everybody knows that *man* means both sexes, and no downgrading of women is intended or implied. Why bother about mere words?"

Everything said in Chapter 1 is applicable here. The words we use express and reinforce attitudes and ideas, so they may never be taken lightly. Often when we say that language isn't important, we mean that the language in question is not hurting *us*. In such cases we need to develop enough sensitivity to the feelings of others to imagine ourselves in their place. If we do this, we discover that many worshipers are offended by exclusive language. Concern for all members of the body of Christ will prompt action to remove such impediments to true community and reality in worship.

There are two main grounds for eliminating male-dominated language from our hymns.

1. Increasing numbers of women are alienated by it, and many male worshipers also are disturbed by its demeaning connotations for persons who comprise a majority in most congregations. When male terms are regularly used to include females, and female words are never understood to include males, women readily receive the impression that they don't matter, or in any case are seen as subordinate to men.

The problem is compounded by the slippery nature of words like *man* and *mankind* as commonly used. They may mean all people or all males, whereas female terms mean only women. The implication of feminine inferiority should be plain. The result is that many thoughtful women suspect that maleness rather than humanness is meant by so-called generic language, and feel deprived of their true identity. As Letty M. Russell has written:

> However much a particular person or organization may protest that the words [man, brotherhood, he, etc.] *really mean* human, human beings, his and hers, humankind, peoplehood, etc., the fact remains that

women are frequently left out of both the mental structures and the social structures of our culture. Their history is not only invisible, they themselves are frequently invisible in the way the male-dominated society speaks its language and makes its decisions.[1]

Christians who may not feel personally threatened by masculine language can hardly be content to have devoted members of the Christian community estranged in the very act of corporate worship that should bind them together.

2. Such language tends to reinforce a social order in which women are cast in a subordinate role. In such a situation they are unable to fulfill their potential or make their maximum contribution. The results are detrimental to men as well as women; all suffer from restrictions artificially imposed on any. When the church through the language of its worship helps to perpetuate an unequal recognition of basic human rights, it undermines rather than advances the abundant life sought by Jesus for all people. This influence may be quite unintended, but it reinforces the notion that maleness is normative humanity, while female humanity occupies a lower level.

We shall now examine typical lyrics that for various reasons have elicited objections from inclusivists, and then consider what steps can and should be taken to achieve the greatest possible freedom from sexist language.

HYMNS THAT SUBORDINATE WOMEN

Male images and pronouns relating to God frequently occur in the same hymn with masculine nouns and pronouns that refer to women as well as men. We shall therefore make no attempt to separate these two forms of male-dominated language, but consider them as they appear.

Isaac Watts extols the Lord Jehovah as the heavenly, universal King. His sovereign power "made us of clay, and formed us men." Hence "men of grace" who love the Lord are called upon to surround his throne. "Happy the man" who relies on his wisdom, goodness, and almighty power. When we praise God as "our help in ages past" we are reminded that time "bears all its sons away." Watts seems to forget that time's daughters are also subject to aging! Charles Wesley likewise summons Christians to praise the great Lord and King, "him from whom all good proceeds." Rejoicing over the risen Christ, "sons of men and angels say, Alleluia!"

Philip Doddridge's "How gentle God's commands!" invites worshipers to "cast their burdens on the Lord, / and trust his constant care," as well as to find refreshment at their Father's throne. We are secure in God's care, for "his goodness stands approved." In Frederick W. Faber's apostrophe to the "faith of our fathers," mothers are not mentioned, and it is mankind that becomes truly free.

Many hymns on the Trinity appear to conceive of the three "persons" in masculine terms. Typical of these are Reginald Heber's "Holy, holy, holy," Ignaz Franz's "Holy God, we praise thy name," and Charles Wesley's "Come, Father, Son, and Holy Ghost." Sometimes identification with the male image is quite explicit, as in Martin Rinkart's "Now thank we all our God":

> All praise and thanks to God / the Father now be given,
> the Son, and him who reigns / with them in highest heaven.

Seen as a whole the hymns of the late nineteenth and early twentieth centuries contain even more sexist language than their predecessors. Ironically, lyrics influenced by the rise of the social gospel are probably the greatest offenders. Written before the Christian conscience had been sensitized to include equal rights for women, these hymns emphasize themes like the brotherhood of man, apparently assuming that women are adequately covered by the phrase. We cite five hymns, all written between 1901 and 1919.

In "This is my Father's world" Maltbie D. Babcock consistently uses male pronouns to describe the one who "shines in all that's fair." He also broadens the male image to declare that "the Lord is King."

In Frank Mason North's "Where cross the crowded ways of life," it is the Son of man whose voice we hear amid the selfish "cries of race and clan," and the Master is called to abide among these restless throngs "till sons of men" learn his love.

Henry van Dyke's "Joyful, joyful, we adore thee" uses male-dominated language to voice its appeal for the love that is our appropriate response to the "God of glory, Lord of love." Singing "Thou our Father, Christ our brother," we learn how to love God and one another. Then we can join the mighty chorus:

> Father love is reigning o'er us,
> brother love binds man to man.

William P. Merrill's "Rise up, O men of God" has sexist language in each of its four stanzas. The men of God—presumably including women—are challenged to serve the King of kings and thus "bring in the day of brotherhood / and end the night of wrong." The church, whose strength is "unequal to her task," is pictured as feminine, but the men of God are summoned to "make her great." In so doing they act "as brothers of the Son of man."

The second stanza of Clifford Bax's "Turn back, O man, forswear thy foolish ways" affirms that "earth might be fair and all men glad

and wise," if only man would "wake from out his haunted sleep."
However, the third stanza moves toward inclusiveness by substituting *people* and *folk* for *men*, though it still speaks of "man's old
undaunted cry."

In the mid-twentieth century, male terms continue to be used to
refer to both God and human beings. The following passages are
taken from lyrics written between 1930 and 1968. A hymn of praise
by John J. Moment opens with the invitation, "Men and children
everywhere, / with sweet music fill the air!" It continues with appeals
to nations and natural forces to bless "the Lord of life and truth and
light," but nowhere mentions women.[2]

In Percy Dearmer's "As the disciples, when thy Son had left them"
the worshipers draw the parallel between their gathering and that
of their early predecessors in the faith:

> So may we here, a company of brothers,
>   make this our love-feast and commemoration;
>   that in his Spirit we may have more worthy participation.[3]

In "Christ is the world's true light" George W. Briggs lauds Christ
as "the captain of salvation" and the bright daystar "of every man
and nation." "Where'er men own his sway," new life and hope
awake.[4]

Albert F. Bayly's "Praise and thanksgiving, / Father, we offer"
acknowledges our responsibility to share with one another the
food that is the fruit of our labors, "so that rejoicing with us, our
brother / may know thy care." With "all men confessing" God's
gracious hand, all will be blessed, and where the divine will reigns
"no man will hunger."[5]

In "Father, Lord of all creation" Stewart Cross prays for grace that
"we may love as brothers / all whose burdens we can share." Where
that happens the divisions caused by selfishness will be overcome,
and "all men" will see the love of Christ.[6]

Fred Kaan prays "for the healing of the nations" by the God whose
great name has been written "on all mankind"; for the banning of
pride and the "dogmas keeping man from man"; and for freedom
from hate and war, that "men may come and go in peace."[7]

These hymns combine high poetic quality with religious depth and
understanding. We can safely assume that none of them consciously
downgrade women. Yet regularly they imply that females as well as
males are brothers, and that women are adequately included and
recognized when men are mentioned.

There are of course some significant recent hymns in which this
identification does not appear, though few in which God is not desig-
nated by male images or pronouns. G. K. A. Bell's "Christ is the King!

O friends, rejoice" tells how "thousands of faithful men and true"
were drawn to Christ in ancient times, but goes on to appeal to
"Christian women, Christian men" today to follow the Way. In an
interesting mingling of male and inclusive language Bell calls upon
Christians to accept their apostleship:

> Brothers and sisters, with one voice
> make all men know he is your choice.[8]

Another exception appears in Percy Dearmer's characterization of
God in a little-known hymn of adoration. He addresses God as Father
throughout, but the opening stanza includes the mother image:

> O Father above us, our father in might,
> all live by thy love, as the flowers in the light;
> our mother and father and maker art thou.
> Forward! Forward ever, forward now![9]

Ironically, some of the popular songs of celebration, which are
cast in a folk idiom especially for Christians who want contemporary expressions of their faith, are as marked by masculine language
as the hymns just cited. Even Peter Scholtes' "We are one in the
Spirit" speaks of guarding the worth and self-esteem of "each
man."[10] The refrain of Ray Repp's "All you peoples, clap your
hands" relies heavily on terms like *mankind, fellow man, every
man,* and *brotherhood.*[11]

The problem surfaces with special clarity in "The Family of Man"
by Fred Dallas. Beginning with the joyful affirmation, "I belong to a
family, the biggest on earth," he speaks of men who do the world's
work, of men who are his brothers, and of the constructive and
destructive capacities of men, always assuming that women are included.[12]

A counterpart of exclusively male images of God and the generic
use of *man* is the custom of using feminine terms to refer to the
church, abstract entities like truth, and physical realities such as
nature and the earth. Inclusivists see in these usages reflections of a
hierarchical social order in which males are dominant and females
are subordinate. The divine power at the heart of the universe is
conceived as masculine, whereas the entities that depend on God are
regarded as feminine.

In "Before Jehovah's awful throne" Isaac Watts pictures the earth
"with her ten thousand tongues" as filling the heavenly courts with
praise. In Joseph Addison's "The spacious firmament on high," the
moon "nightly to the listening earth, / repeats the story of her birth."
In "Once to every man and nation" Lowell describes how noble it
is to side with truth and "share her wretched crust, / ere her cause

bring fame and profit"; and affirms the enduring strength of truth, "though her portion be the scaffold."

Portrayals of the church as feminine arouse the most concern. In exalting Christ as "the church's one foundation" Samuel J. Stone declares that "she is his new creation," sought by him "to be his holy bride." The application of the bridegroom-bride relation to Christ and the church grows out of a patriarchal understanding of marriage, and is therefore felt by many to help perpetuate an inferior status for women.

Timothy Dwight's "I love thy kingdom, Lord" consistently refers to the church with feminine pronouns, as in the third stanza:

> For her my tears shall fall,
>   for her my prayers ascend,
> to her my cares and toils be given,
>   till toils and cares shall end.

"Rise up, O men of God" is especially questionable because its dominant maleness contrasts with the femininity of the church. "Her strength unequal to her task," she waits for the *men* of God to "rise up, and make her great"!

The employment of military and feudal images to refer to both God and human beings has also come under attack. The Vulgate translation of the Old Testament renders the Hebrew *adonai* with *dominus,* and the English translation of this word as *Lord* to designate God or Christ was probably influenced by the medieval relation of the feudal lord to his serfs and dependents. The term is therefore felt by many to reinforce male dominance in human society. Similarly, metaphorical references in hymns to captains, marching, hosts, armor, soldiers, and the like picture the Christian life in terms of functions typically regarded as male, and hence are seen as subordinating women.

Probably hymnists use *Lord* to describe or address God more often than any other term, with the possible exception of *Father.* Military metaphors are more frequently employed than we ordinarily realize. One recalls readily Luther's "A mighty fortress is our God"; Shurtleff's "Lead on, O King eternal," with its day of march, fields of conquest, battle song, and sin's fierce war; Coster's "March on, O soul, with strength!"; and How's "For all the saints," which lauds the Lord who was "their captain in the well-fought fight," and which summons "soldiers, faithful, true, and bold" to join "the countless host" of those who go on to victory.

STEPS TOWARD INCLUSIVENESS

The evidence now before us lends support to five observations: (1) Our hymns contain a disturbing amount of sexist language, which in subtle ways consigns women to a subordinate role in church and society. (2) Wherever possible, offensive words and phrases should be replaced with language that includes both sexes and recognizes their equality. (3) Wide disagreement can be expected regarding the desirability and nature of changes proposed. (4) Consideration of alterations in existing hymns should proceed according to carefully conceived guidelines. (5) The writing of new hymns using only inclusive language should be encouraged.

What can be done to make more inclusive the language of the hymns now available? Basic to the attempt to answer this question are the criteria suggested at the end of Chapter 3 for all alterations. Two guidelines are particularly relevant here.

1. Revision should preserve the basic meaning, meter, rhyme, and poetic style of the original. As Erik Routley has written: "The alteration must not produce something that labels the original author as a bad poet, a shoddy thinker, or an indifferent stylist."[13]

2. Hymns and stanzas should be seen wholistically, rather than only from the standpoint of sexist language. Little will be gained if we remove male-dominated terms while retaining others ethically more objectionable or empty of substance. One list of 51 nonsexist hymns includes at least nine that are seriously defective because of self-centered individualism, irresponsible otherworldliness, questionable atonement theories, or plain triviality. Possible changes in a given hymn should be weighed in relation to its total message.

For examples of revisions thoughtfully carried out, the reader is referred to *Because We Are One People,* an imaginative rendering of 67 hymns in inclusive language; and *Everflowing Streams,* edited by Ruth C. Duck and Michael G. Bausch, which makes nonsexist language a major norm in its rewording of well-known hymns and its selection of other songs.[14]

Words Referring to Human Beings

It is relatively easy to find inclusive equivalents for masculine nouns, the main problem being that of accommodating changes to meter and rhyme. Even where a word with the same number of syllables does not suit, simple changes in phrases may accomplish the end sought. The words *man, men,* and *mankind* may be changed to *men and women, women and men, humanity, humankind, folk, kin, people, all people, all, all of us, one, ones, we/us/our. Man himself* can be rendered *people themselves; man's spirit* by *human spirit.*

By way of illustration, Fred Kaan's "hungry men of many lands" can easily become "hungry ones." In the familiar "Good Christian men, rejoice," *men* may be changed to *folk* or *friends,* or the opening words can be altered to "Good Christians all" or "People of Christ"; while the lines "and man is blessed forevermore" can be personalized to "we are blessed."

One revision completely recasts the fourth stanza of Fosdick's "God of grace and God of glory"—the one that asks for armor of Christlike graces "in the fight to make men free," and for wisdom and courage "that we fail not man nor thee." The first of these lines becomes "in the journey to be free," and the second "ears to hear and eyes to see." However, the changed text is so radically different that it can hardly be regarded as satisfactory. It seems impossible to find a nonsexist equivalent for "that we fail not man nor thee" which preserves the meter and does not change the sense. It may therefore be better to omit the stanza.[15]

Human fathers can be accurately described as parents or forebears. Some contexts may permit a recasting that makes them fathers and mothers. In revising "Faith of our fathers," *Because We Are One People* uses "faith of our ancestors," "God of our parents," and "faith of the ages." In *Everflowing Streams* the first three stanzas are addressed respectively to the faith of "our fathers," "our mothers," and "our brothers, sisters too." In the *Lutheran Book of Worship* "fathers" is retained in two stanzas, but it is "the martyrs" who were "chained in prisons dark."

Sons may sometimes be changed to *children, heirs, sons and daughters,* or *daughters and sons;* while renderings of *sons of God* may incorporate any of these or use *people of God* or *God's people.* In *Because We Are One People* one of Watts's lines is amended quite acceptably: "Time like an ever-rolling stream / bears mortals all [instead of "all its sons"] away." Worthy of note is a fifteenth-century Latin hymn by Jean Tisserand (d. 1494) that forestalls modern inclusivist criticism by beginning "O filii et filiae"—"O sons and daughters." The translators add "Let us sing!"[16]

Brothers can sometimes by rephrasing become *sisters and brothers,* and occasionally *neighbors, friends,* or *kindred* may fit. *Brotherhood* presents serious difficulties, since *sisterhood* is hardly a comparable term. However, in some contexts *kinship, unity, harmony, neighborliness,* or *family* (of faith) may be serviceable. Erik Routley offers a constructive revision of a stanza of "In Christ there is no East or West" which includes both *brothers* and *sons:*

> Join hands, then, all who hold the faith,
> > whate'er your race may be;
> who serves my Father cheerfully
> > is surely friend to me.[17]

In *Everflowing Streams* the second couplet has been changed to read:

> > all children of the living God
> > are surely kin to me.

In some hymns the pronouns *he, his,* or *him* are used in reference to a singular antecedent noun; or *he,* referring to either an individual or humanity, is itself the subject. The simplest way to correct this masculinity is to pluralize the pronoun to *they, their,* or *them.* Thus Richard Baxter's "He wants not friends that hath thy love" becomes in *With One Voice* "They lack not friends who have thy love." Percy Dearmer's "He who would valiant be," adapted from John Bunyan's "Who would true valour see," can be similarly revised. Thus the *Lutheran Book of Worship* begins with "All who would valiant be" and closes each stanza with "to be true pilgrims." These changes still leave a problem for those who are unhappy with "follow the Master." I therefore find it better to revert to Bunyan's first stanza, substituting plural pronouns and a slightly different last line. The opening stanza then becomes:

> Who would true valor see, / let them come hither;
> they here will constant be, / come wind, come weather.
> There's no discouragement / shall make them once relent
> their first-avowed intent / to live as pilgrims.

Words Designating God

Finding inclusive replacements for nouns and pronouns referring to God poses special problems. The divine Spirit for Christian faith is neither male nor female, but transcends sexual differences. Yet mainstream Christian teaching conceives of God according to the analogy of personality. Our total experience is more intelligible if we ground it ultimately in an activity with qualities somewhat akin to what we know as self-consciousness, reason, purposiveness, ability to realize values, and capacity for relationships with other persons. Love, forgiveness, and prayer, for example, are best understood on the personal plane. Hence personal language of some kind, however metaphorical, is most appropriate in worship. The problem, then, is how to find language that conserves the rich values of the personal analogy, without ascribing to God the maleness or femaleness that characterizes all finite persons, yet without making God an impersonal "it."

The difficulty centers in masculine words like Father, Lord, and King; in the maleness of the three "persons" of the Trinity; and in third-person masculine pronouns. The use of *Father* to refer to God has its drawbacks, since the actual human fathers of many worshipers are poor symbols of divine justice and love. For some children a father is likely to suggest abusiveness or tyranny. Yet the teaching and practice of Jesus, the centuries of use of the prayer he taught his disciples, and the time-honored acceptance of ideal fatherhood as a major image of the divine nature make continued use of the Father image inevitable.

There seems to be no adequate synonym. *Parent, ancestor,* and *forebear* lack the warmth and intimacy of the father-child relation. In some hymns slight changes in construction can achieve the desired end. For example, one revision of "This is my Father's world" begins simply with "Our God has made this world"; the use of *our* retains much of the personal relationship of the original.[18]

Another possibility is to expand our thinking to include the mother image. Only deeply entrenched habit stands in the way: we are simply not accustomed to think of God in feminine terms. Our main words for God are the deposit of a still-powerful patriarchal tradition. Theologically, however, the mother symbol is no less warranted than the father image. Certainly the woman's role in giving birth to new life gives her a firm and important place in our thought of God as Creator. The Bible often uses feminine imagery to refer to God, as in Deut. 32:18; Isa. 42:14; 46:3–4; 66:13; Matt. 23:37; Luke 13:34; 15:8–10. Hymns likewise extol qualities in God frequently thought of as feminine, such as mercy, patience, gentleness. These traits are not peculiarly male or female, but both, and we can recognize this by allowing both sexes to symbolize our understanding of the divine Spirit. Then we shall be able to address God the Father also as Mother.

Because We Are One People alters the first line of "Dear Lord and Father of mankind" to "Dear Mother-Father of us all." Such a departure from customary usage will not come easily or rapidly, but if editors and hymn writers explore its possibilities, a change might gradually occur that would enrich our worship.

It seems unlikely that the use of the word *Lord* can be drastically reduced. Some changes can be readily made. For example, in one version of Kethe's "All people that on earth do dwell," the words "sing to the Lord" become "sing unto God," and "the Lord our God" is changed to "Yahweh our God"; while the stanza that begins "Know that the Lord is God indeed," and contains three uses of *he* and two

of *his,* is omitted entirely.[19] Nonsexist nouns can sometimes be substituted, such as Most High, Rock, Mighty One, our Strength, the
Eternal, Liberator. Still, references to God as Lord are so integral a
part of our English Scriptures and liturgies as well as our hymnody
that removal of many of them from our hymns would be virtually
impossible, while a few changes would have little impact. Such alteration in our hymns could not proceed without attention to phrases
constantly used elsewhere in worship: the Lord Jesus Christ, the
Lord's Prayer, the Lord's Supper, and others. In The Psalms alone,
God is addressed or described as Lord 766 times. In *100 Hymns for
Today* there are 15 hymns beginning with Lord.

It is also doubtful whether alteration is in most cases necessary.
Most worshipers are unaware of the original patriarchal connections
of the English word and do not think of it as connoting masculine
supremacy. British Christians are of course familiar with the House
of Lords, but there is little in the experience of Americans today to
suggest that this word supports the subordination of women. In fact,
it seems more likely that the use of the term in common thought to
designate human lordship is derived from its association with the
divine than the other way around. Probably our best course is to use
broadly synonymous terms wherever possible while frequently
pointing out that calling God Lord does not mean that men are
thereby accorded higher authority than women.

Much clearer is the need for close scrutiny of references to God as
King, and to God's rule in terms of a kingdom, since a king is unmistakably male, and since kingly exercise of power has often been the
opposite of the rightousness associated with the Ruler of heaven and
earth. Fortunately, alternative words can often be used. God may be
spoken of as Sovereign, Monarch, or Ruler, terms that designate
queens no less than kings; and the functioning of divine authority can
be described as rule, reign, sovereignty, or dominion. *Everflowing
Streams* avoids both *Lord* and *King* in the opening lines of "Joy to
the world!" by announcing: "The promised one / has come Shalom
to bring." Even if *King* cannot always be altered felicitously, it can
be offset by other nonsexist nouns. "O worship the King" uses some
of these: Shield, Defender, Ancient of Days, Maker, Redeemer,
Friend. At least the last four are quite inclusive.

Serious difficulties remain. The kingdom of God has a prominent
place in Jesus' teachings, and time-honored usage gives the term a
fairly secure status. The adoration of the "King of kings and Lord of
lords" in the Hallelujah Chorus of Handel's *Messiah* and other
church music, along with its rootage in the book of Revelation, lends
authority to the words. However, room remains for removing as
many kings as possible from existing hymns, and for avoidance in
new ones of any reference to human royalty.

The word *kingdom* is less questionable, since it refers to rule or reign, not to a king's geographical domain. A theologian as competent and as committed to women's liberation as Letty Russell speaks without inhibitions of "God's Kingdom."[20] Here again, frequent employment of other metaphors and careful interpretation of meanings may be our best way of eliminating or reducing sexism.

The Trinitarian language often employed in hymns explicitly or implicitly conveys a masculine image of God. This tendency is accentuated by the use of the formula in liturgical responses like doxologies and the Gloria Patri, the classical creeds of the church, and many collects used in corporate worship. Hence revisions of hymns are likely to have little effect unless they can be undertaken as part of a more comprehensive reexamination of the masculinity of traditional formulations of the Trinity. We may hope that church commissions on worship and other responsible leaders will give serious attention to this problem.

In preaching and teaching, alternatives to Father, Son, and Holy Spirit like Creator, Redeemer, and Life-giver, or Sustainer, Reconciler, and transforming Presence, may be constructively used, and occasionally these can be woven into hymns. One version of "Holy, holy, holy" substitutes for "God in three persons, blessed Trinity" the line "who wert, and art, and evermore shalt be."[21] Indispensable is forthright and imaginative interpretation which points out the metaphorical, nonliteral nature of all our references to God and makes plain that none of our analogies accord the slightest superiority to either sex or ascribe human distinctions to the ultimate Source and Ground of all existence and value.

Masculine language cannot be avoided when referring to Jesus Christ. Jesus was a male, and the nouns used in the New Testament to refer to him are masculine: Messiah (Christ), Son, Son of God, Son of man. The Greek noun *logos* is also masculine, though the English equivalent, *Word,* is neuter. In a patriarchal culture it was virtually inevitable that the event which aroused faith in God's distinctive incarnation in a specific human life should be the arrival of a child born as a male. Hence we cannot escape the masculinity of the words that root in the historic Jesus.

Attempts have been made to avoid this restriction, but with little success. One revision of "Angels we have heard on high" invites us to "come to Bethlehem and see / one whose birth the angels sing."[22] The same editors amend "O little town of Bethlehem" to make Christ explicitly feminine. The third stanza assures us that though we cannot see or hear "her coming,"

> . . . if we will receive her still,
> the Christ appears tonight.[23]

Such an attempt to correct the New Testament writings—our only record of the historical Christ event—is unconvincing if not ludicrous. We may regret that God was not made manifest in a woman instead of a man, but we cannot ignore the only accounts we have. However, we can speak of Christ or the Son as the Word, or use other inclusive terms like Redeemer or reconciling Love. We can also emphasize that faith in the incarnation bears witness to God's redemptive action in a *human* life, with maleness or femaleness only incidental. Further, we can stress that divine Love continues to be revealed in manifold ways in human beings, without regard to their sex.

Probably the most frequently encountered form of sexist language referring to God is the use of the personal pronouns *he, him,* and *his.* Often this problem can be solved by the substitution of nouns for the masculine pronouns, or the use of the adjective *divine* for the possessive *his.* Thus *his* power, mercy, or love can become *divine,* though contextual changes may be needed to maintain the meter. John M. Mulder illustrates how sexism can be eliminated from prose by a passage from Reinhold Niebuhr's *The Nature and Destiny of Man.* Niebuhr wrote: "But faith in God as will and personality depends upon faith in His power to reveal Himself." The rewritten sentence speaks simply of "faith in the divine power of revelation."[24]

A stanza from Isaac Watts declares,

> His sovereign power, without our aid,
>   made us of clay, and formed us men;
> and, when like wandering sheep we strayed,
>   he brought us to his fold again.

A perceptive pamphlet by the Community Council of Wesley Theological Seminary offers a revision which removes both *men* and the masculine pronouns for God:

> God's sovereign power, without our aid,
>   formed and created us of clay;
> and, when like wandering sheep we strayed,
>   God brought us back into the way.[25]

"All people that on earth do dwell," a paraphrase by William Kethe of Psalm 100, extends the invitation:

> him serve with mirth, his praise forth tell,
>   come ye before him and rejoice.

In *Because We Are One People* there is a felicitous alteration:

> Come serve with mirth, your praise forth tell,
>   O come ye peoples and rejoice.

Abstract and Personified Entities

Where changes are desired to remove the suggestion of subordination in entities treated as feminine—e.g., truth, nature, the earth, Israel, the church—a neuter pronoun or a definite or indefinite article can often serve. Thus in "For the beauty of the earth" the church can offer *one* or *a* (instead of *her*) "pure sacrifice of love." When we contrast the church's endurance with that of kings and empires, we need not sing, "Immovable she stands." The church as an *it* can stand just as unyielding. The same hymn sings of "her goodly battlements," of "her foundation strong," and of "her unending song." In each case *its* can replace *her,* and if it seems incongruous to speak of an impersonal *it* as singing, we can declare,

> We hear within the solemn voice
> of ceaseless, grateful song.

IF CHANGE IS IMPOSSIBLE

During the present period of transition, when people of faith are seeking wider inclusiveness in all respects, there is great need for openness, creativity, imagination, and sensitivity to sincere differences. With regard to sexist language, it is imperative that a broad spectrum of feeling and opinion be consulted representing both inclusivists and upholders of the status quo, with full opportunity for discussion of the desirability as well as the nature of proposed changes. In local churches individuals may be invited to suggest alternative lines and stanzas. Workshops may be held in which people are encouraged to write original hymns and are guided in the process.

In many instances it will be found impossible to revise existing hymns or stanzas so as to remove all sexist language. Where this occurs, at least five courses of action are open.

1. Stop using the hymn. Erik Routley finds that relatively few hymns would need to be dropped that he would be sorry to miss![26]

2. Omit the offending stanza, provided that the rest of the hymn is poetically and theologically acceptable, and that the deletion does not destroy connected meaning.

3. Use the questionable passage, but carefully interpret the fundamental meanings behind those apparently conveyed.

4. Encourage worshipers to do their own interpretation. This may lead some to omit singing words or lines they cannot honestly voice. Or it may enable them to join in singing while inwardly saying in effect, "Though these are not the words I would use, by singing them

I really mean . . ." Fred Kaan, admitting that in spite of recent efforts
his hymns still contain some sexist language, hopes that people may
sometimes go in for what he calls "back-of-the-head-asterisk singing." He reports that for years, feeling his oneness with the worshiping church family and wanting to be a part of its corporate celebration, he has recited the historic creeds "with a number of mental
reservations and footnotes."[27] Some of us may find mental asterisks
a helpful way of deriving benefit from otherwise bothersome hymns.
Even if we cannot change the words, we can *think* inclusively as we
sing them.

5. In planning worship, balance hymns containing masculine language with a preponderance of inclusivist lyrics, or ask those responsible for leadership in worship to do so.

As writers and singers of hymns wrestle with these issues, uncover-
ing many differences, they will be wise to preserve their mutual
respect and their sense of humor. The spoof of a well-known British
hymnist who signs himself "F. Prater Gent (1981)" offers useful guidance:

> How can we sing the praise of Him
>   who is no longer He?
> With bated breath we wait to know
>   the sex of Deity.
>
> Our Father is our Mother now,
>   and Cousin, too, no doubt:
> must worship wait for hymnodists
>   to get things sorted out?[28]

After a third stanza on the demand to sisterize brotherhood, he
concludes with the hope that God, by whatever name, will "forgive
our stunned ambivalence" and "preserve our common-sense!" These
words may be an appropriate note on which to close both this chapter and the book.

KEY TO ABBREVIATIONS USED IN NOTES

(An asterisk indicates that the book is a supplement to a specific hymnal.)

AHB   *Anglican Hymn Book,* 1965.
AM   *Hymns Ancient and Modern,* revised 1950.
AME   *A.M.E. Hymnal.* African Methodist Episcopal Church, 1954.
BBC   *BBC Hymn Book,* 1951.
BH   *The Baptist Hymnal,* Southern Baptist Convention, 1975.
BHB   *The Baptist Hymnbook,* Baptist Union of Great Britain and Ireland, (1962) 1978.
BHUM   *The Book of Hymns* of The United Methodist Church, 1964, 1966.
BHUM*   *Supplement* to *The Book of Hymns* of The United Methodist Church, 1982.
BOP   *The Book of Praise,* Presbyterian Church of Canada, 1972.
BP*   *Broadcast Praise,* a Supplement to the *BBC Hymn Book,* 1981.
BWOP   *Because We Are One People: Songs for Worship,* Ecumenical Women's Centers, Chicago, 1974.
CD   *Cantate Domino,* an Ecumenical Hymn Book published on behalf of the World Council of Churches, 1980.
CH   *The Church Hymnary,* published jointly by five Presbyterian bodies in the British Isles, 1973.
CHo   *Cry Hosanna,* 1980.
CLB   *The Catholic Liturgy Book* (United States), 1975.
CP   *Congregational Praise,* Congregational Union of England and Wales, 1951.
EACC   *E.A.C.C. Hymnal.* East Asia Christian Conference, 1963.
EcP   *Ecumenical Praise,* 1977.
EH   *The English Hymnal,* 1958.
EHSB   *The English Hymnal Service Book* (abridged edition of EH with 36 additional hymns), 1962.
EP*   *English Praise,* a Supplement to *The English Hymnal,* 1975.
ES   *Everflowing Streams: Songs for Worship,* 1981.
FS   *Fresh Sounds,* 1976.

GH   *Gospel Hymns Nos. 1–6 Complete*, (1894, 1895) 1972.
HC   *The Hymn Book of the Anglican Church of Canada and the United Church of Canada*, 1971.
HCL   *Hymns for the Celebration of Life*, Unitarian Universalist Association, 1964.
HCW   *Hymnbook for Christian Worship*, Disciples of Christ and American Baptist Convention, 1970.
HE   *The Hymnal*, The Episcopal Church, 1940.
HFG   *Hymns for the Family of God*, 1976.
HIV   *Hymns II*, Inter-Varsity Christian Fellowship, 1976.
HLC   *Hymns for the Living Church*, 1974.
HMC   *Hymnal and Liturgies of the Moravian Church*, 1969.
HSM*   *Hymns and Songs: A Supplement to the Methodist Hymn Book*, the Methodist Church in the British Isles, 1969.
LBW   *Lutheran Book of Worship*, Inter-Lutheran Commission on Worship (four bodies), 1978.
LEV   *Lift Every Voice and Sing: A Collection of Afro-American Spirituals and Songs*, The Episcopal Church, 1981.
MH   *The Mennonite Hymnal*, 1969.
MHB   *The Methodist Hymn Book*, the Methodist Church in the British Isles, 1962.
MHSS*   *More Hymns and Spiritual Songs: A Hymnal Supplement*, The Episcopal Church, (1970) 1977.
MHT*   *More Hymns for Today*, a Second Supplement to AM, 1980.
NCH   *The New Catholic Hymnal* (Great Britain), 1971.
NCP*   *New Church Praise*, a Supplement to *The Church Hymnary* and *Congregational Praise*, for the United Reformed Church in England and Wales (founded 1972), 1975.
NNBH   *The New National Baptist Hymnal*, National Baptist Publishing Board, (1977) 1981.
OHT*   *100 Hymns for Today*, a Supplement to AM, 1969.
PCH   *A Panorama of Christian Hymnody*, ed. by Erik Routley, Liturgical Press, 1979 (texts only).
PH   *Pilgrim Hymnal*, 1958.
PL   *Praise the Lord* (Roman Catholic, British Isles), 1972.
PP   *Partners in Praise*, British Methodist Church Division of Education and Youth, 1979.
PT*   *Praise for Today*, a Supplement to 1962 edition of BHB, 1974.
SC*   *Songs for Celebration*, Church Hymnal Series IV, The Episcopal Church, 1979.
SLW   *Sound of Living Waters: Songs of the Spirit*, 1974.
SP   *Songs of Praise*, Vol. I, 1975.
STP   *Songs of Thanks and Praise*, 1980.
SZ   *Songs of Zion*, The United Methodist Church, 1981.
UCC   *The Hymnal of the United Church of Christ*, 1974.
WBP   *The Worshipbook—Services and Hymns*, three Presbyterian bodies in the United States, 1972.
WOR   *Worship II* (Roman Catholic, United States), 1975.

WOV *With One Voice: A Hymn Book for All the Churches,* 1979. Originally *The Australian Hymn Book,* 1977, representing the Anglican, Congregational, Methodist, Presbyterian, and Roman Catholic churches.

WP *Westminster Praise,* Westminster Choir College (United States), 1976.

NOTES

Chapter 1. WHY DO THE WORDS MATTER?

1. CH 16. This one-stanza hymn begins, "Lord Jesus, be thou with us now."
2. Louis F. Benson, *The Hymnody of the Christian Church* (John Knox Press, [1927] 1956), p. 89; see also p. 95.
3. HMC, reverse side of title page.
4. AHB 515; AM 389; BOP 100; CH 540; HMC 549; LBW 446; WBP 633.
5. AME 219; CLB 526; HC 161; HCL 221; HE 548; PH 303; UCC 46.
6. "Am I my brother's keeper?" CD 34; CLB 500; EP* 99; NCP* 2; PL 293; PP 156; UCC 180; WBP 295; WOR 21; WP 58.
7. BBC 409; BHB 21; BHUM 29; EH 52; HCW 283; HE 158; HLC 16; LBW 271; MH 44, 45; MHB 932; PH 39; WBP 529. Some hymnals contain other translations of the Latin hymn "Splendor Paternae gloriae" which begin differently.
8. Augustine, *Confessions*, IX, 6; see also X, 33.
9. *Luther's Works*, ed. by Helmut T. Lehmann (Fortress Press, 1963–75), Vol. 53 (1965), ed. by Ulrich S. Leupold, p. 316.
10. AME 27; BHUM 102.
11. BHUM* 969; LBW 555; STP 12; WP 12.
12. CP 32; HC 90; HLC 52; HSM* 23; NCP* 32; OHT* 33; PCH 490; PP 153; PT* 28; UCC 31.
13. BHUM* 880; EcP 73; HFG 10; LBW 558; STP 6; WBP 354; WOR 69.
14. HIV 15; LBW 416; WBP 498; WOR 200.

Chapter 2. HYMN TUNES AND THEOLOGICAL MEANING

1. Robert McAfee Brown, "Of Horsehair, Catgut and Sublimity," *The Christian Century*, Vol. 96 (1979), p. 911.
2. Corliss Lamont, *A Humanist Funeral Service*, rev. ed. (Prometheus Books, 1977).
3. *Encyclopaedia Britannica, Macropaedia*, Vol. 12, p. 664 d–e.
4. Friedrich Nietzsche, *The Birth of Tragedy*. The Works of Friedrich Nietzsche (Tudor Publishing Co., 1931), Vol. V, p. 202; see also p. 199.
5. Ibid., p. 192.
6. Ibid., pp. 187–189, 174.

7. John Milton, *Il Penseroso,* lines 159–164.

8. "Musical Composition," *Encyclopaedia Britannica, Macropaedia,* Vol. 12, p. 716 c–d.

9. Louis G. Nuechterlein, "The Music of the Congregation," in *A Handbook of Church Music,* ed. by Carl Halter and Carl Schalk (Concordia Publishing House, 1978), pp. 109–110.

10. Louis F. Benson, *The Hymnody of the Christian Church* (John Knox Press, [1927] 1956), pp. 262–263, 264–265.

11. Erik Routley, *Church Music and Theology* (Muhlenberg Press, 1960), pp. 71–74.

12. Ibid., p. 77.

13. Benson, *The Hymnody of the Christian Church.*

14. BBC 309; BHB 631; BOP 420; CH 92; CLB 466; CP 534; HC 262; HE 363; LBW 469; NCH 144; OHT* 61; PH 217; PL 288; SLW 44; STP 66; WOR 169; WOV 546.

15. CH 141; HC 83; HSM* 56; NCH 182; OHT* 78; PCH 469; PL 266; PP 165; PT* 64; STP 69; UCC 45; WBP 512; WOV 103.

16. HC 80; OHT* 36.

17. WBP 616.

18. BHB 60; BHUM 9; CP 8; HC 51; HCW 74; MHB 428; WBP 558; WOV 44(i). This hymn appears also, with other tunes, in HIV 19 and WOV 44(ii) (MONMOUTH) and in MH 25 (NASHVILLE).

Chapter 3. CRITERIA OF EVALUATION

1. *The Book of Discipline of The United Methodist Church* (United Methodist Publishing House, 1980), par. 69, pp. 78–81.

2. Walter M. Horton, in *Revelation,* ed. by John Baillie and Hugh Martin (London: Macmillan & Co., 1937), p. 258.

3. BHUM* 861; BP* 5; OHT* 7; PP 148; UCC 249; WOR 26; WP 39.

4. "As water to the thirsty," PP 96; "As the lyre to the singer," EACC 115; EcP 53.

5. Frederick Buechner, *Telling the Truth: The Gospel as Tragedy, Comedy, and Fairy Tale* (Harper & Row, 1977), p. 21.

6. Erik Routley, *A Panorama of Christian Hymnody* (Liturgical Press, 1979), p. v.

7. BH 150; EcP 81; HC 158; HFG 9; LBW 463; WOR 104; WOV 112.

8. "O Lord of every shining constellation." CH 141; HC 83; HSM* 56; NCH 182; OHT* 78; PCH 469; PL 266; PP 165; PT* 64; STP 69; UCC 45; WBP 512; WOV 103.

9. CP 32; HC 90; HLC 52; HSM* 23; NCP* 32; OHT* 33; PCH 490; PP 153; PT* 28; UCC 31.

Chapter 4. GOD

1. Clement of Alexandria, *Miscellanies,* VII, vii, 38.

2. BP* 24; PP 169; STP 68.

3. AHB 59; AM 480; BBC 14; BHB 68; BHUM 523; BOP 565; CH 145; CP 670; EH 527; HC 206; HE 305; HMC 406; MH 523; MHB 969.

4. BHUM* 880; EcP 73; HFG 10; LBW 558; STP 6; WBP 354; WOR 69.

5. CP 32; HC 90; HLC 52; HSM* 23; NCP* 32; OHT* 33; PCH 490; PP 153; PT* 28; UCC 31.

6. MHT* 160.

7. BH 150; EcP 81; HC 158; HFG 9; LBW 463; WOR 104; WOV 112.

8. MHSS* 20.

9. BH 157; BHUM* 929; BOP 550; CLB 323; CP 601; HFG 5; HLC 553; NCH 159; PH 38; PP 7; SLW 9; STP 7; UCC 29; WOR 179; WOV 91.

10. "Creation's Lord, we give thee thanks." AME 219; CLB 526; HC 161; HCL 221; HE 548; PH 303; UCC 46.

11. HCW 143; WBP 545.

12. Alfred North Whitehead, *Process and Reality* (Macmillan Co., 1929), p. 526.

13. AHB 17; AME 153; BH 13; BHB 444; BHUM 93; CP 442; HFG 318; HLC 28; HMC 358; LEV 76; MH 310; MHB 417; MHSS* 4; NNBH 14; WBP 341; WOV 152. See also discussion of this hymn at the end of Chapter 5.

14. HCW 18.

15. "Sing to him, in whom creation." EP* 43.

16. See, for example, CH 1, 4, 5, 6, 7, 8, and 22–29.

17. This hymn is found in virtually all standard hymnals. For other hymns with a Trinitarian format see Charles Wesley's "Father, in whom we live" (BHUM 465) and "Thou, whose almighty Word," by John Marriott (1780–1825), found in most hymnbooks.

18. BHUM 18; BP* 82; EcP 103; EHSB 83; HC 94; OHT* 90; PT* 78; WBP 580; WOV 339.

19. BP* 56; HC 295; OHT* 60.

20. OHT* 23; WOR 77; WOV 567.

21. ES 4.

22. "The Clock Carol," by Paul Townsend, in *Sing Round the Year: Songs of Praise,* selected and composed by Donald Swann (New York: Galaxy Music Corp., 1965), 10.

23. BBC 23; BH 535; BHUM 476; CH 499; CLB 477; HC 236; HE 269; HLC 494; HMC 261; PCH 544; PH 294; UCC 202; WBP 357; WOR 72.

24. LBW prints all 11 stanzas of the fourteenth-century version.

25. BBC 390; CH 517; CP 577; HC 57; PCH 566; WOV 89.

26. BP* 32; CP 6; EH 404; HC 20; MHB 78; MHT* 39.

27. BHUM 31; WOV 37.

28. AHB 239; AM 175; BBC 26; BHB 194; BOP 88; CH 36; CP 58; EHSB 312; HC 32; PCH 133; WOV 64.

29. See also "Whate'er our God ordains is right," by Samuel Rodigast, cited early in Chapter 1.

30. AHB 523; BH 203; BHB 580; BHUM 210; BP* 35; CH 668; CP 389; HCW 51; HFG 605; HIV 129; HLC 420; HMC 544; LBW 453; MH 314; MHB 503; MHSS* 15; PH 83; WBP 431; WOV 459.

31. MH 77.

32. AHB 530; AM 176; BH 221; BHB 585; BHUM 231; CP 398; HE 443; MH 253; MHB 527; PCH 95; WOV 55.

33. "The man who once has found abode." BHUM 216; PH 91; UCC 270; WBP 594.

34. BH 207; BHUM 521; HCW 30; HFG 89; HIV 103; HLC 41; LBW 474; MH 335.

35. AME 82; BHUM 53; PH 76.

36. BHUM* 895; FS 78; HCW 14; HFG 98; HLC 37; NNBH 153.

37. BBC 299; BHB 492; BOP 104; BP* 3; CH 405; CP 417; EcP 51; EP* 73; HC 134; HCW 20; MH 291; MHB 70; MHSS* 73; OHT* 3; PCH 200; PH 339; PL 278; UCC 167; WOV 465.

38. BHUM 155; HCW 252; HE 563; HMC 443; LBW 498; MH 323; PH 371; UCC 178; WBP 414; WOV 467.

39. BP* 1; CH 148.

40. AME 47; BH 149; BHUM 552; CLB 319; HCW 252; HE 443; HFG 687; HLC 526; HMC 143; LBW 567; NNBH 479; PCH 434; PH 433; UCC 254; WBP 394; WOR 101.

41. BHUM 47; HCW 28; HLC 326; HMC 183; MH 603; PH 97; WBP 395.

42. WBP 396.

43. EcP 112; HC 104; MHSS* 36; PP 162; STP 70.

44. BBC 7; BHB 52; BOP 90; HSM* 222; STP 10; WBP 386.

45. MHT* 163.

46. The paraphrase is by Howard C. Robbins (1876–1952). PH 165; UCC 132.

47. *Break Not the Circle: Twenty New Hymns,* by Fred Kaan and Doreen Potter (Carol Stream, Ill.: Agape, 1975), 4.

48. CP 50; HCW 10; HFG 66; HLC 325; MH 63; MHSS* 29; PCH 42; UCC 279; WBP 477; WOR 182.

Chapter 5. HUMANITY

1. *The New Catholic Hymnal,* compiled by Anthony Petti and Geoffrey Laycock (St. Martin's Press, 1971), p. xiii.

2. HCL 58.

3. "We journey with a multitude." HCL 66; see also 62, 64, 68.

4. PCH 316; UCC 195.

5. HE 299.

6. HC 202.

7. BH 157; BHUM 415; BOP 183; CP 130; HMC 125; LBW 98; MH 170; NNBH 79; WOR 7.

8. ES 10; UCC 35.

9. HC 80; OHT* 36. See also "In Adam we have all been one," by Martin H. Franzmann (1907–1976), LBW 372.

10. J. P. Migne, *Patrologiae cursus completus,* Series Graeca, Vol. XXV (Paris: Garnier Fratres Editores et J. P. Migne Successores, 1884), p. 192.

11. See Nikos Nissiotis, "Interpreting Orthodoxy," *The Ecumenical Review,* Vol. 14 (1961–62), p. 8.

12. WBP 616.

13. LBW 383.

14. BHUM 475; CH 84; CP 586; HC 73; HCW 339; HE 536; MHB 912; PCH 452; PH 451; PT* 89; UCC 63; WOR 251.

15. Thus Josiah Conder refers the "child of the dust" to God's "wise decrees," Isaac Watts ascribes all to the Lord's "sovereign will," and Samuel

Rodigast calls for quiet acceptance of what God ordains. See in the section on "Providence" in Chapter 4.

16. BHUM 118.

17. BHUM 310.

18. See Donald M. Baillie, *God Was in Christ* (Charles Scribner's Sons 1948), pp. 114–124.

19. AME 341; BH 349; BHUM 154; HCW 227; HFG 400; HLC 372; NNBH 125; UCC 170. For biblical use of the potter-clay analogy to express the sovereignty of God the Creator, see Isa. 29:16; 45:9–13; Jer. 18:1–6; Rom. 9:20–21.

20. AHB 602; AM 328; AME 293; BH 407; BHB 461; BHUM 150; HLC 496; HMC 391, 393; MH 350, 351; MHB 578; NNBH 190; PCH 71; WOV 487. See also Charles Wesley's "Soldiers of Christ, arise," found in many hymn-books.

21. HCW 92; HFG 467; HLC 374; WBP 579.

22. HCW 18.

Chapter 6. JESUS CHRIST

1. BP* 74.

2. EACC 117; HC 406; UCC 103.

3. "O Master Workman of the race." BHUM 171; MH 458; PH 412.

4. AME 241; BHUM 197.

5. AHB 611; BBC 347; BH 400; BHUM 252; BOP 432; CP 445; EH 474; HCL 91; HFG 446; HLC 429; MHB 533; PH 336, 530. BOP, CH, and CP place first the stanza here quoted. See Erik Routley, PCH 111, for the full text of the author's revision of 1853.

6. "The great Creator of the worlds." HE 298; MHT* 178; PCH 551; WBP 588.

7. This hymn appears in virtually all hymnals. Translations of all of the original nine stanzas can be found in EHSB 197 and PCH 155.

8. AHB 200; AM 146; BBC 126; CH 302; EH 144; EHSB 162; LBW 300; MH 288; WOV 124.

9. AM 45; BBC 31; BHUM 78; BOP 117; CLB 200; EH 1; EHSB 51; HC 396; HCW 103, 104; HE 6; PH 113; PL 125; WBP 348; WOR 65.

10. *The Interpreter's Dictionary of the Bible* (Abingdon Press, 1962), Vol. II, p. 691.

11. BH 98; BHUM 90; HLC 125; PH 152.

12. BP* 9; EcP 66; HC 119; MHT* 107; STP 82; WOV 191.

13. MHT* 154.

14. *Encyclopaedia Britannica, Macropaedia*, Vol. 15, p. 799e.

15. OHT* 46.

16. The closing line of "Christ is the world's true light," by George W. Briggs (1875–1959). AHB 418; BH 274; BHB 659; BHUM 408; BOP 111; CH 505; CP 171; EP* 101; HE 258; HMC 525; HSM* 9; MH 198; OHT* 13; PH 198; UCC 143; WBP 326; WOV 179.

17. HMC 93; LBW 28; WBP 565.

18. BHUM 373; HC 402; HCW 131; HFG 207; HMC 74; MH 609; PH 118; UCC 107; WBP 315; most English carol collections since 1960. Most hymnals

add a second stanza by Dalton E. McDonald (b. 1910) which exhibits a more Abelardian view.

19. AHB 144; BBC 83; BHUM* 924; BOP 177; HCW 166; HE 59; HMC 101; PH 153; WBP 470; WOR 171.

20. AHB 173; AM 113; AME 312; BHB 144; BOP 187; CH 243; EH 111; HCW 168; HE 74; MHB 187; NCH 175; PCH 212; PH 164; WOV 267.

21. BHB 153; BHUM 438; BOP 191; CH 268; CLB 282; CP 761; HCW 177; LBW 134; MH 611; MHB 210; MHSS* 60; NCH 33; WBP 327; WOR 45; WOV 283.

22. BHUM 446; HCW 173; HE 94; HLC 164; HMC 143, 144; LBW 132; MH 178; PCH 178; PH 185, 186; WBP 344; WOV 278.

23. PH 165; UCC 132.

24. BP* 8; PP 87; STP 77.

25. AHB 504; BHB 208; BHUM 127; BOP 405; CP 470; HFG 268; HIV 87; HLC 241; HMC 327; LBW 302; MHB 370; PCH 56; WOV 137.

26. HMC 330.

27. BOP 356; EH 333; LBW 202; MHB 771; PCH 64.

28. AHB 280; BH 33; BHB 32; BOP 73; CH 374; HFG 363; HIV 16; HLC 40; MH 552; MHB 313; NNBH 23; WOV 85.

29. OHT* 1; WOV 176.

30. AHB 169; BBC 79; BHB 139; BHUM 427; CH 242; CLB 261; HC 454; HCW 169; HE 68; HLC 133; PCH 549; PH 159; UCC 121; WBP 294; WOV 252.

31. HC 459; OHT* 71; WOV 544.

32. BHUM 355; CH 235; CLB 514; HCW 222; HE 522; LBW 421; MH 247; MHB 906; OHT* 54; PH 325; UCC 227; WOV 208.

33. BHB 555; BHUM 86; HE 362; HLC 74; MH 413.

34. OHT* 1; WOV 176.

35. BHUM* 963; SLW 124; UCC 75; WOV 212.

Chapter 7. THE HOLY SPIRIT

1. In the sections on "God as Life-giving Presence" and "The Threefold Oneness of God" in Chapter 4.

2. G. W. H. Lampe, *God as Spirit* (Oxford: Clarendon Press, 1977), p. 116.

3. Ibid. See also Leon Joseph Cardinal Suenens, *A New Pentecost?* (Seabury Press, 1975), pp. 156–157.

4. BHB 230; CH 118; CP 200; EH 156; HE 371; LBW 164; MHB 293; PCH 160; WOR 62.

5. AM 152; HCW 197; EH 154; MH 211; PL 9.

6. CLB 298; HC 246; WOR 205; WOV 329. See also the Ordinal Version, 1929, "Come Holy Ghost, Creator blest," SC* 299.

7. AHB 217; CLB 292; HCW 193; LBW 163; PH 235; WBP 336.

8. BHUM 136; UCC 150.

9. "Filled with the Spirit's power." HC 226; LBW 160; OHT* 26; PL 267; PT* 14; WOV 328.

10. "Of all the Spirit's gifts to me." BP* 70; MHT* 170.

11. BP* 96; HC 237; MHSS* 44; MHT* 189; STP 75.

12. BP* 88; MHT* 182; PP 125.

13. Charles F. Whiston, in *A Prayer Companion,* comp. by Hazel T. Wilson (Abingdon Press, 1958), p. 22. The poetic form is that of the amended version published in *The Mennonite Hymnal* (Newton, Kans.: Faith and Life Press; Scottdale, Pa.: Herald Press, 1969), Additional Worship Resources, Section IV, No. 736.

Chapter 8. THE CHURCH AND ITS MISSION

1. WBP, p. 51.
2. BBC 201; BHB 315; BHUM 307; CH 586; CLB 376; EcP 1; EP* 62; HC 225; HCW 322; HE 195; HSM* 16; OHT* 24; PCH 552; PH 289; PL 69; STP 52; WBP 366; WOR 79; WOV 416.
3. UCC 153.
4. AHB 426; AM 256; BBC 187; BHB 264; BOP 306; CH 424; CP 251; EH 545; HC 152; HCW 356; HSM* 71; PL 273; WOV 389.
5. MHSS* 19; BP* 51.
6. BHB 356; BOP 316; CH 474; CLB 304; CP 365; HCW 355; HE 543; LBW 386; OHT* 12; STP 64; UCC 159; WOR 44.
7. Rudolf Otto, *The Idea of the Holy* (London: Oxford University Press, 1928), p. 10; see also pp. 5–7, 11–15, 20–22, 25–31.
8. BHUM 296; PH 266.
9. BH 241; BHB 260; BHUM 311; BOP 308; CH 490; CP 286; EH 651; HCW 148; HLC 202; HMC 252; HE 233; MH 379; MHB 727; PH 301.
10. BHUM 308; HE 382; HMC 248; MH 378; PH 264; WBP 530.
11. PH 477; UCC 154.
12. AM 258; BBC 173; BHB 255; BOP 303; CH 422; CP 253; EH 375; HC 147; HE 386; MHB 703; PCH 379; PH 261.
13. S. Paul Schilling, *Contemporary Continental Theologians* (Abingdon Press, 1966), pp. 190–191.
14. Ibid., p. 255.
15. AHB 418; BH 274; BHB 659; BHUM 408; BOP 111; CH 505; CP 171; EP* 101; HE 258; HMC 525; HSM* 9; MH 198; OHT* 13; PH 198; UCC 143; WBP 326; WOV 179.
16. HCW 352; PH 268; UCC 160; WBP 468. This hymn also appears in *The Covenant Hymnal* (1973), *The English Liturgy Hymnal* (1965), and *Hymns and Songs of the Spirit* (1966).
17. HE 397; WOV 370.
18. AM 470; EH 166; EHSB 36.
19. HC 226; LBW 160; OHT* 26; PL 267; PT* 14; WOV 328.
20. AM 402; BBC 213; CH 492; CLB 359; EH 324; HC 345; HE 191; PL 79; WOV 443.
21. HC 212; WBP 646.
22. AM 265; AME 216; CP 329; EH 547; HE 254; HLC 472; HMC 270; MHB 801.
23. See Mary B. C. Slade's "From all the dark places," *The Methodist Hymnal* (Methodist Publishing House, 1935), 483; George W. Doane's "Fling out the Banner," AM 268, CP 331, EH 546, HE 259, HMC 296, MHB 817, PH 296; Frank Mason North's "O Master of the waking world," BHUM 407, HCW 210; Jane Borthwick's "Hasten the time appointed," HE

257; Cecil Frances Alexander's "Souls in heathen darkness lying," HMC 267.

24. AME 215; HE 264; *The Methodist Hymnal* (1935), 487.

25. BHUM 406; MH 420; WBP 416.

26. BBC 23; BH 535; BHUM 476; CH 499; CLB 477; HC 236; HE 269; HLC 494; HMC 261; PCH 544; PH 294; UCC 202; WBP 357; WOR 72.

27. BHUM 200; HCW 271; PH 426; UCC 191.

28. BP* 57; HSM* 42.

29. BH 319; BHUM* 981; HSM* 77; MHSS* 40.

30. *Intercommunion;* a report of a theological commission of the Faith and Order Commission of the World Council of Churches (Geneva: World Council of Churches, 1951), p. 29.

31. AHB 368; AM 416; BBC 220; EH 335; EHSB 289; HE 205.

32. AM 397; BBC 198; BHB 307; BOP 344; CH 580; EH 302; EHSB 14; HC 331; HE 189; MHB 759; PCH 249; PH 292; WOV 440.

33. LBW 204.

34. EH 326; EHSB 198.

35. LBW 225.

36. MHT* 129.

37. AM 385; EH 331; EHSB 258; HC 329; LBW 199; WBP 599; WOV 421.

38. MHT* 110.

39. BHUM 314; HCW 309; LBW 200; UCC 214.

40. OHT* 77.

41. BHUM* 971; LBW 207.

42. CD 151.

43. UCC 209.

44. OHT* 19.

45. LBW 218. Adapted from the translation of Charles W. Humphreys and Percy Dearmer, which appears in AHB 201; BBC 215; BHB 328; CH 588; CLB 378; CP 313; EcP 89; EH 329; EHSB 229; HC 348; HE 201; OHT* 88; PCH 181; WOV 417.

46. LBW 221; MHT* 177.

47. LBW 203.

48. BHUM* 904; EcP 84; HC 328; MHT* 140; STP 54; WOV 452.

49. HC 150.

50. LBW 433; STP 78.

51. HCW 335; UCC 183.

Chapter 9. THE CHRISTIAN LIFE

1. BHUM 96; HCW 11; HE 405; HIV 89; MH 228; PH 408, 578; SC* 319.

2. UCC 168.

3. HFG 91.

4. AME 401; BHUM 167; HMC 534.

5. HMC 79.

6. AHB 422; AM 358; BHB 584; BHUM 229; CP 414; EH 468; HE 436; HFG 491; HIV 137; HLC 396; HMC 536; MH 271; MHB 501.

7. AME 79; BHUM 207; HFG 56; NNBH 79.

8. AME 188; HFG 87; HLC 417; LEV 65; NNBH 211; SZ 53; UCC 290.

9. Evelyn Underhill, *The Life of the Spirit and the Life of Today* (E. P. Dutton & Co., 1922), pp. 148–149.

10. "My Shepherd will supply my need" is discussed briefly, with Watts's moving last stanza quoted, at the end of Chapter 4. It appears in CP 50; HCW 10; HFG 66; HLC 325; MH 63; MHSS* 29; PCH 42; UCC 279; WBP 477; WOR 182.

11. "Because the Lord is my Shepherd," Ralph Carmichael (1969), HLC 447; "My Shepherd is the Lord Most High," anon., AME 477; "The God of love my Shepherd is," George Herbert (1593–1633), AM 178; BBC 474; CP 43; EH 93; EHSB 243; HIV 187; MHB 51; NCH 230; "The living God my Shepherd is," J. Driscoll, S.J. (1946), WOR 270; "The Lord is my pacesetter," an anonymous English translation of a Japanese paraphrase by Toki Miyashiro, set by Anthony G. Petti to a plainsong melody based on Psalm Tone II, NCH 235; "The Lord is my Shepherd, I'll follow him alway," anon., SLW 108; "The Lord is my Shepherd, I shall not want," Lucy E. Campbell (1921), NNBH 289; "The Lord is my Shepherd, my guardian, my guide," anon., MHSS* 21, 22; "The Lord is my Shepherd, no want shall I know," James Montgomery (1771–1854), AME 76; HMC 180; NNBH 210; "The Lord is my Shepherd; there is nothing I shall want," from *The Grail* (1956), EcP 5; BHUM* 961; WOR 272; WOV 98; "The Lord my pasture shall prepare," Joseph Addison (1672–1719), AM 179; BBC 477; CP 48; EH 491; EHSB 249; PCH 46; "The Lord my Shepherd is," Isaac Watts, MH 66.

12. BHUM 146; CP 192; EH 483; HCW 15; HE 365; HMC 401; MHB 86; PH 357; UCC 16; WBP 578.

13. "Who fathoms the eternal thought," BOP 518; CH 558; MHB 513; PCH 366; WOV 512; "Within the maddening maze of things," PCH 366; PH 360; UCC 242; "I know not what the future hath," BH 492; BHUM 290; CP 476; HE 441; HMC 539; PCH 366.

14. "Beyond the mist and doubt." EcP 64; HSM* 6.

15. BP* 50; EP* 86; NCH 135; PCH 513.

16. BP* 18; MHT* 124.

17. HSM* 15; MHSS* 5; NCP* 17; OHT* 18; PCH 487; PL 99; PT* 12; STP 71; WOR 61; WP 57.

18. BHB 22; BP* 20; CLB 497; EP* 24; HC 74; LBW 307; MHSS* 9; NCH 60; NCP* 25; OHT* 29; PP 105; STP 47; WOR 84; WOV 564.

19. BHUM 286; HFG 421; MH 293; NNBH 490; PH 353; SC* 322; SZ 76; UCC 232.

20. BHB 380; BOP 489; CD 147; CH 510; CP 560; HC 280; LBW 405; PCH 451; WOV 392.

21. HE 429; SLW 37, 38.

22. AHB 539; AM 367; BBC 325; BHB 12; BOP 476; CH 364; CP 426; EH 424; HC 195; MHB 23; NCH 123; PL 295; WOV 129.

23. EACC 185.

24. BBC 309; BHB 631; BOP 420; CH 92; CLB 466; CP 534; HC 262; HE 363; LBW 469; NCH 144; OHT* 61; PH 217; PL 288; SLW 44; STP 66; WOR 169; WOV 546.

25. *Break Not the Circle*, 3.

26. AHB 550; AM 295; AME 334; BHUM 300; BOP 506; CP 242; EH 373; HE 578; HLC 445; HMC 442; MHB 696.

27. AME 266; BHUM 246; HE 555; HLC 462; HMC 421; MH 321; NNBH 389.

28. AHB 422; AM 358; BHB 584; BHUM 229; CP 414; EH 468; HE 436; HFG 491; HIV 137; HLC 396; HMC 536; MH 271; MHB 501.

29. Louis F. Benson, *The Hymnody of the Christian Church* (John Knox Press, [1927] 1956), p. 170.

30. AHB 602; AM 328; AME 293; BH 407; BHB 461; BHUM 150; HLC 496; HMC 391, 393; MH 350, 351; MHB 578; NNBH 190; PCH 71; WOV 487.

31. LBW 126, which lists Omer Westendorf as translator; *Peoples Mass Book* (Cincinnati: World Library of Sacred Music, 1964), L-25, which attributes the text to C. Clifford Evers; WBP 641, which cites Evers as paraphraser of the hymn in 1960.

32. BBC 380; BHB 636; CP 556; OHT* 55; PCH 449.

33. For examples, see Sydney Carter's "When I needed a neighbor, were you there?" BHUM* 979; CD 37; *Faith, Folk and Clarity,* ed. by Peter Smith (London: Galliard, Ltd.; New York: Galaxy Music Corp., 1969), 30; HSM* 97; MHSS* 38; OHT* 100; PL 298; PT* 97; *Sisters and Brothers Sing!,* ed. by Sharon and Tom Emswiler (Normal, Ill.: Wesley Foundation Campus Ministry, 1977), 102; also "Whatsoever you do to the least of my brothers," by Willard F. Jabusch (b. 1930), *Songbook for Saints and Sinners,* compiled by Carlton R. Young (Carol Stream, Ill.: Agape, 1971), 22; WOR 307; also Kenred B. Rowsell's "As long as you have done it to the least of these my brothers," NCH 262; and Kenneth L. Morse's "Brothers and sisters of mine are the hungry," published by the Church of the Brethren in 1974 and found in *Sisters and Brothers Sing!,* 91.

34. OHT* 97; PP 104.

35. "O who can tell me where Jesus Christ is born today?" CD 61.

36. BHUM* 975; *Genesis Songbook,* ed. by Carlton R. Young (Carol Stream, Ill.: Agape, 1971), 34; MHSS* 35; PL 296; *Songbook for Saints and Sinners,* 5; WBP 619–620.

37. BHB 654; CP 567; EH 566; HE 496; MHB 909; PCH 213.

38. AHB 419; BBC 321; BH 506; BHB 358; CH 514; CLB 522; CP 554; HC 252; LBW 373; PCH 381; PH 275; WBP 358; WOR 73; WOV 513.

39. BHUM* 967; CD 49; EcP 104.

40. HIV 15; LBW 416; WBP 498; WOR 200.

41. UCC 204.

42. OHT* 92; PP 174.

43. Erik Routley, "Sexist Language: A View from a Distance," *Worship,* Vol. 53 (1979), p. 2.

44. BHUM* 857; EcP 54, 55; HC 168; HSM* 3; LBW 436; MHSS* 1; NCP* 1; PP 158; PT* 3; WBP 293; WOV 562.

45. CD 38; HC 125; MHSS* 32; PP 159; PT* 75; UCC 259; WOR 251.

46. EcP 75; PP 21. See also "Lord, bring the day to pass," by Ian Mason Fraser (b. 1917), PP 170; WOV 106.

47. CD 34; CLB 500; EP* 99; NCP* 2; PL 293; PP 156; UCC 180; WBP 295; WOR 21; WP 58.

48. BHUM* 905; EP* 41; *Faith, Folk and Nativity,* ed. by Peter Smith (London: Galliard, Ltd.; New York: Galaxy Music Corp., 1968), 32; HC 106;

OHT* 42; PT* 38; *Songbook for Saints and Sinners,* 18; WBP 426; WOR 128; WOV 183.

49. CD 30.

Chapter 10. CONSUMMATION

1. AM 277; CP 351; EH 392; HE 598; PCH 162.
2. AM 276; EH 495; HE 595; PCH 162.
3. AM 275; BBC 241; CP 350; EH 371; MHB 652; PCH 162.
4. AM 623; AME 471; BBC 247; CH 595; CP 354; EH 638; HE 585; HLC 539; LBW 331; MH 370; PCH 410; PH 312.
5. AHB 437; AM 284; AME 437; BBC 253; BHB 407; EH 486; HE 590; HLC 537; HMC 567; MHB 828; PCH 235; PH 311.
6. AM 206; BH 500; BHB 544; BOP 501; CP 490; HCW 242; HLC 450; HMC 432; LBW 341; MH 319; MHB 624.
7. HE 588.
8. *The Methodist Hymnal* (1935), 525.
9. LBW 351.
10. *The Methodist Hymnal* (1935), 530.
11. Sandra S. Sizer, *Gospel Hymns and Social Religion* (Temple University Press, 1978), p. 31.
12. The stanza on death is included in BHUM 60 and WOV 3.
13. BHUM* 955; *Break Not the Circle,* 19.
14. AM 272; BBC 249; BHB 402; BHUM 302; BOP 312; CH 543; CLB 531; CP 361; EH 428; MHB 824; WOV 370.
15. BP* 65; MH 367; OHT* 69; WOV 395.
16. AHB 334; AM 262; BBC 27; BHB 397; BOP 222; CH 322; CP 534; EH 554; HC 276; HE 544.
17. AM 263; BBC 28; BHB 398; BOP 219; CH 323; CP 585; EH 504; HC 278; HE 391; MHB 742; PCH 388.
18. AHB 89; BBC 419; BH 128; BHUM 468; BOP 118; CH 321; CP 156; EH 492; HE 312; LBW 318; MHB 813; PCH 418; PH 95; WOV 194.
19. BHUM 469; HC 279; HCW 265; HE 532; HLC 516; LBW 413; MH 447; PCH 454; PH 445; UCC 145; WBP 362; WOR 76; WOV 540.
20. BHUM 481; CH 509; CLB 496; HC 160; HE 494; MH 450; OHT* 76; PCH 542; PH 420; UCC 188, 189; WBP 505; WOR 204.
21. BBC 24; BHB 187; BHUM 477; BOP 598; CH 511; CLB 520; HC 275; HCW 266; HSM* 52; OHT* 72; PCH 561; PH 444; UCC 260; WBP 492; WOV 547.
22. BBC 181; BHB 389; BOP 299; CP 347; PH 304; UCC 161.
23. ES 7. The first line originally addressed the "cloud of Yahweh." However, the author now prefers "cloud of Presence," because some people regard Yahweh as a male term, and many Jews are offended by speaking the name of God.
24. LBW 322.
25. LBW 22; WOV 198.
26. HFG 313.
27. "Oh, happy day when we shall stand." LBW 351.
28. AME 106; MH 194.

29. BOP 227; HE 11; HLC 181; LBW 33; MH 196; PCH 185; PH 201; WOR 269.

30. AHB 77; BBC 40; BHUM 366; CH 315; HCW 112; HE 3; LBW 31; MH 118; MHB 255; PH 108; WBP 614; WOR 291; WOV 195. The portion quoted is from the slightly altered version in LBW 31. Other translations appear in AM 55; CP 760; EH 12; HC 394; and PCH 188.

Chapter 11. GOSPEL HYMNS

1. Edward Mote (ed.), *Hymns of Praise: A New Selection of Gospel Hymns* (London, 1936); Ira D. Sankey, James McGranahan, and George C. Stebbins (eds.), *Gospel Hymns Nos. 1–6 Complete* (Cincinnati: The John Church Co.; New York: The Biglow & Main Co.; Diamond Edition, 1894; Excelsior Edition, 1895; reprint of 1895 ed., New York: Da Capo Press, 1972). The contents of the two Sankey editions were the same (739 hymns), but resetting reduced the number of pages from 688 to 512.

2. Sizer, *Gospel Hymns and Social Religion,* pp. 169, 173.

3. Erik Routley, *Twentieth Century Church Music* (Oxford University Press, 1964), p. 198.

4. BH 55; GH 406; HFG 618; HLC 296; MH 551.

5. BH 56; GH 645; HFG 246; HIV 42; HLC 155; MH 561.

6. BH 351; BHUM 433; GH 598; HFG 254; HLC 361; MH 560; NNBH 94; SZ 19.

7. AME 345; BH 178; GH 281; HFG 401; HLC 267.

8. AME 248; BH 183; BHUM 101; GH 587; HFG 629; HLC 258; MH 553; NNBH 146.

9. GH 413; HFG 372; HLC 86; MH 562.

10. BH 423; BHUM 163; GH 584.

11. BH 477; HFG 637; HLC 277.

12. BH 196, 197; BHUM 104; BHUM* 874; CHo 40; GH 670.

13. BHUM 116; GH 658.

14. AME 483; BH 156; GH 588; HFG 273; HLC 232; NNBH 89.

15. GH 574; HFG 70; HLC 400; MH 367.

16. HFG 412; HLC 310; MH 575; NNBH 236.

17. BHUM 179; GH 518.

18. "I'm pressing on the upward way." BH 324; HFG 469; HLC 355; NNBH 309; SZ 39.

19. HLC 362.

20. AME 342; GH 589; HFG 676; HLC 436; NNBH 157.

21. HIV 166.

22. HFG 485; HLC 353; MH 579.

23. BHUM 5; CP 391; HMC 6; NNBH 256.

24. BH 505; GH 567; HFG 550; HLC 275; LEV 92; MH 529; NNBH 22; SZ 3.

25. See the critical discussion of these issues in Chapters 4–6, 9, and 10.

26. *Evangeliums-Lieder: Gospel Hymns,* compiled and edited by Walter Rauschenbusch and Ira D. Sankey (New York: The Biglow & Main Co.; Cincinnati: The John Church Co., 1890).

27. Wyatt Tee Walker, *"Somebody's Calling My Name": Black Sacred Music and Social Change* (Judson Press, 1979), Figure 10, p. 129.

28. Alfred Duckett, "An Interview with Thomas A. Dorsey," *Black World,* Vol. 23, No. 9 (July 1974), p. 13; cited by Walker, op. cit., p. 128.

29. Pearl Williams-Jones, "Afro-American Gospel Music: A Crystallization of the Black Aesthetic," *Ethnomusicology,* Vol. 19 (1975), p. 378.

30. "Yes, God is real," LEV 126; NNBH 249; SZ 201.

31. "God is." Recorded by both Robert Fryson, author, and James Cleveland, with supporting choirs.

32. "I don't feel no ways tired" (Curtis Burrell). SZ 175. Rev. James Cleveland's singing popularized both this song and Fryson's "God is."

33. "Lord will make a way some how." NNBH 286; Walker, *"Somebody's Calling My Name,"* pp. 168–169.

34. AME 333; HFG 611; LEV 12; NNBH 339; SZ 179; Walker, ibid., pp. 164–165; Tony Heilbut, *The Gospel Sound* (Simon & Schuster, 1971), p. 66.

35. "I sent them Men of Old." Walker, *"Somebody's Calling My Name,"* pp. 158–159.

36. NNBH 311; SZ 189.

37. Walker, *"Somebody's Calling My Name,"* p. 158.

38. SZ 173.

39. Walker, *"Somebody's Calling My Name."*

40. SZ 191.

41. SZ 182.

42. SZ 199.

43. NNBH 287; SZ 180.

44. Heilbut, *The Gospel Sound,* p. 322.

45. NNBH 266; SZ 188.

46. SZ 181.

47. SZ 198.

48. Susan Wilson, "Singing About Issues," *The Boston Globe,* Oct. 2, 1980.

49. Pearl Williams-Jones, personal communication, May 16, 1981.

50. Lawrence Levine, *Black Culture and Black Consciousness* (Oxford University Press, 1977), pp. 158, 174.

51. Thomas Morgan, "Gospel Music Enjoying a Dramatic Revival," *The Washington Post,* March 11, 1980, p. C–5.

52. Karl Marx, "Contribution to the Critique of Hegel's Philosophy of Right," *On Religion,* by Karl Marx and Friedrich Engels (Moscow: Foreign Language Publishing House, 1957), pp. 41–42.

53. Thomas Morgan, "Gospel Music Enjoying a Dramatic Revival."

54. James H. Cone, *The Spirituals and the Blues* (Seabury Press, 1972), p. 127.

55. Tony Heilbut, *The Gospel Sound,* p. 11.

56. Wyatt Tee Walker, *"Somebody's Calling My Name,"* p. 144.

Chapter 12. Folk Hymnody

1. BH 106; BHUM 432; CD 79; EcP 46; HCW 157; HFG 283; HIV 38; HSM* 94; LBW 385; MH 163; WOR 306.

2. *Faith, Folk and Nativity,* 14; *Hymns for Now II* (Concordia Publishing House, 1967), 10.

3. Several of the latter have already been discussed: in Chapter 5: Richard G. Jones's "God who created this garden of earth"; and in Chapter 9: Peter Scholtes' "We are one in the Spirit," Sydney Carter's "Lord of the Dance," and Nick Hodson's "It's a long, hard journey."

4. *The Avery and Marsh Songbook* (Port Jervis, N.Y.: Proclamation Productions, Inc., 1972); BHUM* 882.

5. BHUM* 855; CHo 4.

6. BHUM* 917; MHSS* 17.

7. MHSS* 30.

8. CHo 108; EcP 58; LEV 106; PP 160; SC* 298.

9. MHSS* 16.

10. BHUM* 979; CD 37; *Faith, Folk and Clarity,* 30; HSM* 97; MHSS* 38; OHT* 100; PL 298; PT* 97; *Sisters and Brothers Sing!,* 102.

11. OHT* 67; WOR 185.

12. *Dunblane Praises,* Vol. I (1964); EcP 114; PCH 524.

13. EcP 115; *Faith, Folk and Festivity,* ed. by Peter Smith (London: Galliard, Ltd.; New York: Galaxy Music Corp., 1969), 2; PCH 528; PP 47; SC* 296; WOV 214.

14. Avery and Marsh, *Hymns and Carols No. 6,* p. 15; *Sisters and Brothers Sing!,* 13.

15. PP 128; PT* 59.

16. These are part of a wider network, a "community of communities," including two in the British Isles, the purposes of which are closely related.

17. SLW and FS are published by Wm. B. Eerdmans Publishing Co., Grand Rapids, Mich.; CHo by Hope Publishing Co., Carol Stream, Ill.; and SP by Servant Music, Ann Arbor, Mich.

18. Jim Wallis, "Rebuilding the Church," *Sojourners,* Jan. 1980, p. 15.

19. Bob Sabath, "A Community of Communities," *Sojourners,* Jan. 1980, p. 19.

20. Robert Sabath, "The Community of Celebration," *Sojourners,* May-June 1976, pp. 31, 33.

21. CHo 11; SP 34.

22. CHo 77; SP 22.

23. CHo 1.

24. "Fear not, rejoice and be glad." SLW 59.

25. CHo 21.

26. SLW 83.

27. SLW 27.

28. FS 13; SP 68.

29. SLW 16.

30. SLW 82.

31. CHo 30; SLW 64.

32. SLW 76.

33. "Jesus, you're a wonder." CHo 31.

34. "I want to live for Jesus ev'ry day." SLW 40.

35. SLW 49.

36. FS 29.

37. FS 52.

38. "There's a quiet understanding." CHo 37.

39. SP 72.

40. BHUM* 956; SLW 29; SP 73.

41. SLW 69.

42. CHo 109.

43. SLW 90.

44. SLW 58, 66; CHo 67, 93.

45. "Fill us with your love." CHo 88; LEV 32.

46. CHo 92.

47. CHo 52.

48. FS 97.

49. Robert H. Mitchell, *Ministry and Music* (Westminster Press, 1978), p. 87.

50. FS 99.

51. SLW 76.

52. FS 25; see also FS 24.

53. CHo 6.

54. *Songs of Praise* contains hardly a hint of the social evils that blight human lives. Its songs are almost entirely subjective and individualistic. The love that is lauded and urged remains abstract.

55. See the section on "Responsibility for Social Justice" in Chapter 9 and that on "The Kingdom of God" in Chapter 10.

Chapter 13. INCLUSIVE LANGUAGE

(When the source of a hymn is identified in the text of this chapter no number is listed here.)

1. Letty M. Russell, *Human Liberation in a Feminist Perspective—A Theology* (Westminster Press, 1974), p. 94.

2. BHUM 11; HCW 8; UCC 11.

3. OHT* 8.

4. AHB 418; BH 274; BHB 659; BHUM 408; BOP 111; CH 505; CP 171; EP* 101; HE 258; HMC 525; HSM* 9; MH 198; OHT* 13; PH 198; UCC 143; WBP 326; WOV 179.

5. LBW 409; OHT* 82; PP 8; WOV 569.

6. OHT* 23; WOR 77; WOV 567.

7. "For the healing of the nations." BOP 595; HC 210; OHT* 28; PL 294; PT* 20; WOR 82.

8. AM 812; BHB 356; BOP 316; CH 474; CLB 304; CP 365; HCW 355; HE 543; LBW 386; OHT* 12; STP 64; UCC 159; WOR 44.

9. HCW 19.

10. BHUM* 975; *Genesis Songbook*, 34; MHSS* 35; PL 296; *Songbook for Saints and Sinners*, 5; WBP 619–620.

11. *Hymns for Now*, Vol. I, 16.

12. *Faith, Folk and Clarity*, 20.

13. Erik Routley, "Sexist Language," p. 6.

14. *Because We Are One People: Songs for Worship* (Chicago: Ecumenical Women's Centers, 1974); *Everflowing Streams: Songs for Worship*, ed. by

Ruth C. Duck and Michael G. Bausch (Pilgrim Press, 1981). Additional resources: *A New Hymnal,* ed. by Stephen Rose; *The Shalom Hymnal,* ed. by
Grace Moore.

15. BWOP 29; ES 14.

16. AM 130; BBC 110; BHUM 451; BOP 194; CH 277; CLB 279; CP 724;
EH 626; HC 467; HCW 179; HE 99; PCH 168; PH 191; WBP 527; WOR 312;
WOV 281.

17. Routley, "Sexist Language," p. 10.

18. BWOP 20.

19. BWOP 17.

20. Russell, *Human Liberation in a Feminist Perspective,* p. 138.

21. HCL 4.

22. BWOP 43.

23. BWOP 49.

24. John M. Mulder, "A Non-Sexist Style Guide," *Theology Today,* Vol. 34
(1977–78), p. 446.

25. Second stanza of "Before Jehovah's awful throne." "Toward More
Inclusive Language in the Worship of the Church," Washington, D.C.: Wesley Theological Seminary, Feb. 1979.

26. Routley, "Sexist Language," p. 5.

27. Fred Kaan, "Emerging Language in Hymnody," an address at the 1980
Convocation of the Hymn Society of America, Princeton, N.J., June 10, 1980,
p. 7.

28. "Turn Back, You Folks . . . ," *The Hymn,* Vol. 32, No. 4 (Oct. 1981),
p. 217.

INDEX OF AUTHORS
AND TRANSLATORS OF HYMNS

Abelard, Peter, 100, 105
Addison, Joseph, 57, 218, 241n11
Ainger, Arthur C., 170
Akers, Doris, 189
Alexander, Cecil Frances, 103, 239n23
Alford, Henry, 161
Ambrose, Giles, 153
Ambrose of Milan, 26, 100
Andrew of Crete, 158
Appleford, Patrick, 98, 208
Aquinas, Thomas, 133, 134, 137
Avery, Richard K., 198, 201

Babcock, Maltbie D., 216
Baker, Henry W., 144
Banks, Martha Eason, 190
Baring-Gould, Sabine, 158, 181
Barker, Owen, 204
Bateman, Christian Henry, 158
Bathurst, William H., 158
Battles, F. L., 119, 142
Battles, M. D., 142
Bax, Clifford, 85, 216–217
Baxter, Richard, 222
Bayly, Albert F., 39, 48, 59, 65, 127, 171, 217
Beach, Curtis, 82
Bell, George K. A., 120, 217–218
Benson, Louis F., 137, 151
Berg, Caroline V. Sandell, 71
Bernard of Clairvaux, 90
Bernard of Cluny, 160–161, 172
Bevan, Emma F., 46
Bianco da Siena, 114

Bickersteth, Edward H., 143, 150
Blatchford, Ambrose Nichols, 73–74
Bliss, Philip P., 179
Bode, John E., 97
Bonar, Horatius, 121
Borthwick, Jane L., 161, 239n23
Bowers, John E., 134
Bowie, Walter Russell, 107, 169
Bridges, Robert, 73
Briggs, George Wallace, 124, 136, 165, 167, 217, 237 (Ch. 6, n. 16)
Bright, William, 131–132
Brokering, Herbert F., 27, 58, 196
Brooks, Reginald T., 65
Brownlie, John, 173
Brumley, Albert E., 191
Budry, Edmond Louis, 165
Bunyan, John, 36, 73, 158, 222
Burrell, Curtis, 187
Burrowes, Elisabeth, 75

Cameron, Catherine, 48, 59, 196
Campbell, Lucy E., 191, 241n11
Carlyle, Thomas, 73
Carmichael, Ralph, 241n11
Carter, Sydney, 159, 197, 200, 242n33, 246n3
Cennick, John, 91, 150
Chadwick, John W., 154
Chesterton, Gilbert K., 154
Chisholm, Emily, 153
Chisholm, Thomas O., 72
Chorley, Henry F., 153
Christmas, Charles, 204

Clark, Jodi Page, 209
Clark, Thomas Curtis, 60
Clayton, Norman J., 180
Clement of Alexandria, 76, 97, 102, 108
Clephane, Elizabeth C., 25, 151
Clough, S. O'Malley, 181
Clowe, Betsy, 207
Clowe, Jane, 207
Cober, Kenneth L., 140
Coffin, Charles, 172
Collins, Henry, 97
Colvin, Tom, 200, 208–209
Conder, Josiah, 69, 236n15
Cook, Sam, 189
Copenhaver, Laura S., 129
Cosin, John, 112
Coster, George T., 158, 219
Cowper, William, 70
Coxe, Arthur Cleveland, 122
Cramer, J. A., 136
Croly, George, 112
Crosby, Fanny, 104, 179
Cross, Stewart, 66, 217
Crossman, Samuel, 106
Crouch, Andraé, 191
Cushing, William O., 180–181
Cyprian of Carthage, 119

Dallas, Fred, 218
Daniel ben Judah Dayyan, 67
Dearmer, Percy, 73, 80–81, 217, 218, 222, 240n45
Dixon, Jessy, 189
Doane, George W., 239n23
Doddridge, Philip, 72, 101, 158, 215–216
Dorsey, Thomas A., 185–186, 187–188, 188–189, 195
Douroux, Margaret Pleasant, 189, 190
Drese, Adam, 143
Driscoll, J., 241n11
Drury, Miriam, 39, 84
Dryden, John, 113
Duck, Ruth, 171
Dudley-Smith, Timothy, 46
Duffield, George, Jr., 158, 181
Dwight, Timothy, 122, 219

Edwards, Frank, 80
Ellerton, John, 153, 170
Elliott, Charlotte, 81, 179
Elliott, Ebenezer, 153–154
Ephraim the Syrian, 137
Evers, C. Clifford, 242n31

F. B. P., 161
Faber, Frederick W., 50, 101, 162, 216
Fahs, Sophia Lyon, 79
Farjeon, Eleanor, 60
Ferguson, Ian, 157
Fishel, Donald, 205
Foley, Brian, 146
Foley, John B., 204
Forness, Norman O., 84
Fosdick, Harry Emerson, 221
Foulkes, William H., 87
Francis of Assisi, 72, 158, 162, 209–210
Franck, Johann, 90–91
Franz, Ignaz, 216
Franzmann, Martin H., 236n9
Fraser, Ian Mason, 242n46
Frostenson, Anders, 154
Fryson, Robert J., 187

Gabriel, Charles H., 181
Gaither, Gloria, 172
Gaither, William J., 172
Gates, Ellen H., 162
Gaunt, Alan, 96–97
Gaunt, H. C. A., 136
Gladden, Washington, 92, 151
Goodall, David S., 201
Grant, John Webster, 113
Green, Fred Pratt, 15, 27, 96, 115, 129–130, 139–140, 146, 157, 196
Gregor, Christian, 103, 161, 187

Hall, Elvina M., 180
Hardyman, Sandy, 209
Hargett, James H., 155
Harrington, Jan, 205
Hart, Joseph, 180
Hatch, Edwin, 112
Havergal, Frances R., 181

Haweis, Hugh R., 162
Hawkins, Walter, 191
Heath, George, 150, 158
Heber, Reginald, 63, 64, 128, 132, 158, 216
Hensley, Lewis, 167
Herbert, George, 148, 241n11
Herklots, Rosamond E., 59–60, 147
Hernaman, Claudia F., 101
Hewlett, Michael E., 62, 201
Heyden, Sebald, 39
Hodson, Nick, 159, 246n3
Hoffman, Elisha A., 143, 179
Holmes, John Haynes, 129
Hosmer, Frederick L., 167
Housman, Laurence, 168–169
How, William W., 97, 126, 164, 219
Hoyle, Richard Birch, 165
Hughes, Donald W., 145, 146–147
Humphreys, Charles W., 240n45
Hyde, William DeWitt, 25, 60

Ingemann, Bernhardt S., 158
Iverson, Daniel, 207

Jabusch, Willard F., 109, 242n33
Jacobs, Henry E., 133
Jacobse, Muus, 135
Jervois, William H. H., 131
John of Damascus, 102, 164–165
Johnson, Samuel, 122–123
Jones, Derwyn Dixon, 81
Jones, Richard G., 27, 39, 48, 58–59, 82–83, 155, 196, 197, 246n3

Kaan, Fred, 57, 75–76, 77, 115–116, 139, 149, 154, 156, 163, 196, 217, 221, 228
Kerr, Hugh T., 74–75
Kethe, William, 223, 226
Kettring, Donald D., 151–152

Landry, Carey, 207
Laurenti, Laurentius, 172
Lemmel, Helen H., 206–207
Lewis, Howell Elvet, 147
Littledale, Richard F., 114
Littlefield, Milton S., 92

Longfellow, Samuel, 114, 121
Lowell, James Russell, 154, 218–219
Lowry, Robert, 182
Lowry, Somerset C., 104, 108
Lundeen, Joel W., 137–138
Luther, Martin, 26, 73, 98, 101–102, 109, 114, 142, 219
Lyte, Henry F., 61, 98, 163

Macalister, Edith Florence Boyle, 23
McCormick, Scott, Jr., 136
McDonald, Dalton E., 151–152, 237n18
McDonald, William, 180
Macnicol, Nicol, 46
Mansell, David J., 206
Marriott, John, 235n17
Marsh, Donald S., 198, 201
Martin, Civilla D., 143
Mason, John, 68
Matheson, George, 151
Merrick, Daniel B., Jr., 61–62, 87
Merrill, William P., 84, 216
Merrington, Ernest N., 68
Milman, Henry H., 101
Milton, John, 158, 168
Mischke, Bernard, 132
Miyashiro, Toki, 241n11
Moment, John J., 217
Monsell, J. S. B., 158
Montgomery, James, 92, 134, 146, 158, 170, 241n11
Morris, Kenneth, 187, 190
Morris, Lelia N., 182
Morse, Kenneth L., 242n33

Neale, John Mason, 125–126, 158, 160–161, 164–165
Neander, Joachim, 61, 69, 71, 73
Neumark, Georg, 70, 73
Newton, John, 82, 121, 122
Nicolai, Philipp, 173
Niles, Daniel T., 91, 148
Niles, John Jacob, 198
Noel, Caroline M., 94
North, Frank Mason, 155–156, 216, 239n23

Oatman, Johnson, Jr., 181
Oxenham, John, 124

Palmer, Ray, 90, 142
Park, J. Edgar, 96
Patton, Kenneth L., 79
Peacey, John R., 115, 126
Perronet, Edward, 100
Phelps, Sylvanus D., 97
Plumptre, Edward H., 119, 158
Pollard, Adelaide A., 86
Pollock, John B., 121–122
Pollock, Thomas B., 97
Powell, Roger K., 124
Prudentius, Aurelius, 93

Rauschenbusch, Walter, 184–185
Rees, Timothy, 76, 106–107
Reid, William W., Jr., 27, 155
Repp, Ray, 218
Reyes, Nellie, 148
Richard of Chichester, 148
Rinkart, Martin, 64, 216
Rist, Johann, 101
Robbins, Howard C., 102, 236n46
Roberts, Daniel C., 74
Robinson, Robert, 61
Rodigast, Samuel, 25, 235n29, 236n15
Rommel, Kurt, 153
Routley, Erik, 156, 221–222
Rowley, Francis H., 179
Rowsell, Kenred B., 242n33
Rowthorn, Jeffery, 66

Schmolck, Benjamin, 70, 142–143
Scholtes, Peter, 153, 218, 246n3
Schütz, Johann J., 38, 61
Scott, Robert B. Y., 169
Scriven, Joseph N., 91
Sherlock, Hugh, 129
Shurtleff, Ernest, 158, 219
Slade, Mary B. C., 239n23
Sleeper, William T., 179
Small, James G., 179–180
Smith, Samuel F., 122, 128
Smith, Walter Chalmers, 57
Stewart, Alexander, 182
Stocking, Jay T., 92

Stockton, John H., 179
Stone, Samuel J., 121, 124, 219
Stowe, Harriet Beecher, 163
Struther, Jan, 39, 148–149
Symonds, John A., 49

Tauler, John, 46
Tennyson, Alfred, Lord, 49, 144–145
Thomas, Henry Arnold, 152
Thompson, Colin P., 134
Thomson, Mary A., 126–127
Tilak, Narayan Vaman, 46
Tindley, Charles A., 158
Tomlinson, G. A., 135
Toplady, Augustus M., 50
Townsend, Paul, 66
Tucker, F. Bland, 93, 118
Turton, William Harry, 126
Tweedy, Henry Hallam, 67, 115, 129

Utterbach, Clinton, 188

Vale, Alliene G., 205
Van Dyke, Henry, 36, 97, 158, 216
Vanstone, W. H., 76

Walford, William, 47
Ward, Clara, 191
Waring, Anne L., 144
Watts, Isaac, 24, 36, 39, 49, 69, 77, 81, 106, 144, 151, 158, 180, 182, 215, 218, 221, 226, 236n15, 241n10, n11
Wesley, Charles, 26, 32, 37, 49, 50, 81–82, 83–84, 85–86, 86–87, 97, 100, 101, 103–104, 124, 152, 158, 164, 165, 172, 215, 235n17, 237n20
Wesley, John, 26, 103
Westendorf, Omer, 137, 242n31
Wexels, Wilhelm A., 162, 172
White, Estelle, 202
Whiting, William, 63
Whittier, John Greenleaf, 49, 92, 144, 145, 154
Williams, William, 74
Winkworth, Catherine, 90–91, 173

Wordsworth, Christopher, 57
Wren, Brian A., 102, 116, 119–120,
  138, 196
Wright, Priscilla, 204–205

Zinzendorf, Christian Renatus von,
  103
Zinzendorf, Nicolaus Ludwig von,
  25, 103, 161–162

INDEX OF FIRST LINES OF HYMNS

Common titles are in italics

A charge to keep I have, 86, 152

A Christian must by faith be filled, 142

A gladsome hymn of praise we sing, 73

A man there lived in Galilee, 104, 108

A mighty fortress is our God, 73, 219

A new commandment I give unto you, 208

A safe stronghold our God is still, 73

Abide with me; fast falls the eventide, 163

According to thy gracious word, 134

Ah, dearest Jesus, holy Child, 98

Alabaré a mi Señor, 199

Alas! and did my Savior bleed, 49, 81

All creatures of our God and King, 72, 98, 158, 162

All hail the power of Jesus' name, 100

All my hope on God is founded, 29

All people that on earth do dwell, 223, 226

All who love and serve your city, 156

All who would valiant be, 222

All you peoples, clap your hands, 218

Alone, thou goest forth, O Lord, 105

Am I a soldier of the cross, 158

Am I my brother's keeper?, 25, 157

Amazing grace! how sweet the sound, 82

And can it be that I should gain, 47

And now, O Father, mindful of the love, 132

Angels we have heard on high, 225

Arise, my soul, arise, 37

Art thou weary, art thou languid, 158

As long as you have done it to the least of these my brothers, 242n33

As the bridegroom to his chosen, 46

As the disciples, when thy Son had left them, 217

As the lyre to the singer, 46

As water to the thirsty, 46

At the name of Jesus, 94

Awake, my soul, stretch every nerve, 158

Because the Lord is my Shepherd, 241n11

Because thy trust is God alone, 70

Before Jehovah's awful throne, 49, 218, 226, 248n25

Before the Lord Jehovah's throne, 49

Be like your Father, 208

Be not dismayed whate'er betide, 143

Be thou my vision, 39, 74

Beneath the cross of Jesus, 25, 151

Beneath the spreading heavens, 70

Beyond the mist and doubt, 145
Blessed assurance, Jesus is mine, 151
Book of books, our people's strength, 29
Bread of the world in mercy broken, 132, 135
Break forth, O beauteous heavenly light, 101
Breathe on me, breath of God, 112
Brief life is here our portion, 161
Broken bread and outpoured wine, 136
Brothers and sisters of mine are the hungry, 242n33

Children of the heavenly Father, 71
Children of the heavenly King, 150
Christ has for sin atonement made, 179
Christ is alive! let Christians sing, 102
Christ is all, 190
Christ is crucified today, 149
Christ is gone up; yet ere he passed, 125
Christ is the King! O friends, rejoice, 120, 217–218
Christ is the world's light, 96
Christ is the world's true light, 98, 124, 167, 217, 237 (Ch. 6, n. 16)
Christ Jesus lay in death's strong bands, 101, 109
Christ the Lord is risen today, 165
Christ the worker, 200
Christian! dost thou see them, 158
Christian people, raise your song, 134
City of God, how broad and far, 122–123
Come, Christians, join to sing, 158
Come down, O love divine, 114
Come, every soul by sin oppressed, 179
Come, Father, Son, and Holy Ghost, 216
Come, Holy Ghost, Creator blest, 238n6

Come, Holy Ghost, our souls inspire, 112–113
Come, Holy Spirit, God and Lord, 114
Come, let us join our friends above, 164
Come, O Creator Spirit, come, 113
Come, O thou Traveler unknown, 32
Come, risen Lord, and deign to be our guest, 136
Come, sinners, to the gospel feast, 26
Come, thou almighty King, 63
Come, thou Fount of every blessing, 61
Come, thou long-expected Jesus, 97, 101
Come, ye faithful, raise the strain, 102, 164
Come, ye sinners, poor and needy, 180
Come, ye that love the Lord, 182
Committed to Christ, who died but rose, 77
Complete in him, 206
Creating God, your fingers trace, 66
Creation's Lord, we give thee thanks, 25, 60, 235n10
Creator of the earth and skies, 146
Creator of the stars of night, 94
Creator Spirit, by whose aid, 113
Cup of blessing that we share, 132

Day by day, 148
Dear Lord and Father of mankind, 145, 223
Dear Lord, to you again our gifts we bring, 136
Dear Mother-Father of us all, 223
Divinity is round us—never gone, 79

Earth and all stars, 27, 58
Eternal Father, strong to save, 37, 63
Eternal God, whose power upholds, 67, 129

Every morning is Easter morning from now on, 198

Faith of our fathers, 50, 98, 142, 216, 221
Father eternal, Ruler of creation, 168
Father, in the dawning light, 148
Father, in whom we live, 235n17
Father, Lord of all creation, 66, 217
Father, we thank you that you planted, 118
Fear not, rejoice and be glad, 205, 246n24
Fight the good fight, 158
Fill us with your love, 247n45
Filled with the Spirit's power, 115, 126, 238n9
Fling out the banner, 128, 239n23
For all the saints, who from their labors rest, 164, 219
For the bread, which thou hast broken, 135
For the fruits of his creation, 146
For the healing of the nations, 217, 247n7
For thee, O dear, dear country, 161
For you are my God, 204
"Forgive our sins as we forgive," 147
Founded on thee, our only Lord, 122
From all the dark places, 128, 239n23
From Greenland's icy mountains, 141
From the shores of many nations, 155

Give me a clean heart, 190
Give thanks to our God, and let him be praised, 204
Glorious things of thee are spoken, 121
"Glory to God!" all heav'n with joy is ringing, 134
God in his love for us lent us this planet, 157
God is, 187

God is love: let heaven adore him, 76
God is our Father, for he has made us his own, 208
God is working his purpose out, 170
God of concrete, God of steel, 27, 48, 58–59
God of earth and sea and heaven, 80
God of eternity, Lord of the ages, 68
God of grace and God of glory, 36, 221
God of our fathers, whose almighty hand, 74
God of our life, through all the circling years, 74
God of the ages, by whose hand, 75
God the omnipotent, 153, 168
God who created this garden of earth, 39, 82, 197, 246n3
God who spoke in the beginning, 57
God, who stretched the spangled heavens, 48, 59
Goin' up yonder, 191, 193
Good Christian men, rejoice, 221
Good morning, Jesus, good morning, Love, 211
Great is thy faithfulness, 72
Guide me, O thou great Jehovah, 36, 74

Hail to the Lord's anointed, 170
Hark, the glad sound, the Savior comes, 101
Hasten the time appointed, 128, 239n23
Have thine own way, Lord, 86
He wants not friends that hath thy love, 222
He who would valiant be, 36, 73, 222
Heralds of Christ, who bear the King's commands, 129
Here comes Jesus, see him walking on the water, 206

Here, O my Lord, I see thee face to face, 121
Higher ground, 181
Holy God, we praise thy name, 216
Holy, holy, holy, 37, 63, 120, 216, 225
Holy Spirit, truth divine, 114
How beautiful the morning and the day, 204
How firm a foundation, 72
How gentle God's commands, 72, 215
How I got over, 191
How shall I sing that majesty, 68
Hungry men of many lands, 221

I am coming to the cross, 180
I am praying for you, 181
I belong to a family, the biggest on earth, 218
I come with joy to meet my Lord, 138
I danced in the morning, 159, 197
I don't feel no ways tired, 187
I don't possess houses or lands, 190
I have a Savior, he's pleading in glory, 181
I hear the Savior say, 180
I know not what the future hath, 145, 241n13
I love thy kingdom, Lord, 122, 219
I sent them Men of Old, 245n35
I sought the Lord, and afterward I knew, 141
I want to live for Jesus ev'ry day, 206
I was lost in sin and sorrow, 188
I will praise my Lord, 199
I will rejoice in the Lord alway, 205
I will sing the wondrous story, 179
I will sing you a song of that beautiful land, 162
I wonder as I wander, 36, 198
If I had my way, O Lordy, Lordy, 192
If thou but suffer God to guide thee, 70
If you wanna know where I'm going, 191

I'll fly away, 191
I'll praise my Maker while I've breath, 39
I'm pressing on the upward way, 181, 244n18
Immortal, invisible, God only wise, 57
Immortal Love, forever full, 49
In Adam we have all been one, 236n9
In Christ there is no East or West, 124, 222
In heavenly love abiding, 144
In the hour of trial, 158
Is there anybody here like Mary a-weeping, 200
It's a long, hard journey, 159, 246n3
I've found a friend, O such a Friend, 179–180

Jerusalem, my happy home, 161
Jerusalem the golden, 49, 161
Jesu, Jesu, fill us with your love, 208
Jesus, be a fence all around me, 189
Jesus, call thou me from the world to thee, 143
Jesus Christ is alive today, 205
Jesus, humble was your birth, 98
Jesus, I come, 179
Jesus, I look to thee, 86
Jesus, I my cross have taken, 98
Jesus is Lord! Creation's voice proclaims it, 205
Jesus, lover of my soul, 81, 97
Jesus, my Lord, my God, my all, 97
Jesus my Lord will love me forever, 180
Jesus paid it all, 180
Jesus, priceless treasure, 90
Jesus, still lead on, 162
Jesus, the sinner's friend, to thee, 85
Jesus, the very thought of thee, 37, 49, 97
Jesus, thou divine companion, 97
Jesus, thou joy of loving hearts, 90
Jesus, thy blood and righteousness, 103

Jesus walked this lonesome valley, 199

Jesus, with thy church abide, 97, 121–122

Jesus, you're a wonder, 206

Joy to the world, 224

Joyful, joyful, we adore thee, 36, 158, 216

Just as I am, thine own to be, 38

Just as I am, without one plea, 38, 81, 179

Just to behold his face, 191

King of glory, King of peace, 148

Lead, kindly Light, 37

Lead on, O cloud of Presence, 171, 243n23

Lead on, O King eternal, 157

Leaning on the everlasting arms, 143

Let all who share one bread and cup, 136

Let ev'ry instrument be tuned for praise, 15

Let saints on earth in concert sing, 124

Let us break bread together, 138–139

Let us with a gladsome mind, 158

Like a ship that's toss'd and driven, 188

Look around you, can you see, 209

Lord, as I wake I turn to you, 146

Lord, bring the day to pass, 242n46

Lord Christ, the Father's mighty Son, 119

Lord Christ, we praise your sacrifice, 96–97

Lord Christ, when first thou cams't to men, 107

Lord Christ, who on thy heart didst bear, 152

Lord, don't move that mountain, 189

Lord, give us your Spirit that is love, 209

Lord God, by whose creative might, 59–60

Lord, I want to be a Christian, 147

Lord Jesus, be thou with us now, 233 (Ch. 1, n. 1)

Lord Jesus Christ, we humbly pray, 133–134

Lord Jesus Christ, we seek thy face, 182

Lord, make me an instrument of your peace, 209

Lord of all good, our gifts we bring to thee, 65

Lord of all hopefulness, Lord of all joy, 39, 148–149

Lord of light whose name shines brighter, 147

Lord of the boundless curves of space, 59

Lord of the Dance, 159, 197, 246n3

Lord, thy church on earth is seeking, 129

Lord, touch me, 190

Lord, we thank thee for our brothers, 124

Lord, who throughout these forty days, 101

Lord will make a way some how, 188

Love divine, all loves excelling, 26, 50, 83

Make me a channel of your peace, 209

Male and female; God created, 201

"Man of Sorrows," what a name, 179

March on, O soul, with strength, 158, 219

Men and children everywhere, 217

More like the Master I would ever be, 181

Morning glory, starlit sky, 76

Morning has broken, 60

"Moses, I know you're the man," 202

My country, 'tis of thee, 98

My faith looks up to thee, 142

My Jesus, as thou wilt, 142–143

My people need to be redeemed, 211

My Shepherd is the Lord most high, 241n11
My Shepherd will supply my need, 77, 144
My song is love unknown, 106
My soul, be on thy guard, 150, 158

Near the cross! O Lamb of God, 179
Nearer, still nearer, close to thy heart, 182
No use knocking on the window, 200
Nobody knows the trouble I've seen, 159
Now is eternal life, 165
Now thank we all our God, 64, 216
Now thank we God for bodies strong, 81
Now we join in celebration, 138

O brother man, fold to thy heart thy brother, 29, 92, 153
O Christ, our hope, our heart's desire, 94
O come and mourn with me awhile, 101
O crucified Redeemer, 106–107
O day of God, draw nigh, 169
O day of resurrection, 29
O Father above us, our Father in might, 218
O filii et filiae, 221
O for a closer walk with God, 29
O for a faith that will not shrink, 158
O for a heart to praise my God, 83
O for a thousand tongues to sing, 49, 100
O God of every nation, 27, 155
O God of the eternal now, 139
O God, whose love compels us, 87
O holy city, seen of John, 29, 169
O holy Father, God most dear, 135
O Holy Spirit, by whose breath, 113
O how glorious, full of wonder, 82
O Jesus, I have promised, 97
O Jesus, thou art standing, 97

O Lord, all the world belongs to you, 208
O Lord of every shining constellation, 39, 234 (Ch. 3, n. 8)
O Lord of heaven and earth and sea, 57
O Master, let me walk with thee, 92, 151
O Master of the waking world, 128, 239n23
O Master Workman of the race, 92
O Mensch, bewein dein Sünde gross, 39
O Paradise, O Paradise, 162
O sacred Head, now wounded, 32, 98, 106
O safe to the Rock that is higher than I, 180
O Son of Man, thou madest known, 92
O sons and daughters, let us sing, 221
O Spirit of the living God, 115
O splendor of God's glory bright, 26
O thou who at thy eucharist didst pray, 126
O where are kings and empires now, 122
O who can tell me where Jesus Christ is born today, 153, 242n35
O Word of God incarnate, 126
O worship the King, 224
O Zion, haste, thy mission high fulfilling, 98, 126
Of all the Spirit's gifts to me, 115, 238n10
Of the Father's love begotten, 93
Of the glorious body telling, 133
Oh, happy day when we shall stand, 162, 172, 243n27
Oh, the blood of Jesus, 206
Old Ship of Zion, 188–189
On a day when men were counted, 91
Once to every man and nation, 154, 218–219
One holy church of God appears, 121

Onward, Christian soldiers, 158, 181

Our faith is in the Christ who walks, 60

Our God has made this world, 223

Our God, our help in ages past, 36, 215, 221

Out of my bondage, sorrow, and night, 179

Peace, perfect peace, in this dark world of sin, 143, 150

Peace, troubled soul, thou needst not fear, 199

Praise and thanksgiving, Father, we offer, 217

Praise, my soul, the King of heaven, 61

Praise to the living God, 67

Praise to the Lord, the Almighty, 61, 69

Prayer is the soul's sincere desire, 92

Prayer of St. Francis, 209

Precious Lord, take my hand, 188, 194–195

Pride of man and earthly glory, 73

Rejoice, all ye believers, 172

Rejoice, O people, in the mounting years, 171

Rejoice, the Lord is King, 158, 172

Rejoice, ye pure in heart, 158

Renew thy church, her ministries restore, 140

Ride on! Ride on in majesty, 101

Rise, my soul, adore thy Maker, 91

Rise up, O men of God, 84, 216, 219

Rise up, O saints of God, 84

Rock of Ages, cleft for me, 50

Savior, like a Shepherd lead us, 37

Savior of the nations, come, 100

Savior, thy dying love, 97

Seek ye first, 208

Sent forth by God's blessing, 137

Shepherd of tender [eager] youth, 97, 108

Sing praise to God who reigns above, 38, 61

Sing praise to God who spoke through man, 80

Sing to him, in whom creation, 62

Sing to the Lord a new song, 205

Sing we of the modern city, 156

Soldiers of Christ, arise, 158, 237n20

Soon and very soon, 191

Souls in heathen darkness lying, 128, 239n23

Spirit of God, descend upon my heart, 112

Spirit of the living God, 207

Stand up, stand up for Jesus, 158, 181

Still, still with thee, 163

Strengthen for service, Lord, 137

Strong Son of God, immortal Love, 49, 144

Sunset to sunrise changes now, 76, 102

Sweet hour of prayer, 47

Sweet Jesus, 211

Take my hand, precious Lord, 188, 194–195

Take my life and let it be, 181

Take thou our minds, dear Lord, 87

Ten thousand times ten thousand, 161

Thank you, thank you, Jesus, 205

Thanks to God whose Word was spoken, 65

The advent of our God, 172

The Church of Christ in every age, 139–140

The church of Christ is one, 119

The church's one foundation, 121, 124, 219

The Clock Carol, 66

The clouds of judgment gather, 172

The day of resurrection, 164–165

The day you gave us, Lord, is ended, 170

The failure's not in God; it's in me, 189

The Family of Man, 218
The first Nowell, 36
The fullness of the Godhead bodily dwelleth with my Lord, 206
The God of Abraham praise, 67
The God of love my Shepherd is, 241n11
The God who rules this earth, 155
The great Creator of the worlds, 93
The Homeland, O the Homeland, 162
The joy of the Lord is my strength, 205
The King of glory comes, the nation rejoices, 109
The King of love my Shepherd is, 144
The King shall come when morning dawns, 173
The living God my Shepherd is, 241n11
The Lord is King! Who then shall dare, 69
The Lord is my pacesetter, 144, 241n11
The Lord is my Shepherd, I shall not want, 241n11
The Lord is my Shepherd, I'll follow him alway, 241n11
The Lord is my Shepherd, my guardian, my guide, 241n11
The Lord is my Shepherd, no want shall I know, 241n11
The Lord is my Shepherd, there is nothing I shall want, 241n11
The Lord Jehovah reigns, 69
The Lord my pasture shall prepare, 241n11
The Lord my Shepherd is, 241n11
The Lord will come and not be slow, 168
The Lord will make a way some how, 188
The Lord's my Shepherd, I'll not want, 144
The love of God is broad like beach and meadow, 154
The man who once has found abode, 70, 235n33

The market place is empty, 172
The morning light is breaking, 128
The Son of God goes forth to war, 158
The spacious firmament on high, 46, 57, 218
The Spirit is a-movin' all over this land, 207
The strife is o'er, the battle done, 165
The voice of God is calling, 129
The world is very evil, 161
Thee we adore, O hidden Savior, thee, 134, 137
There are some things I may not know, 187
There is a balm in Gilead, 36, 81, 159
There is a green hill far away, 103
There's a quiet understanding, 207
There's a wideness in God's mercy, 142
These things shall be: a loftier race, 49
Thine is the glory, risen, conquering Son, 165
This is my Father's world, 216, 223
Thou, whose almighty Word, 235n17
Through all the changing scenes of life, 148
Through the night of doubt and sorrow, 158
Thy hand, O God, has guided, 119
Thy kingdom come, O God, 167
"Thy kingdom come," on bended knee, 167
'Tis so sweet to trust in Jesus, 142
'Tis the most blest and needful part, 103
To God be the glory! great things he hath done, 104
Today I live, but once shall come my death, 163
Trees don't want to be mountains, 189
Truehearted, wholehearted, 181
Turn back, O man, forswear thy foolish ways, 216–217
Turn your eyes upon Jesus, 206

Under his wings I am safely abiding, 180–181

Veni Creator Spiritus, 112
Victim divine, your grace we claim, 107

Wake, awake! for night is flying, 173
Walk tall, Christian, 39, 84
Watchman, tell us of the night, 98
We are one in the Spirit, 153, 218, 246n3
We journey with a multitude, 79, 236n3
We meet you, O Christ, in many a guise, 75–76
We really want to thank you, Lord, 207–208
We shall overcome, 159
We turn to you, O God of every nation, 115
We who once were dead, 135
We would see Jesus, 96
Wer kann mir sagen, wo Jesus Christus geboren ist, 153
We're marching to Zion, 182
What a fellowship, what a joy divine, 143
What a friend we have in Jesus, 38, 91
What child is this, 32
What God hath done is done aright, 70
What wondrous love is this, 198
Whate'er our God ordains is right, 25, 235n29
Whatsoever you do to the least of my brothers, 242n33

When God Almighty came to be one of us, 201
When I can read my title clear, 151
When I needed a neighbour, were you there, 200
When I survey the wondrous cross, 36, 106, 151
When in our music God is glorified, 15, 27
When the bells chime noon in London, 66
When the church of Jesus, 129
When the load bears down so heavy, 188
When the pious prayers we make, 201
When the storms of life are raging, 158
When wilt thou save the people, 153–154
Where charity and love prevail, 152
Where cross the crowded ways of life, 156, 216
Wherefore, O Father, we thy humble servants, 131
Who fathoms the eternal thought, 145, 241n13
Who would true valour see, 222
Wind, wind, blow on me, 207
Within the maddening maze of things, 145
Won't you come, 208

Yes, God is real, 187
Your love, O God, has all mankind created, 127